Cassette Culture

Homemade Music and the Creative Spirit in the
Pre-Internet Age

Jerry Kranitz

Monger Publications

Acclaim for Cassette Culture

In *Cassette Culture*, Jerry Kranitz has achieved the near impossible, that of summing up the nature, reach and impact of the radical and democratizing technology that was the cassette tape. The invention of the compact cassette wrestled control out of the hands of the record industry and placed it firmly into the laps of you and I, to create, communicate, collaborate and innovate like never before. Drawing on original sources and prime movers in the underground cassette scenes that sprang up all over, Kranitz paints an evocative picture of an era now passed, but whose influence is still with us. The humble cassette offered true emancipation to those seeking to share and exchange music with others across the world and enabled small bands to record and release their own music without the need to go into a studio or chase a recording contract. Kranitz opens the door to this world through the eyes of some of its key protagonists and brings it alive for us through his clear passion for the topic. *Cassette Culture* acts as an eye-opening introduction, a selection box, and a guidebook into the incredible world of the underground cassette revolution, from which once experienced, there is no going back.
- Alan Rider, Outsideleft Magazine/Adventures in Reality

Jerry Kranitz's book evokes the almost-clandestine networks, the home-dubbed love and revolution that snailed its way through the mail, a thing that didn't need permission, a thing that thrived precisely because it was excluded. It was raw, unruly,

and totally outside of the algorithm's grasp. It was rough, slow and amateur, but it built real connections across borders and physical isolation. This is how we misfits found each other, making noise outside of commerce. A countercultural web stuck together with trust, photocopies and international reply coupons.
- Nigel Ayers, Nocturnal Emissions

The humble cassette has received quite a lot of interest of late with a number of books exploring its social and cultural significance across a range of genres, but Jerry Kranitz's book remains one of the few publications to focus on the cassette's significance as a means of DIY music production and distribution. Starting firstly in the heady days of late 1970s post-punk and then outlining the cassette's role in the 1980s and 90s in the development of an alternative network of hometapers. Out of print since its initial hardback publication on Vinyl-on-Demand, this new and updated version is therefore very much appreciated.
- Philip Sanderson, founder of Snatch Tapes

The cassette culture wasn't just about underground music and art, it was a way of looking at the world. Jerry Kranitz's *Cassette Culture* illuminates this grassroots network where kindred spirits were only a letter away and exchanges were always mutual. We created a Christmas Day every day, with quirky packages arriving through mailboxes the world over. This meticulously researched book is full of firsthand information and anecdotes from artists and innovators that join the dots to show how the network grew and interconnected creators and audiences. Embracing the bold challenges of assembling a comprehensive cultural history that straddles countries, musical genres and ideologies, *Cassette Culture* is an engrossing and weighty read. Uniquely, Kranitz roots the artist networks of the cassette scene within earlier fan communities of 1930s sci-fi and the scrupulously DIY approach of 1950s Sun Ra. Kranitz's wide lens contextualizes what emerged with the arrival of the hometapers with foundational concepts from the Dada and Fluxus movements. You will emerge from reading this book not just with an understanding of the

connections of contemporary music and culture but with a thought that maybe, just maybe, there is another way of doing things.
- Martin Franklin, The Cassette Culture Podcast

Jerry Kranitz's entry into music journalism began in the late 1990s with the fanzine Aural Innovations and in 2000 he began an online podcast under the same name. Recently he sent me an advance copy of a fascinating new book titled *Cassette Culture: Homemade Music and the Creative Spirit in the Pre-Internet Age*. This is a fascinating and in-depth survey of indie music artists, labels and music collectors that covers the entire spectrum of music stylistically featuring musicians from all corners of the world. As someone who has been immersed in 'Music from Around the World' since the 1970s, as I read through it there were hundreds of artists, labels, music fans and musicians referenced that I had never heard. I was amazed and overwhelmed by the amount of information contained in the book. *Cassette Culture* is an essential musical reference source. I recommend you check it out.
- Archie Patterson, EUROCK

Cassette Culture is the result of 10 years of painstaking research. It is an enjoyable and captivating read and, although meticulously researched, it thankfully avoids becoming too dry and academic and will appeal to both lay and scholarly readers alike. As someone who was thoroughly immersed in the DIY cassette scene of the late 1970s and early 80s, I recommended this book to anyone who was directly involved and would like to relive those exciting times, or simply wishes to discover more about this fascinating – and often forgotten – period in the history of underground music.
- Richard Rupenus, The New Blockaders

Second edition copyright © 2025 by Jerry Kranitz

Originally published in hardback, 2020, by Vinyl-on-Demand

All rights reserved.

ISBN: 979-8-218-81983-5 (Paperback)
ISBN: 979-8-218-81984-2 (eBook)

No portion of this book may be reproduced in any form without written permission from the publisher or author, except as permitted by U.S. copyright law.

Contents

Acknowledgments	IX
Notes on the Second Edition	XII
Forward	XIV
Introduction	XXV
Part I: The Cassette Recorder: YOU Too Can Be An Audio Artist!	
1. Record Companies	2
2. The Cassette Recorder: Encouraging Creativity and the Impetus to ACT	9
3. Cassettes vs. Vinyl	23
4. The Tape Tax	32
5. Creative Packaging	37
6. The Cassette Recorder as Compositional Tool	53
7. The Plagiarist Path	67
Part II: The Global Network Emerges... and Flourishes	
8. Setting the Stage	80
9. Punk and the UK Scene – DIY!	99
10. The Social Network	115
11. Small Press Publications and Zines	116

12.	Trading, Communication, Collaboration	130
13.	Labels, Distribution and Promotion	165
14.	Radio	191

Part III: Cassette 'Culture'?

15.	Was there a Cassette 'Culture'?	212
16.	An Era in Transition	231
17.	Revolution?	239

Appendix: Cassette Culture Reviews	242
Bibliography	285
Index	294
About the Author	301

Acknowledgments

This is the part of the book I worry about because of the inevitability of neglecting those who are deserving of thanks. The following people provided invaluable assistance, from research material, responding to interview requests, patience with my miscellaneous questions, helpful advice, and facilitated contacts. To you all I owe my heartfelt thanks...

Robin James, Hal McGee, Al Margolis, Carlton Crutcher, Florian Schreiner (helpful fact checking), Bret Hart, Rolf Sonnemann, Ian Abrahams, Peter Bonne, François Haidon, Dave Fuglewicz, Tom Ellard, Frans de Waard, Dan Plunkett, Michael Thomas Jackson, Mason Jones, Tim Jones, Greg Segal, Mike Honeycutt, David Cotner, Michael Chocholak, Charles Rice Goff, III, Andreas Müller, Alain Neffe, Carl Howard, Hessel Veldman, Das, Zan Hoffman, R.Stevie Moore, Karsten Rodemann, Don Campau, Barry Lamb, Peter Ashby, Ken Montgomery, Andy Xport, Mick Mercer, Stephen Palmer, Peter Bright, Rod Summers, George Smith, Arild Bergh, Lord Litter (Jörg Dittmar), Gerard Greenway, Ben Norland, Vittore Baroni, Mick Sinclair, Philip Sanderson, Kevin Thorne, Steve Peters, Richard Franecki, Brian Ladd, Little Fyodor (David Lichtenverg), Amy Denio, John Hudak, Archie Patterson, Ron Lessard, Mark Edwards, Philip Perkins, Didier 'Doc' Pilot, Dion Trevarthen, Jeff Chenault, Michael Gendreau, Ditlev Buster, John Oswald, Bryan Baker, Scott Telles, Alex Douglas, Phillip B. Klingler, Glenn Frantz, Joe Schmidt, Rob Drew, Benjamin Duester, Jed Bindeman, Eugene Chadbourne, William A. Davison, Leslie Singer, Chris Phinney, Joanna Rogers, Tom Sutter, Mitch Rushton, Tom Furgas, Scott Becker, Manny Theiner, Sue Ann Harkey, Ken

JERRY KRANITZ

Moore, Mark Kissinger, Joanna Stingray, Alex V. Cook, Scot Jenerik, Peter Catham, Martin Franklin, Michael Ryan, Richard Rupenus, Mark Lo, Nigel Ayers, and Alan Rider.

Thanks to Charles Rice Goff III for the cover photo and amazing original illustrations that grace the section title pages. And thanks to Sarah Holroyd for the front and back cover design.

Finally, thanks to Frank Maier at Vinyl-on-Demand for publishing the original hardback edition of this book.

All mistakes are, of course, my own...

Jerry Kranitz

Photograph and image credits:

- *Cheap Noise Cassette Compilation* insert scan courtesy of Glenn Frantz

- *Gum* cassette photos courtesy of Peter Catham

- *Dolbied* collage assembled from photos courtesy of Richard Rupenus

- *E-hv* cassette photo courtesy of Scot Jenerik

- *Test Tube Newsletter* cassette photo courtesy of Jeff Chenault

- Test Dept *Ecstacy Under Duress* cassette photo courtesy of Mason Jones

- Crawling With Tarts *Broom* cassette photo courtesy of Michael Gendreau

- Big City Orchestra *We Like Noize Too* cassette photo courtesy of Das

- Pain Clinic *My Dog's Name Is Spot* cassette photos courtesy of Bryan Baker

- Anton Shedlock/Sin Drome split cassette photo courtesy Jeff Chenault

- Wax *Contusions On The Skin Of Sleep* cassette photo courtesy of William

A. Davison

- Eugene Chadbourne *My New Life Vol. 1* cassette photo courtesy of Jed Bindeman

- *Rockin' the ATCO* cassette photo courtesy of Michael Ryan

- Cause And Effect catalog cover courtesy of Hal McGee

- WJHU radio playlist courtesy of Jeff Chenault

- Photo of Ken Montgomery working the Generator counter courtesy of Ken Montgomery

Notes on the Second Edition

This book was first published in 2020 in a now sold-out hardback edition of 500 by Frank Maier's Vinyl-on-Demand imprint. Approaching retirement in 2024, it bothered me that having spent ten years researching and writing the book it was no longer in print. And while I was thrilled with the results of the Vinyl-on-Demand edition, I was anxious for the book to be more widely available.

The research for the first edition took place from 2007-2017. Much has changed. I conducted numerous interviews but also quoted extensively from 1980s and early 1990s small press publications and zines. Revisiting the book revealed quotes from those publications that would benefit from the subject's hindsight commentary. Social media, for all its deserved criticism, has made it easier to find people. I succeeded in tracking down several of these individuals and have added their feedback.

I've also updated and reworked the Introduction. At the time of publication, my book was the only monograph to examine the post-punk era hometaper network. Since then, the literature has been enriched by more books about cassettes, though each takes on the topic from different perspectives, and focuses on scenes/subcultures and uses of cassettes beyond that of the post-punk hometaper network. I broadened the Introduction's literature review to account for these new publications.

The scope of the book has not changed. I am still laser focused on the hometapers and network of communication, exchange and collaboration that blossomed in the post-punk era.

Finally, I took to heart one piece of criticism the original book received and added an Index.

Forward

by Robin James (ed. Cassette Mythos)

Come, let us pay tribute to the noble audio cassette tape. It lives on, but nothing like in the 1980s.

First, as far as the form of the cassette itself, music always wants to be on the best possible medium which, so far, has been changing constantly. This works out really well for merchants. Music lovers will happily buy the same recordings over and over again as the formats change. They have it on vinyl, they have a cassette with bonus tracks, and another cassette that they keep in the basement with the original album. They have an 8-track version in the car. They bought the CD right away

Archival material has to be re-recorded or transcribed every few years as the technology changes and old playback devices are harder to find. The cassette itself as a contemporary phenomenon has come and gone, so let us now remember well its unique qualities. Audio cassettes were easy to use (push the appropriate button), easy to find supplies (pick it up at the store, pop in a new one), and easy to share (mailbox friendly, fits in your pocket). But most of all, they were CHEAP! Everybody had them. Since the early 1960s people were throwing them away as cheap junk. They'd say, "Let the kids play with it!"

My friend Jimmy's older brother Denny had the first cassette recorder I ever saw. You could press the red button and nothing seemed to happen, but then you could rewind it (press the Reverse button and the thing would dramatically rattle and groan and then abruptly snap off a loud CLICKSTOP all by itself), and then press the Play button and you could hear us kids saying that nothing was happening plus the sound of a distant airplane passing that we never noticed before.

Another kid, Johnny C, would make tapes with his siblings and they would read comic books out loud, each taking different parts, and laugh a whole lot and take them to school or mail them to cousins or far away friends who would then laugh themselves silly and try doing it themselves, with some improvised sound effects added this time. The rivalry yielded much hilarity and enthusiasm. Ideas built upon ideas.

Another kid's brother would record himself playing the piano. Homework using a cassette recorder is BORING! There are more interesting ways to use this technology. He would listen to it for hours. His mom liked it even more, and she will play those old tapes forever.

I would make my own radio shows where I was the DJ picking the tunes and introducing them, learning to be tricky with my voice. All I had was a regular little transistor radio for the music source, plus the tape recorder itself. I had to wait until that one song I wanted was played on the real radio, then press Record and do my voiceover on top of the song, my DJ banter delivered leaning close to the cassette recorder, followed by leaning away and putting the little recorder directly on the radio speaker to get the best possible sound, and then trying to stay quiet all through the rest of the song. Maybe the dog would bark and join in the recording.

Most people seem to use blank tapes to make dance or party tapes. Why does this song go after that song and not the other song? That topic is for a different book than this one.

Fast forward to 1985. *Op* magazine (the Lost Music Network's clearinghouse of independently produced music) had completed its A-Z run. I got on board during the O issue as a humble proofreader. They asked me what I wanted my title to be (proofreader was not an option at that time, but assistant to the publisher seemed perfect). I said, 'Assistant Publisher', knowing there was no publisher.

JERRY KRANITZ

So in 1985 *Op* was over and I had a nice pile of cassette reviews that I had written for the *Castanets* column by Graham Ingels, as well as some other magazines (*Transnational Perspectives, Ear, B-Side, Option, Sound Choice*, these are pretty much all long out of business now except for *Transnational Perspectives*) climaxing for me with *The Whole Earth Review* 'Signal' issue (1988).

Anyway, back to my story, a visitor from Boston suggested that I use that pile of cassette reviews to make a book, maybe write a little essay of some kind to go with the reviews, the thousands of pages of reviews, all lost now. All lost, except for a few I found in some old boxes the other day. Because I was reading H.P. Lovecraft at the time, the name for this new project was easily named *The Cassette Mythos*.

Cassette Mythos Cassette Conspiracy (1987)

Citizens of the Cassette Conspiracy: Conspiracies work so much better when there are more conspirators. I tried everything I could think of and did my best to implicate others and get them to think of stuff to write about audio cassettes, or just to keep making more strange audio cassettes because they are not so good at writing. The common communications model of the day was a thing of paper called a zine, derived from the word magazine, or so one rumor has it. A zine is a piece of paper with a unique and usually very personal idea of what a magazine might be if you were making your own and had complete control of the entire process. This was before desktop publishing using the newest home computers so now it seems strange and pointlessly difficult and complicated, and of course expensive. You can skip paper and have lots of color.

Rich Jensen suggested we try sending around some kind of an interview for all the conspirators, so we set about thinking up questions. We would mail those questions to the co-conspirators at large. They would write back with answers to the questions. We would put that into the next mailing. Or so we thought. That was the extent of the plan.

What actually happened was that we got tapes in the mail with co-conspirators sending sounds in response. How is that going on paper? Do I have to transpose the whole thing? Oh, wait, we can make new tapes and skip the paper, or better yet somehow combine it with the paper for even more special effects. It became a whole new thing. From then on we were sending tapes to each other with very little writing. Other people have already tried doing this so it's not really a new idea. There is nothing new, just new combinations of things, which become the new thing.

How does the conspiracy get started? Nobody knows for sure. What I did was to continuously send out updated address lists to everyone I knew in the conspiracy. The spies all learn from each other. I had *Op* magazine to learn from. Remember, this was when there was no email, think of that! Nobody had any idea there would ever be such a thing as email. Up until then, for all time, they had nothing like email and still life went on. Then it got even better. Email is instantaneous, portable and anonymous.

Usually, the tapes coming in would be from a physical address, possibly a post office box. The packages were from musical bands or just groupings of insane people who would make cassette recordings and just send them to strategic and specific other groups of similarly insane people or bands. Some of them had a press kit. Thus floweth the conspiracy.

Enthusiasm is compelling. Zines still show up at certain small but groovy record stores and at concerts or other performance events. Maybe you can find zines at a coffee shop, a newspaper stand, or at a conference or festival. That is where these paper zines would be distributed or just left for discovery.

I had a beat up old reel-to-reel tape recorder. It used 1/4-inch tape, stereo. I had two microphones and corresponding input jacks L-R. Sometimes we would make a cassette master and use that for tape-to-tape sound transfers. We tried different ways, one tape player with one or a chain of cassette recorders, or directly from the reel-to-reel deck to the cassette recorder.

The next level for the conspiracy was finding a place that sells bulk quantities of audio tape. We had a nifty place nearby that would sell large boxes of tape, any kind you want, by the hundreds for a much lower price than most stores offered. And if you drive over there yourself there is no shipping cost. These blank cassettes come with stickers, also blank of course. I found that you can run some formats of blank stickers through some copy machines. We could make those tapes look really interesting. Usually, it was just a black sharpie on the sticker.

Between 1985 and 1990 when I had to get a real job, the Cassette Conspiracy grew to maybe about 200 continuously active members, and it cost too much because I had no clue about making it pay for itself. So, I walked away from it and never looked back. It was easy when I was swapping mail with about 20 or so audio cassette enthusiasts. Here is your tape, now send me one of yours please. Beyond that, managing such a project requires money exchanges.

What is music and what is something else? Music might be what you hear when conventional instruments are played in traditional forms. Who are these contributing musicians? Musical genres mean more to the record stores than to typical home musicians. It's music and these are words.

Consistently the most innovative new forms defy genres or styles or trending. Our people were anyone who wanted to swap tapes. They might play a fiddle or they might play in hip-hop orchestras. There is nothing in our mission or creed about any specific politics or actual advertising. It was just us kids playing with correspondence.

It sure takes a long time to listen to each tape. Right now, I look back and know that I could never muster that kind of passion, listening to tapes day and night, backgrounds to do the dishes (how many dishes can you wash in 90 minutes?), or just free-associating while the tape played on. Each tape I reviewed got listened to a minimum of three or maybe four times. The first time is always the best.

You do not know what is going to happen when you first press Play. When writing reviews, I would play some parts over and over again while I was writing, just to find the right words. I would try to describe the sound, which is impossible really, marks on paper to describe something invisible? I would listen to the most interesting song titles, or band members, or musical instrumentation, or just make stuff up based on what I was hearing, sort of a whimsy of impressions. Sometimes I was able to write more than one review for a recording. I would listen to a recording one day and it would make me think of one thing and feel a certain way, and maybe I was influenced after that by something else that happened so that another day the same recording might make me think of another thing and feel a different way. Both valid in my opinion.

Most of the recordings were of baby musicians flailing away. Some were really sophisticated. Mostly the tapes were classic rock monsters, making a huge noise in the basement. We accepted and asked for the strangest ones. That was our edge. There are no limits. We received rock operas, poets in the rain, guitars in the bathroom (they insist that the tile walls have the best acoustics for recording), band practices, studio masterpieces, scratch tapes, poetic or theatrical performances, artist sketches used for composition purposes, as well as recordings of actual performances.

JERRY KRANITZ

CLEM, the *Contact List of Electronic Music*, attracted lots of electronica interests. Folk singers had *Sing Out* with lyrics and charts and concert schedules. Punk rockers had *Maximum Rocknroll*. *Factsheet Five* was the best inventory of zines ever. If a tree falls in the woods and nobody hears it, what sound does it make? Does a zine exist without an audient (audience/participant)?

Thus, was born the *Audio Alchemy Digest*. ADD turned out to be already copyrighted as an acronym in the music business, so I kept looking for the best names for the project. The Wildear. Riding the wildear. I still like *Audio Alchemy Digest* the best. Using the only available equipment at the time I made what I intended to be a bunch of audio zines, taking bits of tapes I had gotten recently and blended them into my own audio program. Stuff I liked and wanted you to hear. I wanted the whole world to hear it. It turned out to be just a few other cranks who were actually able to hear it anyway.

So, there I was making little tape shows based on bits I stole from the cassettes I was getting. I called it *A Feast of Hearing* and built it as a 29-minute radio show containing music samples, contact information and some electronic spicey bits, thanks to Stuart Hallerman. Then came the *Cassette Mythos Deathpack*, three 90-minute tapes with a huge poster. I made the cassette stickers with a rubber stamp pad. It was a smeary mess. It fit carefully folded into a manilla envelope. They all went around by way of the mail. Mail art. When you say mail art out loud, it sounds like 'male art'.

From that there came a special edition of the *Deathpack*. There were going to be 12 commissioned in advance by 12 intrepid pre-purchasers. I think I ended up making about 20 in all. I did all this in 1985. The name *Deathpack* is intended to reach the practitioners of a certain style of music or a certain bold rock and roll approach to life. The name worked very well at the time and still does. We knew what it all really meant (celebrating adolescent passion) and those that were cosmically meant to find it did so. It was rad. Nobody got hurt. Well, certainly nobody died in making or distributing the *Deathpack*. It was for fun. If the name

Deathpack bugs you then probably lots of other things bug you too. Get over it. It's our art form, all others keep out.

One guy made me some special cedar boxes. I worked at a place that threw away photographic paper boxes when empty so I got a supply of nice big sturdy cardboard boxes with lids. A really awesome logo came from this amazing person in California named Suz Dycus. I made a stencil of that logo and later some t-shirts and ultimately it became the cover of the *Cassette Mythos* book.

Anyway, back to the special edition of the *Deathpack*. I painted it all black, applied the stencil using white spray paint, and put them all together with special gee-gaws and cards from games, playing pieces for an unidentified board game, Cracker Jack type prizes, pretty pebbles and brass bullet shells, and spent cartridges. There was a guy who made cards like baseball cards of local bands, with band photo on one side and band stats on the other. I put in some random one-of-a-kind photographs. We put anything and everything that would fit into the 20 boxes. Mariko painted the interiors of the cedar boxes, one of a kind.

At the last minute we added actual live cedar green cuttings. Bad idea. Those live cedar cuttings sure do smell great that first few days or so. The sap that comes from cedar cuttings kept getting all over the place, followed some dry months later by the crumbling organic matter itself, as that invariably falls into those three audio cassette tapes and becomes lost somewhere in the inside of whatever tape player you have, and ultimately jammed into all sorts of interesting places.

We tried a video bicycle tour. Meaning, I bought a video cassette, borrowed a home video recorder, and made a 5-minute thing. I then mailed it to the next person on the pre-arranged list. The list of co-conspirators who agreed in advance to accept the video, to record something for 5 or 10 minutes, and then pay the postage for sending it on to the next person on the list. I set up and sent out a bunch of such tapes, and one came back! I want to share it with everyone, maybe find some new conspirators. Things are getting modern, with new technology and new ways of using old technology.

IRONY. We put a lot of effort in getting the contact information (mailing addresses) right. Most of the folks who sent me tapes were in rock bands (one or more people usually using goofy names). Their mailing addresses are only good for as short as a few hours. Sometimes it was good for a whole academic term. Some just might still be in the same place now, over 30 years later. Don't count on it. I suspect that most really do not want their children to find out what they were doing in the 1980s. None of the carefully cultivated artist contact information is any good now, for the most part. Back then that was the only reason to participate in the conspiracy, to swap tapes or otherwise acquire them, directly from other conspirators. If you got the zine on Friday night and you sent your own stuff to some addresses found in the zine by Monday, you might just hear back in a week or two. Now you upload to post the recording and maybe ten minutes later start getting responses.

That mail business was a big thing that is most different, comparing the tools of the 1980s to the age of the internet. You little bastards are all spoiled and you don't even know it. It took us lots of time to make the recording, then to dress it up somehow, then to make a pile of them, one at a time, then you put it in the mail and it could be a few days or it could be Never Heard From Again and you have lost your investment totally. Your tape and life blood went out to a strange address and maybe it got returned or more often got lost or thrown away, or maybe the artists are working away on a response to you but it's not done yet. Or maybe they are just laughing too hard.

If you were to ask to join the conspiracy, I might know what to say. Go for it. Show us your new visions.

THE QUESTIONS

1. HOWDY: What is your earliest memory of using cassettes? What do you do with them now? How did you get started?

2. BEST: What are some of the best ideas that you have heard for using

cassettes? Don't limit yourself to music, or even commercially available material.

3. WORST: What are, if any, the worst ideas that you have heard for using cassettes?

4. OWNERSHIP: Do you have any comments about legalities regarding home taping (copyrights, taping records, distributing cassettes, taping other people's tapes)?

5. DISTRIBUTION: How do you get your cassettes around? Do you trade? Do you have distributors? Do you send them to magazines or people that you like?

6. WHAT THE HELL IS A NETWORK: What does the term 'networking' mean in the context of our subject matter (audio cassette art exchanges)?

7. BEST AGAIN: Who has produced outstanding cassette creations and utilizations? What did they do?

8. INTERNATIONAL: Do you have any observations about the uses of cassettes in different parts of the world: Africa, Japan, South America, Europe, Australia, etc. (marketing techniques, amateur/home activity, etc.)?

9. GEAR: Do you have any comments about the technology surrounding cassettes? Do you use Dolby?

10. MAKE MONEY: How can people make money with cassettes (for example, some bands sell their tapes at shows, etc.) Do you? How much do you charge? Does it work?

11. YOU: Do you have any other comments that you would like to make regarding the general topics we have discussed? What have we missed? Do

JERRY KRANITZ

you have any tips to share? What do you do with cassettes?

Introduction

What is this book about?

The internet is a royal banquet of options for music fans. If I want to discover new music, I simply go to Google, type in keywords or a band name and the results will keep me busy for hours. When I started researching this book in 2007 my website of choice was Myspace. Each page typically included information about a band or artist, including music samples. Myspace has long since faded and as of 2025 I regularly visit Bandcamp, though there are numerous other options that I make little attempt to keep up with. Regardless of individual preference, the internet offers instant search results and immediate gratification.

But what if you were a music fan in the pre-internet age? Someone with eclectic tastes, wondering what alternatives there might be to the albums the major record companies were releasing? Well, you had to be willing to roll up your sleeves and break a sweat. Among the necessary resources were independent or used record stores in your town, college radio with freeform formats, or awareness of some obscure mail order source.

Growing up in the 1970s, I spent countless solitary hours listening to records and went to nearly every concert that came to town. I would spend entire weekend afternoons crate digging in used record stores, seeking out new music and hoping to find previously unknown treasures.

Even the commercial record stores were goldmines. Throughout the 1970s it was possible to find adventurous music released by the major record companies. Until punk and new wave exploded in the latter half of the decade, myriad flavors of progressive and hard rock were my sources of inspiration. The import sections, though more expensive, included a diversity of esoteric music from Europe, unlike anything I could dream of hearing on the radio.

And then came punk and its first cousin new wave. Increasing numbers of albums by smaller labels began to appear in record stores. These labels were independent (though often subsidiaries of the major record companies) and had secured sufficient distribution to ensure relatively easy availability of their records.

With the passage of the 1970s into the 1980s, the pioneering progressive musicians sought more commercial opportunities, hard rock became hair metal, electro-pop dispensed with the guitars, and MTV taught us that if it looked good it tasted good.

On the surface it seemed like popular music was hurtling toward a vacuous abyss. Yet a cauldron of activity was bubbling underneath. Musicians around the world were creating exciting music in the electronic, rock, jazz, punk, industrial, noise and experimental/avant-garde realms. This music was being released by small labels tapping into distribution networks that functioned independently of those controlled by the major record companies.

Punk is far more than the Sex Pistols, Ramones and guitar/bass/drums screaming hardcore. Punk is an ethic: Do-it-Yourself, or DIY. In the mid-1970s punk era, cassette tape recorders were increasingly adopted by the public to make home recordings of music and audio art. Adopted by musicians and non-musicians alike, home taping on cassettes revved its engines in the late 1970s and slammed into overdrive in the 1980s.

People have been forming bands since the dawn of rock 'n' roll. But the cassette recorder, along with affordable electronic equipment and sheer creative muscle flexing, was a key player in the democratization of audio recording. Cassettes were cheap and portable. If you didn't like what you heard, you could record over them.

And if you could get your work reviewed, included on a compilation tape, or played on the radio, then you had publicity.

For many musicians and audio artists the motivation was more about creation than sales figures, and the variety of music and sounds produced was stunning. If you didn't care about selling millions of albums, scoffed at the idea of fame and fortune, and wanted to create for the sake of exploring the possibilities and making the music and sounds you were passionate about, then the sky was the limit with cassettes. Adding to the excitement was a global community of fellow travelers, many wanting to communicate with you, trade tapes of each other's recordings, and even collaborate. For many, sales were not even part of the equation.

How did they do this? Why did the cassette recorder inspire so much creativity? How did these 'hometapers' find each other and how did they communicate and collaborate? And what kinds of recordings did they create? That's what this book is about. Through the old-fashioned postal service and small press publications, these audio artists - some called them audio 'anarchists' - built a loose network of communication that covered the US, UK, Europe, Australia, Japan and other countries.

Since science fiction fans began communicating through fanzines in the 1930s, people with shared interests have always managed to find each other. Compared with the relative ease of internet publishing, the effort it took to record and distribute one's own music and communicate with others about it was significant. You had to type or write letters by hand, mail them, and wait for them to reach their destination. And then you hoped for and WAITED for a response.

The small press publications commonly included contact information. Consequently, if an audio artist or music fan was intrigued by a review they would, in many cases, be communicating directly with the artist. If a cassette was purchased the money went directly to the artist. No managers, no lawyers, no middlemen. Even when a label was involved, it was usually the only layer between the artist and consumer. But you had to be aware of and have access to these publications, and effort was required to write letters and place mail orders.

Audio artist Hal McGee had a radio show on WMNF in Tampa, Florida where he played hometaper cassettes. When listeners called and asked at what record store they could buy the tapes, records and CDs played on the show, McGee had to explain the need to write the artist or indie label and order it (McGee, 1991, p. 5). This takes time and effort! On the internet, the search engine reigns supreme, the average search takes seconds, and placing orders or downloading can be accomplished in a few clicks.

This is the story of an important but overlooked component of post-punk and DIY music history - the first wave of true audio artist independence. This is also a neglected chapter in the ongoing history of 20th century independent arts movements, with roots in Dada, Fluxus and mail art. It is about the creative spirit and the individuals who, often unintentionally, challenged the status quo, simply in the name of following their muse. A universe of creative work was produced by homemade musicians around the world, and many were on the cutting edge of the audio avant-garde.

There is also an important social element to this story. This book is just as much about 'networking' as it is about cassettes and the recordings they facilitated. For many it was about more than creating their own work and making it available. It was about seeking connections with like-minded individuals in the same spirit as seeking fellow travelers to share one's passions with when joining a topic specific internet discussion group.

What is 'Cassette Culture'?

Cassette Culture can have different meanings, depending on the network and/or use of cassette tapes. By surveying the available literature, we can define these varied networks and uses of cassettes, identify common characteristics, and more clearly articulate the hometaper network that is at the heart of this book.

An early book was Peter Manuel's 1993 *Cassette Culture: Popular Music and Technology in North India*. Manuel's goal was to study the impact of cassette technology on popular music in North India and survey several genres of music:

"The low expense of cassette consumption renders the medium accessible to rural and lower-income groups. At the same time, the lower costs of production enable small-scale producers to emerge around the world, recording and marketing music aimed at specialized, local, grassroots audiences rather than at a homogenous mass market. The net result is a remarkable decentralization, democratization, and dispersal of the music industry at the expense of multinational and national oligopolies" (Manuel, 1993, p. xiv).

Manuel, to an extent, describes exactly what the hometaper network of this book is about. However, while essential reading for anyone studying the democratizing role of the cassette recorder, the Manuel work is a case study limited to the specific experience of North India and the music and culture of that country, which did not participate in the cassette culture that is the subject of this book.

Similarly, Andrew Simon's 2022 book *Media Of The Masses: Cassette Culture in Modern Egypt*, details the social, political, economic, and cultural impact of cassettes as their use became widespread in that country. In an environment of state-controlled media, Simon explains how "cassette technology and its users would later democratize sound, subvert state-controlled Egyptian radio, and decentralize other 'big media' dominated by local gatekeepers" (Simon, 2022, p. 11).

Simon identifies components of Egyptian cassette culture that share commonalities with yet sharply contrast with the post-punk hometaper network. As elsewhere in the world, the use of cassettes exploded in Egypt because their low-cost and portability empowered anyone to be an artist. Distribution occurred in thousands of kiosks and stores throughout Egypt. In addition to introducing 'unapproved' artists and styles of music, cassettes were valued for their ability to spread Islamic sermons, making them "vessels for militant messages by scrutinizing the technology's part in the fashioning of moral sensibilities" (ibid, p. 6).

A critical aspect of Egyptian cassette culture Simon details is broad concern among state officials, including censors and members of the taste culture over Egyptian cultural production and who has the right to create it. The parallels with western record company control over production and distribution and the challenges cassettes posed are fascinating. But the motivations differed:

"From the perspective of many local observers, audiotapes empowered anyone to become an artist, resulting in a diffusion of suspect voices that degraded the ears, the morals, and the taste of Egyptians. The individuals popularized by cassettes, critics maintained, did not deserve to be heard" (ibid, p. 80).

Simon, like Manuel, describes a scenario with features similar to the post-punk hometaper network, though the Egyptian artists and producers did not participate in the global cassette culture that is the subject of this book.

Closer to our theme is the 2012 book *Unofficial Release: Self-Released and Handmade Audio in Post-Industrial Society* by Thomas Bey William Bailey. The book's focus is networked/participatory/at-a-distance experimental audio networks, including audio and mail artists. Though the book's timeline includes the internet era, Bailey interviewed several artists with roots in the 1980s hometaper and mail art networks. These interviews form the basis of several chapters, focusing on the subjects' activities and network experiences, their motivations, and in some cases the conditions of doing so in their respective countries. Bailey also surveys the technologies that have, over the years, and to varying degrees, enabled audio artists. Though broad in its coverage, the book is a valuable resource for its insights into hometaper history from a contemporary perspective.

Three recent books focus exclusively on cassettes, partly covering the post-punk hometaper network, but approaching the cassette from various angles and enriching the literature since the original 2020 publication of this book.

Marc Masters' 2023 book *High Bias: The Distorted History of the Cassette Tape* covers a range of cassette use. Masters provides a history of the medium. He addresses anti-piracy efforts as embodied in the major record companies' 'Home Taping Is Killing Music' campaign and ensuing legislative attempts. Chapters are devoted to the network of live concert ('bootleg') traders, and international cassette 'hunters' who travel the globe seeking unique tapes in such places as Syria, Cambodia, Vietnam, Thailand and Ghana.

Mixtapes are collections of previously recorded music copied to cassette, rather than cassette albums of original work. Masters identifies two distinct mixtape subcultures:

One is DJs dubbing mixes of their club performances to sell and their role in the rise of hip-hop. It's a fascinating story and the tapes could be lucrative for their assemblers. Masters describes how wealthy customers, "sometimes drug dealers or 'hustlers' – would pay DJs to 'shout out' their name during sets, then buy a tape from them and blast it around town. It was an easy way to boast that not only did you have the hottest mixtapes but you were also tight with the DJs themselves" (Masters, 2023, p. 35).

The second details collections of existing music that were more than mere compilations. In 2004, Thurston Moore of the band Sonic Youth published a book titled *Mix Tape: The Art of Cassette Culture*. The book is a collection of mixtapes submitted to Moore by their owners and the personal stories behind them. Masters provides a detailed analysis of this use of cassettes to create personally curated collections of songs, describing how people "selected and arranged sounds for friends as gifts, for crushes as courtship, for fellow music fanatics in impassioned exchanges of art and information that spurred learning and discovery" (ibid, p. 134).

Masters also devotes a chapter to the international network of hometapers who recorded original works of music and audio art. He concludes his survey by profiling contemporary cassette labels.

'Sharing' is the key to Rob Drew's 2024 book *Unspooled: How the Cassette Made Music Sharable*. Drew concentrates on "independent rock music scenes, wherein the cassette was adopted both as a format of first release and a token of interpersonal exchange" (Drew, 2024, p. 8).

Taking pre-2000 indie rock as his focus, Drew identifies common characteristics and distinctions between the 1980s hometaper network and the indie rockers of his study: "What I tried to argue was that there were continuities between what became known as the cassette underground (itself a broad term for a lot of different things) and the uses that indie rock musicians/scene makers like Calvin Johnson, Bruce

Pavitt and a lot of others put the cassette to. Those musicians liked the accessibility of the cassette, but they also had larger ambitions and ultimately didn't want to be tied to cassette releases. Mostly these were working bands, acts that played bars or played out in clubs, things like that. And they had a certain amount of ambition, maybe to get a record contract. So, the cassette was a holdover format on the way to success for them" (personal communication, 2025).

The indie rockers differed from the hometapers in their priorities and motivations. Yet, as Drew further points out: "But those musicians also came to see symbolic value in the cassette, as it was a format that connected them to the underground and to values of creative independence, community and gifting that they admired" (ibid).

While the post-punk hometapers prioritized the crafting of their recordings and interacting with other hometapers, the indie rockers used cassettes as a launching pad to wider recognition, while functioning as genuinely grassroots DIY operations.

Dovetailing with indie rock, Drew discusses mixtapes, which he sees as having its roots in the indie world. Curating mixtapes could be done for both sharing of musical tastes and for romance: "Those two metaphors, on the one hand, is this kind of curated thing where you're showing off your tastes. Not necessarily these are the best songs, but these are the songs I love and I'm wagering you're the kind of person who would love these songs too. And then on the other hand, wooing somebody, which is in some ways an entirely different function." (ibid).

Benjamin Duester's 2025 book *Tomorrow on Cassette: Tape Jams in the New Media Age* studies cassette tape use from a twenty-first century, post-millennial perspective. At the heart of his study is a reaction to what Duester saw as the press hailing a cassette 'revival', having dismissed cassettes as obsolete when in fact they had never gone away.

Duester explains the ongoing use of cassettes in various scenes and subcultures (e.g., noise artists) but also provides granular examples like elderly consumers reluctant to adopt CDs or mp3s. Critically, though Duester argues against the revival of a perceived obsolete format, he acknowledges a resurgence of cassette tape use.

Duester argues that while cassettes are used across a broad age range, a younger generation has discovered the physical release, providing people with a personal connection to a band, label or scene, even though they may stream or download the music to listen. As Duester says: "Even if an album has already been available in digital form for a while, a physical release on cassette functions as a means of maintaining cultural integrity in DIY music scenes" (Duster, 2025, p. 93).

Even though the owner may not play the cassette, there is a sense of satisfaction via supporting the artist or label or connection felt to a particular scene. Duester provides the interesting example of "entire Facebook groups such as Underground Metal on Tape/Cassette dedicated to sharing photos of tapes, whether they be new releases or rarities from members' collections" (ibid, p. 95).

Significantly, these tapes are largely manufactured, and Duester contrasts this with the post-punk era hometapers. Speaking of tape manufacturers like National Audio Company, Duester notes: "As these companies also offer printing services for cassette shells and j-cards, tape releases in the 2010s exhibit a professional aesthetic that directly contrasts with the homemade coarseness of 1980s cassette culture" (ibid, p. 25-26).

When this book was first published in 2020, the only previous book to have targeted the global hometaper cassette culture network remained *Cassette Mythos*, compiled and edited by Robin James. James' experience writing cassette reviews for *Op* magazine inspired him to broaden his activities. He circulated a list of interview questions to hometapers, published *The Audio Alchemy Digest* and produced accompanying compilation tapes. The resulting book was a collection of essays by participants in the network detailing how to get involved in the cassette scene, how to make one's own cassettes, case studies, personal reflections and strategies. Though published in 1992, the essays had been written in the mid-late 1980s, precisely when the scene was in full bloom.

JERRY KRANITZ

With nearly four decades of retrospection, the time is ripe for a historical-analytical examination of this era in DIY music history. Because of the internet, more people than ever are interested in independent music, even if they have not made a deliberate effort to seek an alternative. The impact of the internet is nothing less than the upheaval of the established music industry business model. Where is it going? I don't know and that question is outside the scope of this book. But I do believe it does make now the perfect time to tell this pivotal yet less than comprehensively documented chapter in the larger post-punk and 20th century independent arts movement stories.

Despite the *Pre-Internet Age* of the title, this book is, ultimately, very much about the internet. There is a direct lineage from cassette tapes, to CDRs and mp3s. All have empowered the individual. A 1983 editorial by *Op* magazine publisher John Foster proved to be prophetic. Talking about how *Op* reviews are just a starting point for investigation he says, "Unfortunately, until the advent of *dial-a-song* on your home computer hookup, there just aren't that many ways to find out what you're missing" (Foster, 1983, p. 52). Prophecy indeed...

Much of the research for this book was conducted using primary resources. Small press publications and 'zines' published in the 1980s and early 1990s were goldmines of information, as were personal interviews with participants in the cassette culture of that era. Some of the participants also maintain internet web and blog sites on which they have documented their contributions to, and experiences in the hometaper network. Many have digitized their recordings and made them available for download on the internet.

Readers schooled in this topic should not expect an index of artists and labels. Several artists are profiled, but the intent is to be representative rather than comprehensive. The sheer number of people who released home recorded cassettes makes indexing a task I shudder at the thought of undertaking. My goal is to document the existence of hometaper cassette culture and its place in the larger stories of punk, networking and independent arts movements.

Though the hometaper cassette culture lasted well into the 1990s, the era I cover extends through the early 1990s, when a period of technological and associated cultural transition began. This was the period when the public began to use online services and the internet, and when CDRs and digital sound files came into use. Though it took some years for these technologies to become widespread, I made the choice to conclude before this transition commenced. I consider that to be a new era and, consequently, a new chapter in the story.

Part I:

The Cassette Recorder:
YOU Too Can Be An Audio Artist!

Chapter 1

Record Companies

I was a child of the 1970s and an insatiable music fan. Rock music locked me firmly in its grip at a young age. I spent countless hours shut away in my bedroom listening to records and gazing at the album covers, fully absorbed in the sounds pouring from the speakers. And while multiple interests have come and gone over the years, my passion for music has never waned.

My love for music has endured because I've always hungered for something new. American hard rock was exciting. But I soon learned about bands from England and Europe and sought those out. Eventually the hard rock styles became less satisfying, and my quest led to progressive rock. These bands drew their inspiration from classical and other influences to produce what seemed like an endless banquet of variation. This, in turn, led to explorations into jazz and experimental music and, later, punk and new wave.

In the 1970s I obtained nearly all this music in commercial record stores, and most of it was released by the major record companies or their subsidiaries. My favorite record stores had three general sections: new releases, imports, and cut-outs. The cut-outs were inexpensive gems, while the imports were more costly but yielded obscure treasures from overseas. I still possess a tattered 1976 JEM import catalog that the owner of a small record store had given me, and which served as my bible for British and European bands.

As the 1970s progressed, a convergence of developments generated whirlwinds of change. Popular music experienced some innovations, but also some disappointments. Many are still scratching their heads over disco, progressive rock morphed into bland arena rock, and punk and new wave arrived, briefly injecting new life into a rock history that seemed to be losing its creative edge.

After the initial punk explosion, popular music seemed to become increasingly formulaic. With the arrival of MTV in the early 1980s, visuals came to dominate and drive music's direction. Following trends in popular music through the decades, music made available by the major record companies reveals a downward trajectory toward designer brand styles, uncontaminated by innovation, excitement or risk.

One wonders if the major record companies ever really supported creativity and innovation. Record companies are revenue generating entities, and the ever-increasing pressure to maximize profits dictates their decision making.

Virgin Records is an example of a record company fully focused on maximizing profits which, nonetheless, provided a platform for some of the most innovative and experimental bands of the 1970s. Virgin's roster included, among others, Henry Cow, Faust, Tangerine Dream and Gong, artists on the cutting edge of developments in rock music. And while Virgin began life as an independent record company, they secured sufficiently wide distribution that their releases were readily available in commercial record stores. In a 1981 interview, former Henry Cow guitarist Fred Frith shared revealing thoughts about his experience with Virgin:

"Virgin never had any idea as a company other than to make money. They were quite a straightforward business concern. They wanted to make a profit. It's just that initially, at the very beginning, there was a certain naïve and idealistic idea that they could make this money that they wanted to make out of music they really liked. But because they had no experience they were fairly inept and it took them a long time to get their operation going. The idealism of the first year was very rapidly evaporated. Since then the company has done a number of 180 degree turns. I think they were also partially, shall we say diverted, by the fact that Tubular Bells sold so many copies. Tubular Bells more or less kept the company afloat for the first three or four years of its existence" (Fisk, 1981, p. 10).

Frith goes on to explain how Virgin started moving into whatever genres appeared to be making money. Reggae, for example: "I remember a time when Richard Branson flew to Jamaica and was signing anybody who was prepared to put pen to paper" (ibid). Virgin is also enshrined in punk history for its role in the release of The Sex Pistols *Never Mind The Bollocks* album.

An important example for the cassette culture story is Rough Trade, whose attempted innovations in distribution will be examined later. In his history of Rough Trade, Neil Taylor describes the company as "an ethically minded, idealistic, radical record business that set out to redefine the market on its own terms – and did so spectacularly successfully – only to be knocked back by a combination of overly rapid growth and naïve business management, to then once more rise up again in an altered form and have even more success than first time around" (Taylor, 2010, p. xi).

Founded in 1976 by Geoff Travis, Rough Trade began as a shop on Kensington Park Road in West London, eventually becoming a record label and distributor. Structured on a cooperative basis, business practices were less than conventional. One former employee reported that all business was conducted for a time on a cash basis.

From big name bands like the Smiths, to lesser known but influential artists like Swell Maps and Cabaret Voltaire, Rough Trade was all over the punk and pop stylistic map. Speaking from a 1981 perspective, Fred Frith compares Rough Trade to 1973 or '74 era Virgin: "Rough Trade, I think, has a much more political idea of what it is doing, although this has to be modified to a certain extent depending on the actual financing. I think Rough Trade has a much clearer idea of being separate from the business and not having a particular profit motive in the operation" (Fisk, 1981, p. 10).

Frith's comment speaks to the informality and idealism with which Rough Trade conducted business, and many bands in the punk era benefited from the association. Initially run as a collective with equal pay for all employees, the company was very much a product of the DIY punk era. Geoff Travis viewed the company's lean and informal structure as a strength, in opposition to the crushing bureaucracy and overhead of the major labels.

The major record companies undoubtedly have music lovers in their employ. Many bands have been signed because they were championed by an enthusiastic A&R (Artists & Repertoire) representative who believed in them. But the larger problem for artists who wish to have their work heard, and consumers who buy music, is the control that record companies have over the means of recording production and distribution.

Because of this control, record companies can dictate who is worthy of signing and what styles of music will be offered to the public. The record companies are positioned to feed on an artist's eagerness for success, be it a simple desire for their music to be heard or a full-blown hunger for fame and fortune. This provides a powerful incentive for bands to play what is marketable, resulting in music that is compromised because it's not what is in the artist's heart. Creativity is sacrificed, and ultimately becomes dishonest, when the hunger for success results in conformity. And, for the record buying public, the choices are limited because they're only aware of what is available in the record stores and broadcast on radio and television.

In his study of trends in popular music and technology in North India, Peter Manuel observes what can easily be applied to the music industry in the West: "Before the advent of recording, a singer could no more be separated from his song than could a dancer from his dance. Recording technology effected such an alienation, presenting a fixed rendition of a performance as a tangible, salable entity. Acquiring commodity status, the recording takes on a social life of its own, subject to new dimensions of economics relating to commercial mass-market pressures and incentives" (Manuel, 1993, p. 7).

Regardless of whether one subscribes to Manuel's neo-Marxist analysis, the essential point is that the 'music-industrial complex' commodifies the music that artists create, leaving the public dependent on the choices they make available. This is further complicated by the limitations the media impose as they choose which bands to spotlight.

In addition to its impact on the music that is created, there are numerous pitfalls for artists signed with a record company. Stories abound of artists losing the rights to their music. Many have sold millions of records and made no money from the sales. In his study of the music business, journalist Hank Bordowitz charts a hierarchy representing the typical record company: The artist at the top and 20 entities between him/her and the consumer, including lawyers, managers, promotion, distribution, radio, video, and so on. Bordowitz states that the average major record label needs to sell between 250,000 and 500,000 copies to break even (Bordowitz, 2007, p. 67).

Even if these numbers aren't completely accurate, they are good indicators of the costs involved in producing and promoting a record, and the considerable sales required before any profits for the record company or royalties for the artist are realized. The numbers are less of a surprise when adding in the layers of bureaucracy and bloated costs that often go into making a record. It wasn't uncommon for bands like Pink Floyd and the Rolling Stones to spend months on expensive studio time recording albums. This doesn't count the money subsequently spent on promotion, costs that skyrocketed in the video age.

By the early 1980s there were a large number and variety of independent record labels. These independents, or 'indies', functioned at a more grassroots level, operating with less overhead and bureaucracy then the majors.

In contrast to the major record companies, Bordowitz notes that the average break-even range for an indie is sales in the 10,000-25,000 range (ibid, p. 68). While considerably more reasonable than the requirements of a major label, these are still staggering numbers. Even at the low end, having to sell 10,000 albums before any profit can be made is by no means trivial.

Furthermore, artists signed to an indie label were not necessarily protected from the hazards of dealing with a major record company. Barriers to entry remained. And getting paid could still be a problem.

A 1991 issue of *Electronic Cottage International Magazine* includes an interview with the founder of the Coalition for Independent Artists, formed by musicians on indie labels selling 1000-5000 copies and not being paid royalties due by the labels. The coalition published a survey, the intent being to document problems musicians were having with their record companies, and tabulating the responses, organized by record company. Ultimately the hope was to have the coalition take action against record companies on behalf of the artists (Kastov, 1991, p. 14-15).

Whether the coalition represented multiple artists or was a mechanism for action on its founder's behalf is unclear. But countless artists have been taken advantage of or simply swept up in the maelstrom of the music industry, and this has occurred even in the so-called indie world. Some of the artists impacted by their brushes with the 'big time' came out of the experience with a life-long commitment to DIY independence.

Jazz iconoclast Sun Ra was a pioneer of complete, if haphazard, pre-punk self-sufficiency. In his biography of Sun Ra, John F. Szwed explains how having registered as a record company with the Musicians Union in 1956, Ra's El Saturn Research purchased no advertising, gave out no promotional copies for review, and had no distribution channels except mail order, hand delivery to record shops, and sales from the bandstand after performances (Szwed, 1997, p. 170).

Ra's experience provides a crystal ball glimpse into what many punk bands would undertake with their own records and tapes: "By handprinting the covers, they could avoid printing costs altogether. Often the covers carried only a simple title, or only the location of the recording in black ink; but at times they became more elaborate, with multicolored grids, rainbows, or astral scenes; or there might be photos of Sun Ra pasted on, hand-tinted, the whole cover laminated with a piece of textured plastic shower curtain. Sometimes every cover of a single record was different (ibid, p. 201).

Szwed's account of Ra's distribution methods is remarkable. Being wary of conventional record business practices, "everything was done by hand, face to face, cash on the barrelhead, even if it meant flying to upstate New York or even Utrecht or

Amsterdam to trade records for American dollars, on the tarmac if possible, and catching the return flight home. It could mean loading five or six boxes of records onto tiny commuter flights where the ticket seller might also be the baggage handler; or talking their way through customs on a bus driving from West Germany through East Germany to get to Berlin; or more often than not, flying to Europe with records in one box, covers in another, labels in a third, and meeting purchasers in hotel lobbies after staying up all night assembling the records and hand-lettering the labels and covers (ibid, p. 273).

Countless musicians can relate to the rigors of the rock 'n roll life and the requirement to pay one's dues. But paying dues carries a high price in terms of the sacrifices made, the obstacles hurled in the artist's path, and the regrettable lack of reward, all for the opportunity to gain an audience the only way the aspiring musician knows how.

So, if record companies, even the independents can't be relied on, what is an artist to do? A turning point was on the horizon in the late 1970s. The birth of punk and growing numbers of indie labels took place concurrently with declining record company support for genuine alternatives. And for the artist whose goal was, quite simply, to 'create', opportunities of seismic proportions were available.

Chapter 2

The Cassette Recorder: Encouraging Creativity and the Impetus to ACT

Thomas Edison could not have predicted what he was setting in motion when in 1877 he made the first recording of a human voice on the first tinfoil cylinder phonograph. 'Mary Had A Little Lamb' may not have been the most imaginative piece to record. But the ability to make an exact duplicate of a sound, or combination of sounds, would prove to be one of the monumental innovations of the 20th century. Among the more significant subsequent developments was the introduction by Columbia in 1948 of the 12" 33 1/3 rpm vinyl LP, and RCA Victor's introduction the following year of the 7" 45 rpm vinyl record.

But it was Philips' 1963 introduction of the compact audio cassette recorder that would prove to be momentous for independent artists. Reel-to-reel tape recorders were already in existence but were too cumbersome and expensive for the general consumer market. Philips originally designed the cassette for use as dictation machines and other professional purposes, but the convenience of the compact cassette led to its breaking into the domestic market.

A further development was the 1979 introduction by TEAC of the Portastudio 144, followed by Fostex in 1983 with the Portastudio X-15, which were mini recording studios in a single unit. Available in 2-track and 4-track versions, these machines used standard cassette tapes and came equipped with built-in mixing boards. By the early 1980s, a Fostex X-15 could be obtained for as little as $400. Music magazines in this era commonly published articles instructing readers how to make their own home recordings. The following excerpt from a 1984 home recording article in *Objekt Magazine* is representative:

"A lot of the tapes that we receive & review are made in home recording studios, and you know what? Some of 'em sound as clean and as professional as many studios and some of 'em sound BETTER than recordings done in a 'professional' recording studio! Often the pressure that is created in a studio can be detrimental to the health of your musical endeavors, especially if you're paying upwards of $35 an hour! So the best thing is to record it yourself - at home. How do you do this? Well, there are a number of mini-studios & porta-studios on the market which enable you to record up to 4 individual tracks at once or a single track at a time on a cassette tape. Yes, cassette tape! Don't let the purists try to fool you. You can make very impressive sounding demos on a cassette recorder" (Ladd, 1984).

The article goes on to detail the various cords and jacks that are needed, what gets plugged into where, tips, tricks and more. Individuals were empowered to create their own recordings, at home, with minimal investment. And provided that the goal was to create their own music and audio art, there was no requirement to rely on external business concerns.

The cassette recorder is only one in a long line of technological advances that facilitated artistic possibilities. Film, radio, television, the Xerox photocopier, and the personal computer all represent technological milestones. Yet the cassette recorder is the one that facilitated widespread participation. Xerox copiers may have been readily accessible, but the cost and portability of the technology made cassette recorder ownership available to all.

Record companies had long enjoyed a near monopoly on the means of producing, distributing and publicizing records. For individuals functioning outside the sphere of the major record companies, the cassette recorder meant ownership and control of the means of recording production. This would result in a wildly diverse variety of music and audio art that often defied genre or stylistic classification.

Home recording represented a rebellion against record company dictation over who gets to record and what gets recorded. The cassettes produced may not have been up to the standards of an Abbey Road studio, but impressive sound quality could be achieved if the artist was attentive to detail. Furthermore, the lo-fi sound that characterized many cassette recordings was in harmony with the punk revolt against professionalism. As UK based hometaper Andy Xport says:

"I think it was one of the best things to ever happen in my life and was the most powerful tool for getting a message to people ever. It was liberating and anarchic and gave people the freedom to express themselves in a way that was just the privilege of an elite few at the time. Don't forget that the music industry at the time (like today with mp3s) claimed it was destroying music. The slogan read - 'hometaping kills music'. Myself and others put out flyers with the slogan on but with a line underneath - 'good fucking job!' and 'hometaping kills capitalism'" (personal communication, 2008).

American hometaper Hal McGee described it in more politically caustic terms: "The cassette is the counter-cultures most dangerous and subversive weapon. The mass media and big entertainment companies feel their monopoly on information and its dissemination slipping away - cassettes truly are the most democratic art form. Cassettes turn passive consumers into producers" (McGee, 1992, p. vii-viii).

The cassette recorder represented democratization of the means of production by putting it in the hands of individuals. According to Alain Neffe, founder of the Belgium based Insane Music label: "The best thing about the cassette was that it was democratic. Because of the cost, everybody could record. And you could record good sound quality if you were careful, even if you only had a guitar and your voice. Sometimes I released things that were recorded in the kitchen. And it was allowed by the network and by the fans. It was a real democracy of the cassette system. We had our own small world that was based on honesty" (personal communication, 2007).

Barry Lamb, cofounder of the UK based Falling A label, echoes a similar sentiment of permissiveness and acceptance as regards the lo-fi nature of their recordings: "I think our unique sound has been largely shaped by our lo-fi ethos. I am very grateful for it. If we had access to money I am sure we would have been lured by expensive equipment in our earlier days and we may have ended up sounding the same as everyone else. The whole cassette culture thing really started as it was the only medium we could afford to work with. We couldn't afford studio time until at least 1981, so we couldn't record anything of sufficient quality to even submit as a demo. However, the cassette culture audience was much more forgiving and interested primarily in the adventure contained in the music" (personal communication, 2009).

Hometapers could be a prolific lot, releasing several cassette albums a year. R. Stevie Moore had by 1987 amassed a catalog of 180 tapes, which he characterized as everything from quirky pop songs to noise collages: "My cassettes are a diary of sound, a very personal kind of thing; this is what I do, writing songs and building soundscapes. It's almost a kind of sickness. You know, I just did a whole instrumental album yesterday, on a whim. How else could an unknown have 180 releases in print?" (Pareles, 1987).

Moore was not unusual in the quantity of his output. Hometapers functioning without regard to sales or profit could create to their hearts content. Zan Hoffman describes the creative momentum he built in the 1980s: "When I got the ball rolling - I'll say it was 1985, '86, '87, '88 - the ball is rolling and it's rolling really fast. I was just pumping out release after release. In 1988, by the first five months, I had done 90 releases. It's all a big blur. I ended up doing like 112 releases that year" (personal communication, 2008).

It must be emphasized that though the cassette was considered by many to be ideal for demo work and audition purposes, dedicated hometapers treated them as finished products - cassette 'albums'. Philip Sanderson, a participant in the late 1970s UK cassette network notes that, "The Philips cassette recorders were invented in the late 60s and in the 70s bands were using the cassette for demos to try and get a deal. But what was good about the DIY tape scene was I think it was the first time people said, 'no, this isn't a demo, this is it!' And I think that was the important paradigm. This is it, and this isn't going to be re-recorded" (Pinsent, 2007-08).

Hal McGee is firm on this point when he says, "I want to stress at the outset that our cassette releases in the 80s and 90s were not demos. 'Demo' is a dirty word in my book. These were fully-realized works of audio art."

Punk commonly conjures up images of the Sex Pistols and the Ramones, spiked hair and safety pin studded jackets, and guitar/bass/drums thrashing hardcore. The record companies co-opted punk by facilitating fame for a handful of bands and happily marketed it to the masses. 'God Save The Queen' and 'Anarchy In The UK' growled rebellion and were hit singles.

There certainly was a punk rock scene associated with these bands, images and music. But the significance of punk to history was epitomized by the motto: 'Here's one chord, here's two more, now go form a band'. Punk meant that anyone could do it. Anyone could 'create'. And placed within a larger historical context, the implication was that anyone could be an 'artist'.

DIY became a battle cry and call to action as use of the cassette recorder by individuals spread in the late 1970s and exploded in the 1980s. The 1980s became the post-punk period when people created on their own initiative and established their own networks of communication. Some came from the punk rock scene, others from the industrial/electronic and experimental/avant-garde scenes, and others were motivated to get involved by reading about it. Consequently, the 1980s was a creatively fruitful decade for music, even if much of that music only reached the ears of family and friends.

With the ability to record open to all, there was naturally a great deal of mediocrity. But with record companies and money removed from the motivational equation there was little incentive to conform. Thus, the true artists could thrive by experimenting, learning and honing their craft. In a 1989 editorial, Hal McGee envisioned cassette culture as a form of folk art:

"I'm convinced that today's hometaper/home artist is our modern folk artist. He/she creates personal reflections of the world around him/her in an intimate, 'home-made' fashion that is meant basically for the enjoyment and edification of her/him-self and a few close friends. I'm reminded of the 'cottage industries' of a bygone time when I see today's independent cassette labels - people creating and distributing their work from their homes. In folk art lifestyle and creativity are inextricably linked" (McGee, 1989, p. 5-6).

Punk represented a rejection of professionalism and proficiency, and amateur status in no way necessitated a deficit of talent or creativity. Technical skill without inspiration and proficiency without imagination can be a lifeless corpse, however compelling it may appear on the surface. Many a guitarist has achieved fame and loyal followings by producing music that is thrilling due only to the flash of the musician's technique. Yet a close listen reveals only the technique, and a cold, generic repetition from one song to the next.

Alternatively, pure imagination can be a potent force, regardless of any lack of instrumental proficiency. The imagination, free to roam, is a testament to the power of the creative spirit. As Paul Hegerty has observed:

"Many punk bands made a virtue of an actual lack of skill. Ineptitude is a strong, fundamentally noisy anti-cultural statement, and, pleasingly, comes in many forms (believers in the importance of technical mastery might imagine that only such a skill can permit variation, the emergence of personal styles, and so on, but just as there are many 'wrong notes', so ineptness is an opening of sound). To many, ineptness is very directly noise: the playing of incorrect notes, or the wrong kind of playing maybe even offending the delicate sensibilities of the elite listener/performer. The inept player will make many mistakes, or what are perceived as such. He or she will make choices and create combinations that are 'wrong', and this is what has led to the belief in the creativity that comes from a lack of preconceptions and a willingness to try out anything, even if badly. The results can be taken (and in punk, were) as more authentic, the lack of preconceptions allowing a greater creativity and personal expression to emerge" (Hegerty, 2007, p. 89).

In addition to recording his own music, Andy Xport released 15 volumes of the *International Sound Communication (ISC)* cassette compilations from 1984-89, featuring a variety of music and audio art by hometapers from around the world:

"With ISC I would accept any quality, and it was purely a means of communication. But on the whole most songs/sound pieces were of surprising quality. I always remember one guy sent a piece entitled 'Lipstick', and in the piece he punched a typewriter whilst chanting 'Lipstick lipstick lipstick!' As much a classic as 'Stairway to Heaven' ever was. To me it was always about participation. Most people cannot play guitar like Jimmy Page. But then who cares? Why sit back and let others make music when it's very easy to do yourself. DIY not EMI. The whole world watches a select few create. Passive sheep that consume anything that's given to them. With the cassette culture we did it ourselves. Sometimes it was bad, but mostly it was great and exciting to boot. I never use to be able to get out of bed in the morning. I just lay there waiting for the thud on the doormat of all the mail the postie would drop through the letterbox. Every day was like Christmas with packets to open and surprises to find. The only dull day was Sunday because the royal mail did not deliver on Sundays" (personal communication, 2008).

Similarly, when asked if he found the volume of submissions received and the task of identifying quality from mediocre music challenging, German hometaper and radio show host Lord Litter is emphatic:

"NO!! EVERYTHING was new in those days. For the first time I heard sounds I NEVER heard before. Whether a pop singer with a very strange/unique voice or a tape with 90 minutes of hiss, EVERY package brought a new surprise. Every day I RAN to my mailbox after I saw the postman in the street – so that REALLY was completely different! This does not mean that all the sounds presented very good worked out concepts. BUT more or less ALL the sounds broke down barriers set up by business rules and regulations - so tapes with 90 minutes of hiss were good and needed in those days!" (personal communication, 2009).

It's a natural inclination to feel that making our own music is beyond our reach when a record collection consists of music played by proficient musicians recorded in state-of-the-art studios. The hometapers shed this thinking and discovered a boundless universe of possibilities that only required imagination and dedication as its core tools.

The lo-fi nature of many hometaper recordings was not only acceptable but conveyed a confident charm, demonstrating that lack of access to professional studios could never obscure genuine talent and creativity. In many cases, hometapers were blatant flag wavers for the limits of the technology, as evidenced by a 1983 call for submissions to a compilation:

"*Cheap Noise Cassette Compilation* is to be made up of music intended for cheap, noisy cassette tapes. Interested persons are invited to send contributions (any sound) on a cheap cassette with return postage; pieces will be compiled (using a cheap tape machine) and copied onto the cassette, which will be sent back to the contributor" (*Op* 'Notes', Issue T, 1983, p. 11).

Compilation organizer Glenn Frantz reflects on his intent: "In 1983 I was 19 years old and had been doing a lot of musical experiments on cassette tape using ordinary consumer equipment. I was unhappy with the poor audio quality of the results. Sonic details and high frequencies got washed out, and I also figured no one would take my music seriously if it was so badly recorded. But I had neither the money, nor much inclination, to invest in more professional gear. So, I decided to try to make a virtue of necessity by going to the other extreme, by embracing and celebrating the crummy sound and all the tape hiss and other noise as an integral aspect of the music and part of the aesthetic. Thus, the emphasis on cheapness. And in addition to a change in attitude, I would need to create music appropriate to the medium. The response I got was almost exactly what I was hoping for. I received enough submissions to make up a good compilation without leaving anyone out, and the types of music submitted pretty much covered the range that I expected" (personal communication, 2025).

CASSETTE CULTURE

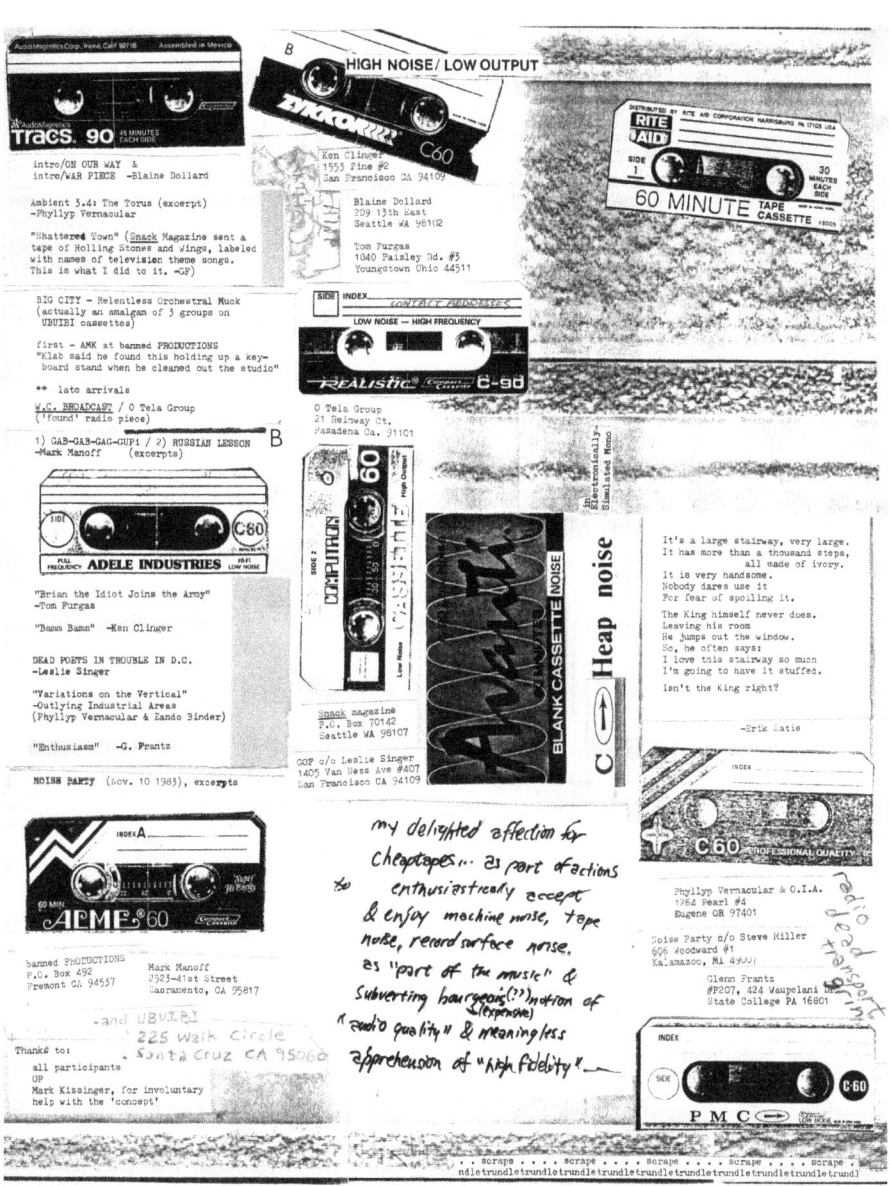

Cheap Noise Cassette Compilation insert

If cheap and noisy was *Cheap Noise Cassette Compilation*'s intent, the results were a success. Introductory hiss and fumbling are followed by lo-fi singing and guitar strumming. And from there we hear an array of chaotically intriguing collage/cut-up and other tape manipulations, plus sundry noise workouts, freeform musical noodling and more.

Home recording was open to all. The creative possibilities for those who didn't play conventional instruments burst open as synthesizers and other electronic equipment became affordable and scalable for home use. Brian Eno's records were released by major record companies, but he was nonetheless a substantial influence on the hometapers due to his non-musician status and the groundbreaking music he created. In his biography of Eno, David Sheppard gives an account of how the artist had access to the tape recorders at Ipswich Civic College:

"He quickly mastered the technology, not by reference to manuals but by throwing himself into trial-and-error recording experiments. Almost immediately he began to subvert the machine's basic function by running reels backwards and experimenting with the vari-speed control, which altered the rotational velocity and thus the pitch of the recorded sound. His first ever recorded 'piece' was the sound of a pen striking the hood of a large anglepoise lamp, multi-tracked at different speeds to form a shimmering, bell-like cloud of tones, over which a friend read a poem" (Sheppard, 2008, p. 42).

With the support of Island Records, Eno founded the Obscure label to release experimental/avant-garde records. Sheppard explains how Eno "sought to use his imprimatur to more widely disseminate music that would otherwise languish in relative anonymity, appreciated only by a tiny cognoscenti. He, rightly, thought much that was composed in the name of experiment would in fact be eminently accessible to a rock audience if they could only be persuaded to listen to it" (ibid, p. 208).

Persuading people to listen to something they might otherwise not have paid attention to is a testament to the way in which the Eno name conferred a form of 'legitimacy' to the music, providing exposure that resulted in Eno becoming one of the most influential non-musicians in the rock world. Hometaper Tom Furgas spoke for many of his peers when he described Eno's impact in a 1991 interview:

"What he did is brought the 'non-musician' angle into it. And he showed that you didn't have to be particularly well-skilled in an instrument in order to... you know, there are other ways of making and shaping sounds than just virtuosic finger-play and so forth. He brought a sort of naïve, untutored approach that I thought was refreshing and it sort of made me want to limit, to a certain extent, the degree of schooling that I would have in it, 'cause I wanted to keep it fresh and I knew that if I got too deeply into it, it would be like... discovering how the magician did all his tricks or something. It would lose that potency for me" (Kissinger, 1991, p. 12).

Eno's records were recorded in state-of-the-art studios, yet his ability as a creative non-musician to make music by mastering the technology, and the imaginative ambient excursions he created, inspired many hometapers to create similar works with limited resources.

Equally influential, though more directly linked to the larger cassette culture story was Throbbing Gristle. Concurrent with the emergence of punk, Throbbing Gristle launched their Industrial Records label in 1976, along with what became the Industrial Music genre. The band began in true hometaper spirit. To minimize costs, most of their first LP, *The Second Annual Report*, was recorded on a Sony cassette recorder with a condenser microphone and a home stereo Wharfdale cassette, at a cost of approximately £15 (Ford, 1999, p. 7.20-7.22).

Band member Genesis P-Orridge claimed that the choice of equipment was both economical and ideological, and in reference to the sound quality said, "Don't be surprised by surface noise crackles, they are all like that, it's one in thee eye for hi-fi freaks" (ibid, p. 7.22).

Combining live and studio material, *The Second Annual Report* sounds like a disturbing, full force Frankenstein's laboratory in space. Rushing noise waves combine with wildly blasting synths, buzzsaw psychedelic guitar, high intensity atmospherics and twisted vocal rants. Throbbing Gristle create a densely sinister montage assault of chaotically intriguing electronics plus sundry voices and sounds all glommed together into a creepy, spaced out psychedelic stew. The lo-fi aspect is not only a key element of the experience, but also potently demonstrates how deeply moving, unorthodox music can be created without the need for state-of-the-art recording studios.

Through their Industrial label, Throbbing Gristle released both vinyl records and cassettes, with several albums by themselves, Cabaret Voltaire, Richard H. Kirk, Clock DVA, The Leather Nun and Monte Cazazza being cassette only releases. The band also recorded and released nearly all of their live performances on cassette and allowed fans to record the shows.

Throbbing Gristle were a seminal influence in that they were essentially hometapers who created music that wasn't being released by the major record companies and successfully marketed this music through an independent label. Speaking in 1980 of the *Heathen Earth* album selling 10,000 copies in its first three weeks of release P-Orridge said:

"The big companies try to perpetuate thee myth of public disinterest in our area of music and ideas and tactics whilst thee public response and sales figures show steadily increasing real interest on a global scale. Thee big companies are scared, only their corruption remains, they can still hype idiot fodder into thee charts, can still convince us all to purchase their wares, butter it's a separate world now from the new underground and this time art imitates business and is more effective for it" (ibid, 10.7).

Hometapers unconcerned with making a living from their work operated with unfettered freedom, independent of censorship, and no regard for mainstream commercial concerns. They could choose not to attempt the hurdle of trying to 'make it' or deal with the music industry in any capacity. No rejection letters or 'don't call us, we'll call you' responses. Hometaping also alleviated the need for skills required to market one's music and organize live performances and tours. Hometapers were free to let the creative juices flow.

In a world where the media spotlight is on the 'stars' and albums selling in the millions, it can be difficult to grasp the idea of creating art as a labor of love. Dutch hometaper and head of the Exart label, Hessel Veldman, says:

"It was the feeling of being part of something big in creating new sounds in music. Not being part of the world of big music companies, whose only interest was money. Every contract that came my way in the 1980s (EMI, CBS and Warner) was destroyed. Even the good proposal by a commercial television station was for me something against my principles. At that time, I never made music on demand of any organization. I wanted complete freedom of creativity. It was completely the principle of not being involved in money making projects and being independent on all levels. Everything was done with low budgets and only earning back the money we used for new projects. And it's still my principle for all music lovers around the globe. Copy my music free and do with it whatever you want. If you want to earn money with my music, go for it! It's my decision to be free from copyright" (personal communication, 2007).

English singer-songwriter Martin Newell, one of pop music's true craftsman, expressed similar sentiments in a 1988 interview. Negative experiences had left him feeling disenchanted with the music business. Consequently, when his band Cleaners from Venus formed in 1979 the musician decided to go the homemade route. Newell described how Cleaners From Venus tapes would include anti-copyright messages along the lines of, "no right reserved... if you have money, buy it... if you don't, copy it" (Bradberry, 1988, p. 66).

In 1981 Newell and partner Lol Elliott sent 18 of their songs to *Sounds* magazine with a note that anyone who wanted a copy had to send a blank tape or 50 pence, which garnered a good response. Newell goes on to explain how their 1985 album *Living With Victoria Grey* was picked up by a small independent tape distributor in the US and the band were beginning to gain a following in America. Yet Newell was still reluctant to sign with a record company:

"We were offered contracts by at least two major companies, but I was fed up with the music industry. I'd been reading a lot of anarchist literature and was sick of being ripped off. I wanted to try a new way without 'big daddy music biz' getting in the way, so I simply released tapes and didn't bother to talk to anybody in the business. If asked, I simply used to say, what if they started a record company and nobody signed?" (ibid, p. 67).

The hometaper network did include individuals with major record company opportunities and even direct experience. Nevertheless, people like Veldman eschewed the industry in favor of artistic passion and Newell from pure disgust with his experience. Both decided to continue creating with limited resources, even if it meant giving their music away for free.

Chapter 3

Cassettes vs. Vinyl

Cassettes offered multiple advantages over vinyl records. Most cassette artists were not against releasing records. The foremost problem was cost. Audio cassettes were inexpensive and accessible. You could go to the store and buy blank tapes, which was vastly different from having a record pressed and released. Furthermore, cassettes were easier to package and cheaper to ship than records. Cassettes could be duplicated one at a time, unlike records which were only economical when pressed in quantity. Al Margolis, head of the US based Sound of Pig label, described his brand of ingenuity in the early years:

"It was all real-time. In the mid-1980s I worked as a shipping clerk, by myself for a small company. And I had in the back, by me, three dubbing decks. And while I was at work all day I would dub. Those things ran all day. In an eight-hour day I probably ran 24 tapes at work. And I'd come home and I'd be dubbing tapes. It was all by hand, one at a time. I did look into what 50 or 100 cassettes would cost to be made and it was too expensive. In 1984 or '85, to go to a place that would dub 50 cassettes for you could cost a couple hundred dollars. And as far as I knew I didn't need 50 or 100 cassettes on hand anyway. You had $150 dubbing decks back then that did the job. The Sonys, the Tascams, the TEACS" (personal communication, 2007).

Dubbing tapes by hand all day may not have been efficient, but it was effective. However cumbersome it may have been, hand dubbing was a means to an end that allowed people to accomplish what they were committed to.

Andy Xport gives an admirably mind-boggling account of how his band APF Brigade made their music available: "It all started for us when the band Crass put an ad in *Sounds* music paper for bands to send in tapes for possible inclusion on their *Bullshit Detector* compilation album, and to our surprise Crass chose one of our tracks, 'Anarchist Attack'. Each band got a square of cover to do their own artwork, and on this we put our address and the fact that if people sent us a blank tape and S.A.E. we would record our demo live. We were flooded with mail! I am talking sacks of it every day for months!" (personal communication, 2008).

Andy goes on to describe how the band would fill orders for their first album by recording them live to blank cassettes people sent in, with the intent being to personalize each tape:

"It was a stupid idea that even got a mention in the big music papers. We received about 5000 before it eventually fizzled out, and we did a 40-minute set which we honed down by playing faster and faster until it was under 30 minutes. By that time, we had seven mono recorders we had got by hook or crook and we set them all going at once and went for it. This went on every night for the best part of six months until we said enough is enough, and we just duplicated them on these new tape-to-tape machines we bought" (ibid).

The power of cassette technology encouraged imaginations to run wild yet facilitated a simple freedom by virtue of their availability. Alain Neffe speaks to the freedom that cassettes offered:

"It was two different worlds. I was raised with vinyl. And I like vinyl because of the cover sleeve. It's something I can feel. It's like a book vs. the internet. But cassettes allowed you more freedom. That was the main difference. It's very expensive to release vinyl. To release a cassette, you can do only 10 copies if you want. And if I needed more copies, I copied them. So, I had no money tied up in stock. With vinyl if they don't sell you can do nothing with them. With cassettes, if a cassette doesn't sell well you can erase it and reuse it for another release. Very easy. You can make modifications, make improvements to it. Once the vinyl is made, it's made. So, the main difference is freedom. Because it's cheaper and there's less money involved. Sometimes almost no money involved. In the beginning I was making cover sleeves on a photocopy machine. It didn't cost a lot of money. You weren't limited by the cost as you were with vinyl" (personal communication, 2007).

One point that Neffe makes in this description is the interactive nature of cassettes. They key functional distinction between cassettes and vinyl records is that cassettes can be used to record, as well as play back. A cassette that couldn't be sold, or contained undesirable content, could be erased or recorded over with different content.

Lord Litter elaborates on the cost benefit of cassettes over vinyl: "I think the main difference was the investment. To release vinyl was expensive, so to release on cassettes would allow a constant flow of releases. One would only copy as many cassettes as one needed. Once you had enough songs to release a new cassette you would stop copying the prior cassette and start copying the new one. Vinyl had to be sold to get the money back to invest in another vinyl release. This (probably) led to two results: More 'careful' vinyl releases and more 'careless' cassette releases" (personal communication, 2009).

The length of cassettes facilitated a creative benefit in that they inspired hometapers to stretch out and explore. The early 1970s albums by electronic pioneers like Tangerine Dream and Klaus Schulze commonly included recorded works that took up entire album sides, and in some cases comprised entire albums. An extended piece would have to end at roughly the 20-minute mark, perhaps representing a forced stopping point. If it continued on the B-side the listener's experience was interrupted to flip the record.

With up to 90 minutes available, each cassette side was as long, or longer, than the typical record album, offering a sweeping sonic palette to improvisors, creators of ambient works, and anyone with a penchant for experimentation. Multitudes of sound explorers, infected with pioneering enthusiasm, took advantage of this opportunity to create longer audio works than could be heard on a record album.

Lengths of greater than 90 minutes were available. However, they were not commonly used as the tape was too thin and wore out quickly. Among other problems was not all cassette motors had the torque to accommodate the longer tapes, and some couldn't play them at the correct speeds (Thanks to members of the now defunct Yahoo Cassette Culture list for this information).

In the Letters section of a 1981 issue of *Op* magazine, Philip Perkins writes in to say: "From reading *Op* I see that you all are mostly interested in records, but I think that more and more small producers like us will be turning from records to cassettes as record quality continues to plummet and costs soar. Also, many of our pieces, for technical reasons, cannot be made into discs" (*Op*, Issue F, 1981, p. 1).

Explaining the technical reasons that his music could not be made into records, Perkins confirms the value of the extended length that cassettes facilitated: "Cassettes had much longer uninterrupted durations for long pieces, especially something environmental or ambient and perhaps made for playback in a gallery installation" (personal communication, 2016).

Perkins elaborates on the technical drawbacks to vinyl: "Vinyl does not allow the 2 channels of stereo to have audio out of phase with each other below about 100 Hz. Disk masters cannot be cut unless the low bass is mono. Oddly enough, I ran into exactly this problem again this year, trying to premaster a piece by Maggi Payne for an LP, and the solution was the same as it was in 1980. All bass below about 100 Hz has to be summed to mono. Back in 1980 or so we weren't willing to compromise on this for some pieces we wanted to publish, so cassette was the way to go" (ibid).

Alain Neffe describes related drawbacks to vinyl: "For a record sometimes you have a bad surprise if the pressing or the master is not done well. You might have treble or bass frequencies missing. We had a record released on Dead Man's Curve in London with a lot of bass frequencies and when the record was released it sounded very flat. On a cassette it doesn't have that as you can control the quality" (*ND*, Issue 10, 1988, p. 39).

Despite the benefits and accessibility of cassettes, records were not considered taboo and were even desirable for many hometapers. Ladd-Frith cassette label co-founder Brian Ladd was instrumental in the production of the 1983 *The Gift Of Noise* LP. Ladd explains how the album came to be:

"I was in contact with various music labels. I was always trying to get them interested in Psyclones. I wrote to Sordide Sentimentale (Psychic TV, Ludus, Tuxedomoon) in Rouen, France after reading about them in the *Industrial Culture Handbook* and JP Turmel wrote back. He liked Psyclones and wanted to do an LP with us. He introduced me to Yann Farcy at L'invitation au Suicide who was doing Virgin Prunes and Christian Death records. This paved the way for the first compilation LP we ever produced, *The Gift Of Noise*, which we compiled for L'invitation au Suicide. We included all our hometaper pals like Smersh, F/i, Senseless Hate and No Trend (who we met when we played with them at Club Foot in San Francisco)" (personal communication, 2010).

Hoping to reach those who may have been unaware of or dismissive of cassettes, Alain Neffe made an exception to his long running *Insane Music for Insane People* cassette compilation series by having Volume 13 produced as a vinyl LP. Neffe characterizes vinyl and cassette consumers as two different audiences:

"The vinyl lovers hated cassettes and the cassette lovers hated vinyl. I wanted to attract the vinyl lovers to cassettes. So, I released *Insane Music for Insane People*, one a more easy side and one a more difficult side. And I put a paper inside listing all the previous cassettes and asking them why they won't buy cassettes? Cassettes are cheaper. You will have one hour of music for less money" (personal communication, 2007).

The album is a potpourri of diversity. The 'easy side' consists of quirkily propulsive electronica, dreamy synth-pop, King Crimson-ish tribal grooves, melodic synthesizer ditties, frantic paced new wave, and a cool grooving melodic instrumental. The 'strange side' is not a dramatic turn, featuring music that is largely accessible, while venturing into more experimental territory. It has dark synth-pop, bewitching electronica with tribal speak-in-tongues operatic vocals and a spacey Philip Glass-like minimal flow, Dadaist vocal and sound gymnastics and bizarre tape manipulations that create a variety of craftily alluring tunes, at times like the Residents and Laurie Anderson.

The 1987 set is an outstanding reflection of the decade's more exciting post-punk. Yet, as Neffe explains: "But it didn't work at all. That LP compilation was pressed in 500 copies and didn't sell well. I still have some copies. And I was known for cassettes and not for vinyl" (ibid).

The small press publications that supported hometapers notwithstanding, it was widely recognized that cassettes suffered a promotional disadvantage. American hometaper Andrew Szava-Kovats felt strongly about records as a goal:

"Making the leap from cassette to vinyl was important, because that opened a lot of doors that were closed to cassette. For instance, the radio scene, college radio was much more apt to play vinyl than cassette. And record stores would take records - even if they were weird stuff - on vinyl, whereas they might not on cassette. So that transition to vinyl was really important if you wanted to expand your audience base" (Szava-Kovats, 2014, p. 38).

From 1987-89 Szava-Kovats produced four volumes of *Grindstone* compilations featuring a variety of American artists and an impressive array of genre bending electronica. With what seemed like a nod to the ethic that permeated much of the hometaper network, a note on the *Back To The Grindstone* LP says: "By all means tape it! Play it for your friends! But please encourage further support!"

Dutch hometaper Frans de Waard supports the point that vinyl was desirable if it could be fit into a budget: "The whole cassette thing wasn't a principle per se, so when Abo of Petri Supply/Yeast Culture said he knew a pressing plant where you could get vinyl for a good price, I looked at my money and thought it would be good to release a one sided 7" by Kapotte Muziek. That sold quickly. After that I did some more 7" records and when I wanted to release an LP by Jos Smolders I sent out a note and asked people to pre-pay and I managed to sell all 100 in advance. I still kept releasing cassettes on Korm Plastics though, until 1990, I think. With Kapotte Muziek I kept releasing them on other labels until 1995 or 1996, mainly to get rid of quick ideas or concepts.

Depending on the format, listeners could sometimes expect different types of music from artists whose work appeared on both cassettes and vinyl. American musician Eugene Chadbourne has long experience with both cassette and vinyl releases. In a 1987 interview Chadbourne bemoaned the long and detailed process of completing an LP, be it self-released or through a label, noting both the challenges of the process and the benefits of cassettes:

"Even the most rushed album will take at least 6 weeks to be pressed, yet when I am done with this I will take my banjo, do a 60-minute solo tape, run the master through my machines, and hopefully have a sale made while you're eating breakfast tomorrow" (Chadbourne, 1992, p. 59).

Chadbourne expands on the practical advantages of cassettes: "Cassettes offer a change in how people are able to communicate their ideas. I put out cassettes that I don't think anyone is going to release on record or I'm practical and I realize that convincing someone to release a specific thing is going to take a year, maybe two years before somebody finally gets it together and decides this is worth releasing. In the meantime, why should people wait to hear it? In the meantime, I make it available on cassette for people who are really following the developments of music and want to hear everything that comes out. Or the cassette means I can go on the road and I can have my latest material I've written and recorded available to fans who come to the concerts" (Ciaffardini, 1987, p. 37).

Chadbourne is not only addressing the practical advantages of cassettes but also revealing that the music he released on cassettes could differ from what was heard on his vinyl releases. Comparing his LP to cassette releases, Chadbourne says the material on the cassettes is much more revolutionary, as well as less expensive (Chadbourne, 1992, p. 59).

Chadbourne is also referencing an audience that was interested in these alternatives. The "people who are really following the developments of music" were those who were interested enough to make the effort to find alternatives, and open-minded to something different. In the 1980s there were no quick internet searches offering treasure troves of results that could be downloaded or streamed immediately. Music fans had to be interested in alternatives, aware of their existence, and willing to make the effort to seek them out.

Responding to a question about the use of pornographic imagery in the packaging of his music, Japanese sound artist Merzbow makes an artistic distinction between his cassette and vinyl releases:

"I have two directions in the use of pornography. In my early cassettes and mail art projects I used lots of pornography. I made many collages using pornography as it was a very important item in my mail art/mail music. I thought my cheap noise cassettes were of the same value as cheap mail order pornography. These activities were called "Pornoise". In this direction, I would say that I used pornography for its anti-social, cut-up value in information theory. I soon started to release Merzbow vinyl which was very different from the cassettes of the same time period. I think my vinyl works concentrated more on sound itself because I think vinyl is a more static medium. So, Merzbow went in two separate directions in the '80s - a cassette and a vinyl direction" (Hensley, 1999).

For some, cassettes and vinyl were components of a larger artistic vision. Vittore Baroni describes the multi-media aspect of his TRAX label: "TRAX was not simply a label or a group of artists but a 'modular system' composed by Central Units (those who actually coordinated and produced TRAX items or events) and Peripheral Units (those who would contribute to an item or event). In seven years, from 1981 to 1987, TRAX involved 13 Central Units and approximately 500 Peripheral Units from all corners of the world. The final report of the TRAX project, *Last Trax* (that enclosed a vinyl EP, postcards, stickers, stamps), is a sort of commented catalog of all the activities produced by TRAX: audio-magazines, cassettes, records, exhibitions, performances, concerts, festivals, copy art portfolios, comics, t-shirts, handbags, etc. As you can see, TRAX was not just related to music, but more an attempt to mix all the media available. We would use cassettes, for practical reasons, usually for products under 500 copies, while we would use vinyl when we printed a thousand copies or more of an audio project. But the conceptual frame was exactly the same. There was always a theme and an audio-visual element both in the cassette release and in the vinyl release. We did not value vinyl as 'better' than cassettes, we loved both media, what we chose was simply a matter of economic convenience" (personal communication, 2008).

Chapter 4

The Tape Tax

The cassette recorder may have been mana from heaven for hometapers, but the major record companies were not happy. Downloading music has been a source of near hysterical worry for the music-industrial complex in the internet age. But the download controversy is only the latest in a long line of technological advances to put media giants on the defensive, threatening their control over the reuse of content due to consumer ability to copy media at home.

Though the legislative trouble began with the introduction of the Sony Betamax video recorder in 1975, cassettes were an earlier nuisance for record companies because they allowed consumers to record, or as the industry so dramatically characterized it - 'pirate' - LPs. With the muscle flexing assistance of the Recording Industry Association of America (RIAA), the business and lobbying trade group of the record companies, 'Home Taping is Killing Music' became the recording industry mantra, along with a frenzy of attempts starting in the early 1980s to legislate the taxing of cassette recorders and tape.

The timeline and details of the bills introduced in the US House and Senate is a larger story. But what these bills represented was a campaign by the major record companies to legitimate, through the legislative process, their control over duplicating mediums. With a single-minded focus on pirating, the justification for taxing was to recover sales revenue allegedly lost due to consumers taping records.

1979 was a watershed year in the debate. The record industry followed the previous year's record high sales of $4 billion with a sharp drop-off in profits. Adding fuel to the fire was the introduction that year in Japan of the Sony Walkman player, which spread in availability and grew dramatically in sales over the next year due to its portability. Add to these factors the quality issues with high speed duplicated, pre-recorded tapes, and the result was a lack of cognition and response to emerging trends by an industry which chose to focus exclusively on pirating.

Writing in the *Washington Post* in June 1981, Richard Harrington reported on a record store that attempted a record rentals model, which the industry objected to because it argued that the practice encouraged piracy. Harrington noted that "cassettes have become the cheapest optimum means of listening to music; portable cassette players in particular combine technological and social advantages - the fact that you can take it with you weighs heavily in the minds of an increasingly mobile population." Harrington went on to say that "tapes, besides holding up better than vinyl, offer one distinct advantage that the record industry can't counter: they are reusable, adaptable to the transient nature of music. Records, unfortunately, tend to be unalterable artifacts - you can't erase a record" (Harrington, 1981).

While neglecting the creative component, the report hit squarely on key benefits of cassettes. And here we see rumblings about taxing tapes. Harrington went on to quote Stanley Gortikov, president of the RIAA: "Stanley Gortikov admits that the ultimate solution may be legislative. There has been talk about a levy or royalty on blank tape and hardware" (ibid). Though their efforts would never secure them the hoped for legislation, the music-industrial complex fought hard.

Industry and trade group calls for a tax on the sale of all audio and video tape recorders and every blank tape resulted in 1982 tax proposals in the U.S. legislature (the Mathias Amendment, S.A. 1333 in the Senate and the Edwards Bill, H.R. 5705 in the House). Reporting in the *New York Times* in August of that year, Hans Frantel noted that American lawmakers wished to take a permissive stance toward home taping with the attitude: "Let's make it legal, but let's tax it. The underlying theory, highly regarded in legislative circles, is that generating cash flow causes happiness" (Frantel, 1982).

A crucial precedent had been a 1981 California appeals court decision to declare it illegal under US copyright law to tape television movies off the air. As Frantel further reported, "by extension the ruling could be construed to apply to taping music from the radio. The effect was to make instant criminals of millions of audio and video fans using their cassette machines to tape broadcasts" (ibid).

Sony Corporation, the key defendant in the California suit, had appealed to the Supreme Court, hoping for a ruling that would exempt all forms of private, non-commercial home recording from the strictures of copyright.

A 'Special Report' by Michael Schrage in a September 1982 issue of *Rolling Stone* came out swinging, declaring his conclusions early in the article:

"The record industry's claim that home taping alone is responsible for a loss of $1 billion a year is greatly exaggerated. The results of studies conducted by record companies in their case against home taping have been distorted. Any imposition of a royalty on blank tape would most deeply penalize the record companies' best customers. Other factors - including record quality, high prices, a dearth of creative talent and insufficient marketing - would appear to have caused more damage to the record industry than has home taping" (Schrage, 1982, p. 59).

Schrage made the succinct case that the record industry was ignoring multiple factors that went into diminished record sales, attributable to the blinders behind which it chose to view the situation.

The battle heated significantly two years later with the results of the copyright infringement suit brought against Sony and its Betamax video recorder. In 1984 the U.S. Supreme Court ruled in Sony's favor, citing the 'fair use' codified in the 1976 Copyright Act.

This led to the next legislative salvo to be hurled in the form of the 1985 Home Recording Act (H.R. 2911), calling for an amendment to the 1976 Copyright Act, which sought to impose license fees on manufacturers and importers of audio recording equipment and blank tape.

The concept of fair use was the key argument against these laws - copying LPs to cassette for the purpose of preservation, custom programming in the form of mix tapes, for listening on a Sony Walkman or car stereo, and other non-copyright uses such as business dictation and college lectures.

One problem was that a mechanism for collecting taxes and distributing them to record companies and copyright holders was conspicuously omitted. Furthermore, while the law was to exempt those individuals taping records they had purchased and those buying tape recorders for personal use, no details accounted for how subsequent use would be determined at the time of purchase.

Writing in a 1986 issue of the *Fordham Law Journal*, Teresa E. Sulyok made an argument against the proposed legislation that correctly focused on fair use. Yet, like the majority of mainstream press reporting, Sulyok was ignorant of the concept of hometaping as a creative endeavor, unrelated to record industry copyright complaints. Itemizing distinguishing fair use factors, Sulyok did indicate "musicians who tape their own original music" and "persons who correspond via cassettes", and in a footnote cites a statistic that "forty-eight percent of tapers surveyed used blank tapes for taping music performed by their family, friends or themselves" (Sulyok, 1986, p. 455).

Ultimately, however, this scholarly journal article, which argued to reject the proposed bill, concluded to the disadvantage of those using cassettes for creative use by conceding the use of tape recorders for piracy: "A more equitable approach to the home taping dilemma would be a uniform surcharge only on cassette recorders containing two or more cassette wells. This approach could be implemented by imposing a license fee only on double or greater capacity cassette recorders capable of copying from one tape onto another tape in the same deck" (ibid, p. 476).

Tape recorders with dual cassette wells were precisely what enabled hometapers to make multiple copies. And yet the 'Hometaping is Killing Music' slogan, purporting to characterize the fight in the name of protecting artists, completely disregarded the use of the technology as a home recording studio and duplicating mechanism for original home created music. Moreover, it wasn't only the record industry that ignored this use. It was only nominally considered by a largely ignorant opposition and mainstream press. It was left to the underground press to put the spotlight on home taping for creative purposes. As Pennie Stasik so eloquently stated in a 1986 article:

"Whether by deliberate intent or ignorance, the opinion that 'Home Taping is Killing Music' is a direct insult to anyone who does not agree with the notion that the entire world of music is embodied in major corporate labels' products. The implication that 'music' will die is an affront to the very spirit of the independent musician (and let us not forget the countless others who make music simply for their own enjoyment). If anything, music thrives because of homes and the tapes which they contain - and not the 'copied' kind, but the kind recorded for the purpose of self-expression. The statement by Stanley Gortikov, President of the Recording Industry Association of America (RIAA), that the tape industry 'is a predatory, parasitic industry' (Rolling Stone, September 16, 1982) should make most independent musicians bristle and flinch at such a short-sighted view. The fact is that from the most blinding-glitter superstar to the dark closet synthesist, everyone starts making music by noodling, and the cassette is the perfect noodling agent - and still in its tiny infancy" (Stasik, 1986, p. 3).

Chapter 5

Creative Packaging

Some cassette artists took great care in the packaging of their releases, with cassettes presented as full-blown works of art. The ornate and often confounding packaging was done in the spirit of mail art.

The imaginatively designed packages commonly resembled Fluxus 'multiples', which were three-dimensional objects or assemblages that Fluxus founder George Maciunas reproduced like prints. As Fluxus historian Owen Smith explains:

"The multiples consisted of found objects purchased in the junk shops that lined Canal Street at that time. They were housed in a variety of boxes, the most uniform thing about them being the labels which Maciunas designed and had printed in some quantity. 1964 also saw the publication of the first Fluxus Yearbox – which consisted of approximately twenty envelopes bolted together, each containing work by a different Fluxus artist. Although ostensibly a multiple, each copy varied slightly in content" (Smith, 1998, p. 57).

What the Fluxus artists created is precisely how many cassettes were packaged, assembled, or otherwise adorned, being yet another example of the environment of unrestrained freedom that hometapers operated in.

Robin James humorously describes the lengths he went to with his compilation tapes: "My first *Cassette Mythos* compilation in 1985 was called *The Box*. I made 12 of them. It had three tapes and was a bit bigger than a cigar box. I had access to a bunch of components: a cedar box that a friend hand painted the interiors of, that was the inner box, and the outer box was a larger box originally used for photographic paper. I spray painted it black, a nice white stencil went on top, and I put some cedar boughs in there. Big mistake. Cedar boughs smell great, but they dry out and crumble and get into the cassettes and from there into the cassette players and do all kinds of interesting things to the delicate mechanisms therein. My lesson from that: Never use things in the packaging that will break up and get lodged inside components" (personal communication, 2008).

An *Unsound* magazine review notes the contents of Peter Catham's 1983 *Gum* cassette: "Peter's second cassette release, packaging by Christopher Grace. The cassette comes in a box with various titled photos relating to the pieces and a special listening device (assembly required). This tape is more complex both in composition and packaging than Cathum's first release" (*Unsound*, Vol 1 No 3, 1983, p. 44).

Catham characterizes the package as having been a cross between 'art' and 'intent'. The tape was housed in an open-reel box with several photos. But there was also a practical component, where he devised the 'Eavesdropper' as his way of enhancing the listening experience. Catham explains that "the idea was to bring the sound into your head. Put your hands behind your ears and hear the sound. I wanted it to be a total experience" (personal communication, 2025).

Peter Catham - Gum tape (1983)

CASSETTE CULTURE

Peter Catham - Gum eavesdropper (1983)

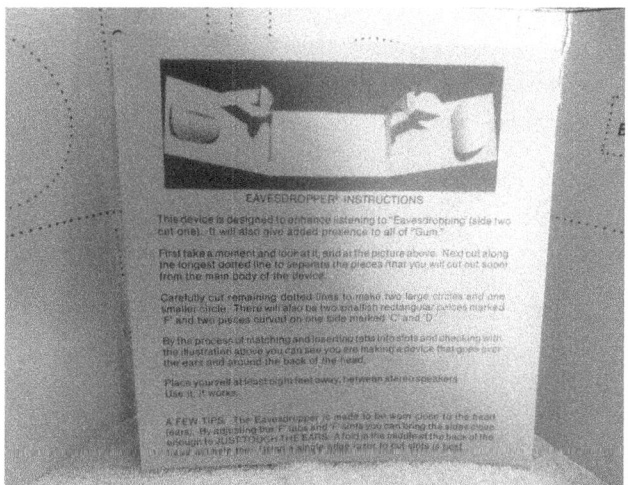

Peter Catham - Gum instructions (1983)

Richard Rupenus describes a 1984 collaboration tape between his group The New Blockaders, Coil, and Vortex Campaign: "Each cassette was housed in a cloth bag made from various types and styles of fabric that were unique to each of the 50 tapes produced. Although the collaboration is untitled, it is often referred to as *Dolbied*, due to the fact that one of the inserts included *Dolbied*". "As of 2025, original copies of the tape have sold for as much as $1200 on Discogs" (personal communication, 2025).

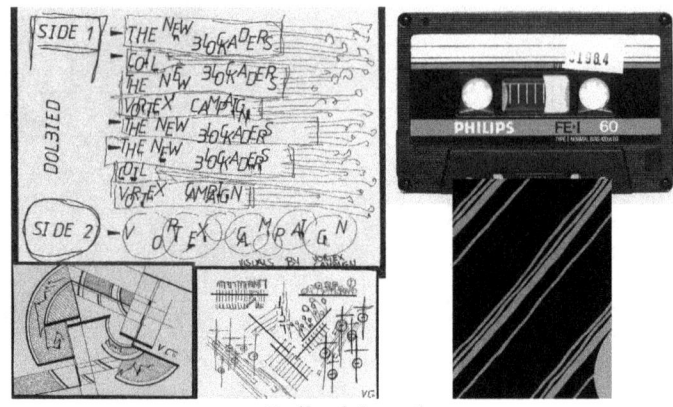
Dolbied (1984)

Don Campau describes a 1986 collaboration titled *Pinata Party*: "It all became part of this sprawling two tape set which was housed in a clear strawberry container that included the tapes, candy, confetti, stickers, little toys, etc. I sent it in the mail in a brown paper lunch bag" (personal communication, 2007).

An *ND* magazine review marvels at the packaging of Scot Jenerik's 1990 *E-hv* cassette: "The package itself is a real beauty; cast in a cement case with an etched steel lid that is bolted on. The music has at times a churning like rhythm which is hypnotic and inspiring" (*ND*, Issue 17, April 1993, p. 61).

Jenerik explains the ambitious intersection of concept and packaging that went into the release: "The recordings are interpretations of theoretical and quantum physics through noise, rhythms and sonic frequencies. The two sides of the cassette are based on the theory of opposing hemispheres in a closed universe. Hitting auto-reverse on one's tape deck would immerse one in the same spot in the universe, though heading in the opposite direction. The intent of the release is not purely related to sound. The physical object is as integral to the overall concept as the composition. Physics explains the fundamental building blocks of matter and our observed universe. In our modern world, concrete and steel have a similar purpose upon which contemporary life is constructed. The weight and physicality of a concrete brick and steel plate lid bolted into place, encasing the aural matter, transforms the container from a simple vessel into a symbolic representation. Symbolism relating to density, permanence and the physical restraints of existence" (personal communication, 2025).

Scot Jenerik - E-hv (1990)

A 1986 issue of *Sound Choice* magazine included an article in which James Hill shared the joys of hunting down mailers that will comfortably hold cassettes: "A few weeks ago I was strolling down the street when my eye caught this two-foot disengaged doll leg lying in a pile of trash on the street corner. The thought occurred that this doll leg would make a great mailer. Much to my joy, a tape fit perfectly into the upper portion of the leg allowing the rest of the leg to be filled with all sorts of other stuff such as puffed yellow corn, buttons, and an assortment of other mail art" (Hill, 1986, p. 19).

Hill does the same when he finds a 90-cent pair of red plastic high heel shoes in a thrift store: "Once again I brought my find back to the studio and wouldn't you know it, a tape fit snug as a rug in those shoes. I wrapped a little clear plastic tape around those puppies, slapped an address on them and off they went. One to London and the other to Frankfurt" (ibid).

Zine reviews often highlighted the packaging of tapes, with bizarre and sometimes hilarious descriptions:

"Robin Rose (ex synth player for Urban Verbs) sent in a piece called Reliquary that was inspired by the catastrophic Air Florida plane crash into the Potomac River in January 1982. The 'fossilized' cassette came mounted on a silk-screened board and the tape contains some quietly spooky sounds (a reliquary is a compartment for keeping religious or sacred objects)" (*Op*, Issue Q, May-June 1983, p. 17-18).

"Innersleeve Distributing sent in two tapes by Hideous in Strength. Each comes with a booklet scented with Egyptian or Moroccan essence. These are really 'mood' tapes: you're supposed to listen to them on headphones while reading the booklet (one even comes with incense) to heighten the experience" (ibid).

"When I opened the envelope that contained Dliefkoorb's *Fall*, it (and the cassette itself) was completely filled with dry leaves, providing a seasonal touch. The eccentricity just began there – this was recorded in 'Dlief-o-vision': all the information is in the right channel. The left is up to you mentally. No doubt" (*Op*, Issue U, Jan-Feb 1984, p. 24).

"Best Packaging of the Month Award goes to the Legendary Pink Dots this time, for their *Kleine Krieg* (Little War) tape, which comes nestled in a box containing a dinky model of a jet fighter (according to the picture on the box mine was a Japanese Air Force version of the McDonnell Douglas F-15 fighter [1/144 scale] and it even included decals). Besides all that, it's a credible and enjoyable electronic excursion" (ibid).

"Packaging of the Issue Award will have to be divided among the following two (group) entries. (First): Trance Port Tapes' latest 2 releases both come wrapped in folded cardboard sleeves beautifully silkscreened in silver. The other half of the Outstanding Packaging trophy goes to PPP in France for the white polystyrene medical specimen beaker (? – my best guess) that cylindrically encased their *Assemble Generale #4* international compilation" (*Op*, Issue V, March-April 1984, p. 16).

"From James Hilltcab of TCAB Sound in San Francisco: This one came with a pipe cleaner and a pin that says 'The Bible Only'. Free to anyone interested. Instrumental synth bed for horn. Wins by default the coveted 'stuff falls in your lap when you open the cassette box' award" (*Op*, Issue W, May-June 1984, p. 9).

"Mark Murrell easily walks off with the Best Packaging honors this issue for sending in his letter on a 7-foot long, 1/2 inch wide strip of paper wound into a scotch tape dispenser. The cassette, letter, poster, envelope, and everything were painted with beautifully airbrushed textures, a real impressive piece – shame I couldn't frame and hang it. *Dangling Ganglion* it's called and contains some very rich audio collage work with clever musical ideas added. Altogether a heady experience" (*Op*, Issue X, July-August 1984, p. 13).

"ASP-AMP, Crawling with Tarts. Tape is nice noise, not dense, understated; voice, percussion, minor electronics. The packaging is outstanding! WOW!!! Lots of effort airbrushing and Xeroxing and cutting paper. I can't say enough about it, and for $3 too. Came with a Xerox collage artzine called *4* which is fifty cents" (ibid).

"Untitled is the name of a tape by Jarboe (Atlanta, GA), a solo effort that comes wrapped in white gauze with some black paint minimally applied. Inside the cassette is wrapped in white sticky bandage tape which had to be removed to listen to it" (ibid, p. 14).

"The Young Schitzophrenics, *AMOL OBOL 1#*: An interesting packaging job on this one. The cassette was totally wrapped in electrical tape, making it a very dicey job getting the tape off without cutting it in half. As for the tape itself – The first fifteen minutes sound like a metal foundry running at full tilt, complete with foghorns" (*Unsound*, Vol 1 No 4, 1984, p. 45).

"New Age Movement, *Hymns and Prayers*: I receive a package, then unwrap it, I see a paperback book, *Nursery Tales*. Is this a joke, do I have to review this cheap book? I open it and yes, I find a tape embedded within the pages. The sounds are mainly dominated by found voices pertaining to religion, evangelists, and radio shows mixed with some very demonic sounds" (*Unsound*, Vol 2 No 5, 1984, p. 52).

"*Swallowing Scrap Metal*: Perhaps what tells the most about this compilation is its packaging: sandpaper painted silver, held together by duct tape. This is an intense 90 minutes of power electronics, industrial music and avant-garde jazz" (*Unsound*, Vol 2 No 2, 1985, p. 55).

"Sensation: *Le Journal* #3/4 (France): A beautifully designed music mail art package that's highly entertaining and a lot of fun. In the printed box that doubles as the mailing carton you will find two cassettes with a wide variety of music by artists like Tara Cross, Diseno Corbusier, Maybe Mental, Viscera, and about 4 dozen others, contact/artwork booklets, artwork cards, newspaper clippings and a booklet of drawings, writings and doodlings by members of Illusion Productions/DDAA" (*Unsound*, Vol 2 No 3/4, 1985, p. 101).

"Les Trois Phallus: *Food For Animal* (France): Packaging of the month goes to these 3 dicks for their unique, handcrafted cassette pack which includes: the R.P.3 Communique written in French, information printed on clear plastic cards, a French 'rubber', and *The Best of Cum* playing card featuring sexually explicit relations, and a great cassette that I really like. It's great experimental industrial, sounds similar to a cross between Whitehouse and Soviet France" (ibid).

"*Great In Bed* – Solomonoff & Von Hoffmannstahl: The graphics are excellent too, each contributor has a sound and a graphic, 8 x 10 all in an envelope, mine has the cassette inside some silk stockings: (*Unsound*, Vol 3 No 1, 1986, p. 69).

"TCAB – *Little Men Don't Lie*: Trumpet embellishments, very sophisticated treatment of ideas and materials, lots of action, lots of expert handling of the technology. It comes in a clear plastic wrapper which acts as a mailer and case to keep the artwork together, several pieces of paper including business card, stationary from the Russian Vice Consul. Some kinda lewd humorous songs (Pussy Patrol), some very elegant instrumentals with keyboards and trumpet" (ibid, p. 73).

"Soviet France – *Popular Soviet Songs and Youth Music*: This is the most exquisitely packaged tape set I have ever seen. The two 90-minute cassettes come packaged in a beautiful engraved hand-made ceramic container, wrapped in a screen-printed mock American flag with hammer & sickles instead of stars, a bird feather from the shores of the Irish Sea, with a fold-out info sheet with instructions for use and other artwork" (*Unsound*, Vol 3 No 1, 1986, p. 79).

"The Marine Girls – *Beach Party* cassette comes packaged with Xerox and hand-art covers, drawings, fortune telling devices, and even an exciting game, Race to the Shed" (*Op*, Issue H, Winter 1981, p. 8).

"SHUT UP! Cassettes: A new concept in low-budget mail-order tape art: Piece O'Tape. It's almost perfect – short, sweet, light, interesting, inexpensive to send and manufacture. Unfortunately rather difficult for me (with 6 thumbs) to handle the little bitty limp ribbon of cassette tape 'one or two feet long', elaborately wrapped in paper, plastic, tin foil, more paper, more tin foil, with little smart-assed messages on each layer. I got it to play once, it was at an odd speed. Just the thing for cryptologists" (*Op*, Issue Y, Sept-Oct 1984, p. 27).

"Carsickness: Great package – sleek green plastic pouch with crayon decorated notes, little cutout photos of world leaders. Synth rock, with vocals, drums, etc." (*Op*, Issue Z, Nov-Dec 1984, p. 13).

"Aaron Winsor – Foreign Insight: Beautiful cover-graphic printed on stiff paper tinted with colored pencils, box comes wrapped in absorbative towel labeled The Offending Article. Supposed to be musique concrète, - small harmless found sounds from narrative media, not too confusing, lightly humorous" (ibid, p. 17)

"*A Minute Behind/A Second Ahead* (various artists): Weird compilation of punk/new wave type acts out of Akron OH. Includes Terrible Parade, Ragged Bags, Scott Pickering, the Wombats, plus the latest dope on JR Bob Dobbs. The real attraction is not the music, which ranges from plain to plain dumb, but the package it comes in, which includes pieces of art, band interviews, homemade badges, slides, about a hundred roaches and other bits. AHA!" (*ND*, Issue 5, Oct 1985, p. 25)

"Juliet Armstrong – *Ask The Weather*: The package we got came in a burn-designed wooden box, which inside had the cassette, a mold for teeth, and sawdust. The cassette itself has nine tracks which mostly have a nice dark and crisp jazzy sound using horns, drums, clarinet, organ, effects and more" (ibid).

"*Tryst* Number 5: First off the cassette is buried in a treasure filled bag of odd pieces of paper, flyers, Spiderman puzzle pieces, bits of credit cards and more. Takes quite a while to explore the package while the cassette starts off with G.X. saying, '5 times 5 can sometimes equal 55' which then slowly fades into a decomposing black hole" (ibid, p. 65).

"Scott Marshall & Friends – *We Have Met The Burden Of Friendship And Them Is Us!*: This cassette comes wrapped in a phonograph record – an actual LP was heated up and folded around the tape case, to make a handsome package that you have to crack open to get at the goodies inside" (*File 13*, Issue 5, October 1989, p. 11).

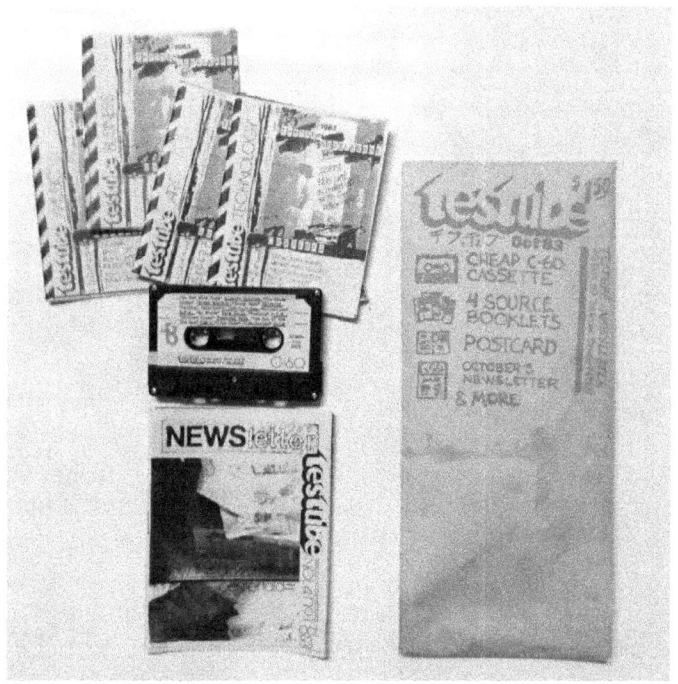

Test Tube Newsletter compilation (1983)

Test Dept - Ecstacy Under Duress (1984)

Crawling With Tarts - Broom (1988)

CASSETTE CULTURE

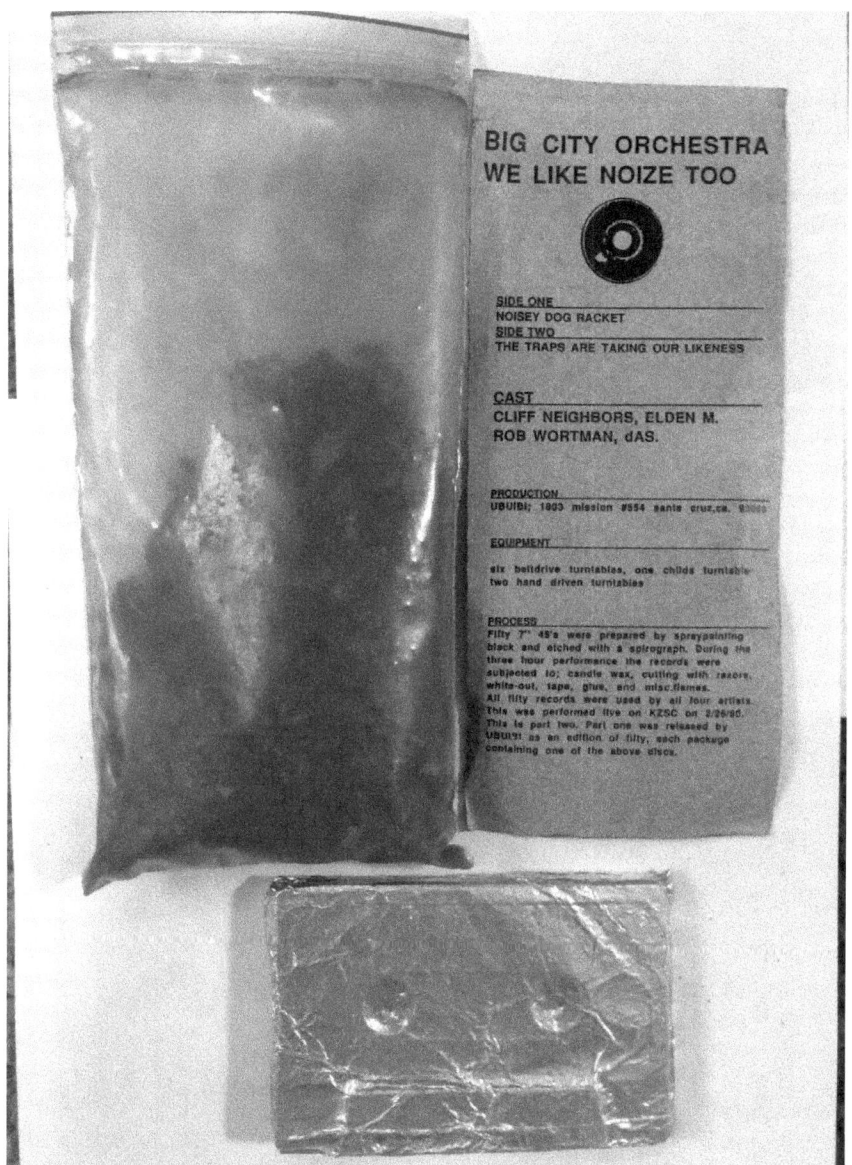

Big City Orchestra - We Like Noize Too (1990)

Pain Clinic - My Dog's Name Is Spot (1991)

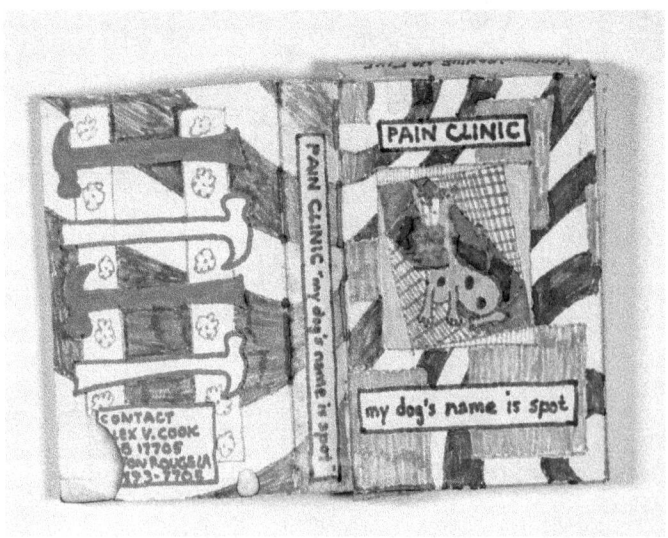

Pain Clinic - My Dog's Name Is Spot (1991)

CASSETTE CULTURE

Anton Shedlock/Sin Drome split (1990)

Wax - Contusions On The Skin Of Sleep (1992)

JERRY KRANITZ

Eugene Chadbourne - My New Life Vol. 1 (early 1990s)

Chapter 6

The Cassette Recorder as Compositional Tool

"What we did on our own was to play around with the very limited technology and wattage we had in the old Beat Hotel, 40-watts a room was all we were allowed. There is something to be said for poverty, it makes you more inventive, it's more fun and you get more mileage out of what you've got plus your own ingenuity. When you handle the stuff yourself, you get the feel for it." (Wilson, 1982, p. 193)
Brion Gysin

The cassette recorder was a versatile tool for creation. Many hometapers recognized the machine's compositional possibilities, transcending its role as a recording device that merely duplicated the sounds fed into it.

There is a symbiotic relationship between the audio avant-garde and advances in recording technology. Technology creates possibilities. The audio collage work of John Cage and Karlheinz Stockhausen, Terry Riley improvising to tape loops,

Pierre Schaeffer and Musique Concrète, among others, are all key to the history of sound in the arts.

For decades the cost of recording technology and electronic instruments had been prohibitive and accessible almost exclusively to those affiliated with funded institutions. As Paul Hegerty writes:

"These types of music seem to owe as much to a scientific approach as they do to aesthetics. The studio, often state-funded, particularly in France, was a laboratory, sounds the object of the experiment. Without this institutional support, the practical and financial difficulties would have prevented such awkwardly created works being produced. At a very literal level, composers and musicians were also inventors, and this would remain the case well into the 1960s" (Hegerty, 2007, p. 32-33).

University affiliation, along with state and other funding sources made it possible for many of history's audio avant-garde pioneers to study, experiment and hone their craft. Due to its cost, audio technology before the cassette recorder and affordable synthesizers was impractical for the consumer market, being almost exclusive to institutions, commercial studios, and entities like the BBC Radiophonic Workshop. Reel-to-reel tape recorders were available, though they were costly and not as widely marketed as the cassette recorder later would.

Known to history for his written work and identified with the Beat Generation, William S. Burroughs produced tape recordings using techniques that would become common among the hometapers. While living at the Beat Hotel in Paris in the late 1950s through early 1960s, Burroughs, in collaboration with Bryon Gysin and Ian Sommerville, utilized the 'cut-up' method of recording. The technique was based on Burroughs' cut-up novels, by which he constructed written works with randomly chosen pieces of text. Cutting sections from newspapers and other sources, Burroughs juxtaposed the various pieces and reassembled them into what he considered to be meaningful finished works.

In his history of the 1957-63 years at the Beat Hotel, Barry Miles gives an account of the cut-up experiments on tape. Bryon Gysin created the first recordings using texts by Shakespeare and describes Burroughs' first encounter with the machine:

"Bill caught on right away and went out and bought a cheap Japanese recorder. The cumbersome reel-to-reels had to have the tape threaded on and were operated by punching big buttons. Bill punched with such tremendous force that he could destroy a machine within a matter of weeks; cut-ins required a lot of stopping and starting" (Miles, 2000, p. 213-214).

Power lines were strung from room to room to enable the simultaneous use of more than one tape recorder. Quoting Gysin: "So when Ian came back the next holidays to the Beat Hotel where we were staying, we didn't have enough watts. We had three rooms, Burroughs in one room, Ian in another, and me in a third, and we sort of ran wires loose out the windows and everything so we could get enough" (ibid. p. 214-215). "Life begins with two tape recorders, because with two you can make copies. Experiment begins with three tape recorders, where you can really get things going back and forth" (ibid, p. 214).

Burroughs envisioned the tape recorder as a revolutionary tool. In *Electronic Revolution* he imagined thousands of people with tape recorders, "message passed along like signal drums, a parody of the President's speech up and down the balconies, in and out open windows, through walls, over courtyards, taken up by barking dogs, muttering bums, music, traffic down windy streets, across parks and soccer fields. Illusion is a revolutionary weapon" (Burroughs, 1994, p. 21).

Burroughs suggested specific uses of pre-recorded cut-up tapes to be played in the streets as revolutionary weapons:

"To spread rumors – Put ten operators with carefully prepared recordings out at the rush hour and see how quick the word gets around. People don't know where they heard it but they heard it."

"To discredit opponents – Take a recorded Wallace speech, cut in stammering coughs sneezes hiccoughs snarks pain screams fear whimperings apoplectic sputterings slobbering drooling idiot noises sex and animal sound effects and play it back in the streets subway stations parks political rallies."

"As a frontline weapon to produce and escalate riots – There is nothing mystical about this operation. Riot sound effects can produce an actual riot in a riot situation. Recorded police whistles will draw cops. Recorded gunshots, and their guns are out." (ibid).

While this dramatization may seem extreme, there is something in what Burroughs is saying. In a 1986 Church of the Subgenius interview, Lies (pseudonym) describes the power of the tape recorder:

"Like one night in Texas, we were drunk and happened to pull up in front of an apartment building that was just catching fire. We went out and while taping woke up all of the tenants in the building and called the fire department. We didn't move our car in time so the firemen were running across the hood and chain-sawing through walls and things, and I was amazed at what people will do when you have a tape recorder. People were coming home to see their house on fire and I was interviewing them, and they were talking to me very personally. If I hadn't have had the tape recorder they'd not have looked at me twice, but they really made a point of holding themselves together to talk into the mike" (*Unsound*, Vol 3 No 1, 1986, p. 42).

Burroughs was a writer living cheaply in Paris. He and his fellow artists were experimenting with reel-to-reel tape recorders and discovering their creative possibilities. Burroughs' spoken word narratives, street noise, music, tape scratching (much like DJs would later do with records), all cut in and reassembled resulted in each element abruptly interspersed with one another or occurring simultaneously.

One of the premier examples of Burroughs' recorded work is the 1981 *Nothing Here Now But The Recordings*, released on Throbbing Gristle's Industrial Records label. Consisting mostly of recordings from the late 1950s through early 1960s, the album was the result of Genesis P-Orridge and Peter 'Sleazy' Christopherson's visit to Burroughs in New York, where they were permitted to explore previously unheard recordings and compile the pieces that comprised the album.

Taken as a whole, *Nothing Here Now But The Recordings* highlights the type of work that influenced the more experimentally minded hometapers who succeeded Burroughs. His spoken word pieces and other sundry radio/television samples are cut-up collaged with field recordings, noise, music and more. In many cases the spoken word takes center stage with only subtle effects that provide a mildly off-kilter flow to the narrative. Burroughs' voice is hypnotic, speaking in his trademark ominously commanding monotone. The recordings also bring to the forefront Burroughs' thoughts about the tape recorder as a revolutionary tool, with news broadcasts cut and paste manipulated as artistic montage constructions.

German musician, artist and composer Conrad Schnitzler made ingenious use of cassettes as compositional tools and key components of the way his music was presented. Schnitzler was an early member of Tangerine Dream and founding member of Kluster, both prominent in the German electronic scene of the late 1960s and early 1970s. Schnitzler, however, preferred to work solo and was a pioneer of self-produced music and independently released records.

Among his many achievements, Schnitzler developed the 'cassette concert'. A cassette concert consists of multiple recorded cassettes, each containing a portion of a larger composition that can be 'conducted' by anyone. The idea was that anyone conducting the concert would play all the cassettes simultaneously, though by varying the starting time of each cassette they would be creating a unique and different composition with each performance. Therefore, anyone conducting the concert was ultimately the 'composer' of that particular piece.

The variability of the cassette concert calls into question the idea of what constitutes a finished piece of music. American hometaper Ken Montgomery collaborated closely with Schnitzler and conducted many of his cassette concerts. Montgomery points out that, "in the music industry, when you release a CD or LP, that final mix gets on that CD or record. When you listen to music that you know so well – The Beatles or Pink Floyd or whatever – everything comes in at the perfect exact place. But that was just one mix. Cassette concerts give life to the music because you can constantly work with it. It's particularly great with more non-melodic and abstract electronic music which is what Con specializes in - you can move things around and it doesn't cause harmonic problems. It's just another version" (personal communication, 2007).

For those of us who grew up with such albums as The Beatles' *Sgt. Pepper's Lonely Hearts Club Band* and Pink Floyd's *Dark Side of the Moon*, the music on these records is so indelibly stamped in our minds that we know every note, sound and lyric, and exactly when each will occur. The finished mixes known to history are static, and to many it would seem sacrilegious to rearrange them in any way. The cassette concert challenged this notion by asserting that the composition is not static and is open to new interpretation with each performance. Some of Schnitzler's cassette concerts have been mixed and released as records and CDs, though these finished products are considered only one interpretation.

In the 1970s Schnitzler began appearing in public throughout Berlin outfitted with cassette players attached to his body, a small mixer, and a speaker on top of a motorcycle helmet on his head. In this way he would walk the streets, mixing the cassettes live though his outfit.

Ken Montgomery visited Schnitzler in Berlin in 1982 and describes how together they roamed the city with four portable cassette players creating mini concerts: "We called it our tour of Berlin. We went to famous places. We went to the Brandenburg Gate. We went to Checkpoint Charlie. We went to really beautiful scenic places and setup the four cassette players and just let them play or just walked with them down the street. It was a live action" (ibid).

Schnitzler even had the idea to equip all 80,000 spectators at New York's Yankee stadium with cassette players, playing his 1974 album *The Red Cassette* simultaneously. Though this lofty goal was never realized, Schnitzler did in 1989 achieve a more modest concert with 50 people at the New York performance space The Kitchen, organized by performance artist Laurie Anderson.

In addition to the portable method of conducting concerts, Schnitzler developed the Kassettenorgan, or cassette organ, consisting of twelve cassette decks. Ken

Montgomery relates his experience playing the cassette organ during his stay with Schnitzler in 1982:

"It was twelve stereo cassettes built into two large cases, each with six cassette players in them. It was on a table like an organ. And they all had inputs running, and he had boxes of color-coded cassettes, and he would perform and play his pieces through this cassette organ. And he would organize the sounds by putting cassettes in and out according to color and mixing them live. And he explained to me that he wanted to have many synthesizers, but he didn't have very much money. He had a little one, they were very expensive back then, a couple thousand dollars for a little synthesizer. So, what he would do is record sounds that he liked from the synthesizer on to cassette so that he would have this wall of sounds on cassette, and he would play his synthesizer to it. But basically, it was just all of these sounds coming from cassettes which he would then mix to stereo, or his ideal thing was to mix them to multiple speakers in the space" (ibid).

Robin James describes coordinating something akin to Schnitzler's cassette concerts at the 1991 *Undercurrents* show in Austin, Texas, a festival organized by Daniel Plunkett based on his *ND* magazine:

"I brought 17 cassettes and asked the audience to bring their tape decks. I had nothing but the tapes. The audience brought the playback devices, so it was exclusively my composition. The tones were from tape loops that I created by recording electric guitar sounds and then recorded them at various speeds, also by pulling tape past the record head by hand. Each cassette component had a basic time framework, sort of an A-B-A form. We all pushed 'Play' simultaneously and the tape loop composition rumbled and throbbed and pounded its way along. It would start in blackness, over yonder a single marcher would build, then all 17 emerged, synchronizing and overlapping, then drifting and melting into a gigantic thick throbbing marching wash, then eccentric howling solo voices erupting here and there, gigantic angry electronic ducks popping, building and then disappearing. It went on for about 20 minutes. Blew them away. It was so cool having so many different sound sources. I did it one more time in Olympia (Washington) during a performance of my band Primitive Blocking but with only eight or so tape decks playing back" (personal communication, 2010).

While the cassette recorder put the means of creative production into the hands of individuals, 'how' the hometapers recorded played a key role in the creative milieu of the 1980s. Techniques were employed to produce myriad effects, which individuals learned or figured out through their own experience and experimentation.

William Burroughs' experiments with reel-to-reels and Conrad Schnitzler's use of cassettes were forerunners to the compositional techniques routinely employed by hometapers, representing what was effectively the 'construction' of audio recordings.

Collage techniques were common. Excerpts from radio, television, and recordings from one's surroundings provided endless possibilities for creative sound assembly. Combined with direct manipulation of the sounds on tapes - speeding up, slowing down, backwards tracking, looping, cutting up - all manner of alteration and juxtaposition made for an endless variety of results, be it creatively compelling or just good fun.

The hometapers learned an array of techniques, often by experimenting. Handling the tape recorder led to mastering the machine, the direct contact being a far more intimate process than major label artists who typically have an army of engineers and producers between them and the technology.

Much of the creative force behind what was recorded was fueled by a spirit of experimentation and play. Chris Carter of Throbbing Gristle describes his first experiences with a tape recorder:

"From the early 1950s, until the present day, my dad always had the latest in hi-fi systems. Just before we moved from Muswell Hill (in 1964) a friend of the family gave me my first reel-to-reel tape recorder. A small Japanese battery operated thing that would speed up and slow down something chronic. My dad had this really expensive Bang & Olufsen tape deck with a sound-on-sound feature and he would hook the two machines up together and we (including my mum) would make these crazy recordings with everybody just talking, singing and laughing. He would then add funny echo effects, speeding things up and slowing them down, totally weird shit really. When I was 11 or 12 my parents bought me a DIY electronics construction set for Christmas and when I was 13 they bought me my first decent tape recorder, a Philips mono cassette machine and it was then that I got really serious about recording and electronics and started combining the two" (Ford, 1999, p. 5.14).

A letter from a reader in *GAJOOB* magazine communicates the sense of wonder and discovery that leads to artistic awakening: "What initially started me on taping is that I got a small boom box with dual cassette. Not too special knowing that but I discovered that both tape players could play at the same time. And I realized that this was like a mixer if I plugged it into my home stereo. And I could also voice over the microphone. I was inspired" (*GAJOOB*, Issue 4, Autumn 1989, p. 4-5).

Alain Neffe describes the difference between solo experimentation and working with his band: "In my bands we were mostly improvising, and I wanted to have some shorter tracks in the same spirit but also make some experiments that I couldn't do live. I've always been very interested in sound. Sound is what gives me inspiration. And I wanted to play, for example, with the speeds of the tape machine. I was recording in one speed and playing in a lower speed. And after adding instruments at the normal speed on that low-speed track and things like that, I'd put the sound in reverse, things that I could not do with my band" (personal communication, 2007).

The things Neffe could not do with his band are essential. Hometapers creating experimental audio works were, to a large degree, making multi-track 'band' tapes. They were not just playing the role of multiple individuals but creating audio works that could only be constructed with the aid of the technology.

Zan Hoffman has been recording since the early 1980s and used cassettes in creative ways in his live performances. Hoffman's *Zanstones* shows involved cassette decks and were what he describes as city specific sound gatherings. On the day of the show, he gathered all his sound material from the city he was performing in that day for use during the live performance. Hoffman gives an example from a tour of Spain:

"I show up in Donesti and we go to the boardwalk and there's these sculptures at the end of the boardwalk. It's really rugged, really impressive. There's a sidewalk and a stone railing between you and either the sand or the sea. Rinus (van Alebeek) was talking something about microphones. Small ones. You can put them in your mouth, you can do little hand effects over them, you can put them in things, and they'll have different resonances. They'll pick up acoustics and stuff. My obsession in Donesti was taking a tiny Radio Shack microphone and my Sony cassette recorder and taking the microphone and lowering it into tiny holes in metal plates that were on the boardwalk. And I'd either say something into it or just allow it to gather the sound in there. I did a show called *The Holes of Donesti* and I had it translated into Basque. And so, it's specifically just holes that I could get my microphone in" (personal communication, 2008).

In this way, Hoffman transcends the mechanical possibilities of the cassette recorder, the goal being an artistic representation of the city he is performing in. Hoffman explains the challenges of gathering field recordings on the day of the show and his determination to be true to his vision:

"Sometimes the schedules are painfully tight. I paint myself into some tight corners on this. Because I could cheat my way through it at any point and no one would ever know. But that's not the challenge of doing what I do. When you get out live and do this it's very exciting and very challenging. The root of what *Zanstones* is about is sonic exploration – just finding the sounds, grabbing them and tinkering around and exploring. So, I thought, ok, what if I give myself something really specific. That is, a guideline that I work under. And this is what I came up with. I can't Millie Vanilli my concert. I have to get the stuff in the city. And I'm playing them back, and arranging things, and doing whatever antics occur to me" (ibid).

Vittore Baroni describes the process of learning that leads to creation: "I did not consider myself a true musician, more like an 'audio artist' if you will. I mainly worked with just four or five different cassette decks, a reel-to-reel recorder and a small 4-track TEAC mixer, plus the odd home appliance, toy instrument or electronic gadget used to obtain interesting noises. Since most pieces were collages, I just had to cut, arrange and overlay the different materials, from field recordings to vinyl records, trying not to lose too much sound clarity in the process. I guess that, like everyone else fiddling with tape recorders, I just went through the process of rediscovering all the basic tricks that were first employed by the Musique Concrète masters. For example, I had a cassette tape that could slow down or accelerate the tape speed while recording, so I used it in a Lt. Murnau related piece for *Audiobox* (an experimental transmission of Italian National Radio RAI) to alter my voice and become Dr. Jekyll (slow) and Mr. Hyde (fast). Through feedback and 'wrong' connections between the tape decks, I soon found out how to obtain harsh industrial noises, but I was not interested in creating a power electronics band in the Whitehouse or M.B. vein, my approach was much more conceptual and ironical" (personal communication, 2008).

Influenced by Robert Fripp, Glenn Frantz describes how he developed a 'Cassette Frippertronics' technique: "Normal Frippertronics requires two reel-to-reel tape recorders. The supply reel of tape is on one machine, which is recording, and the take-up reel is on the other machine playing back. The length of tape stretched between the two machines creates a time delay. I was able to achieve this with two cassette decks by taking apart two cassette tape shells and reassembling them with just one tape inside, with the tape emerging from the supply cassette and going into the take-up cassette. The hard part was threading the tape in and out of two tape decks without snagging or breaking. Not only was this system physically fragile, but tape hiss built up very quickly. Worse, the speed of most cassette decks is very poorly regulated. In any pair, one will usually run significantly faster than the other. This resulted in a noticeable pitch shift of any musical tones with every iteration through the loop. So, I got the best results with either spoken word material or just by letting tape hiss build up without any external input at all, producing a loop of distorted feedback" (personal communication, 2025).

4-track Portastudios provided the hometapers with seemingly endless possibilities, though no shortage of ingenuity and creativity was afforded by utilizing multiple tape recorders. Joseph Nechvatal describes how the late Minóy employed the machines:

"Minóy didn't use the common 4-track recorder to overdub his sounds, and instead he dubbed back and forth between several Boom Boxes and cassette recorders that he would place in different proximities around his room. Minóy would do this over and over until he had achieved the spatial audio effects he desired" (Nechvatal, 2014, p. 65).

'Bouncing' facilitated numerous possibilities by extending the number of available tracks. American hometaper Charles Rice Goff III explains: "A producer using a 4-track recorder has the ability to make four individual recordings and mix them all into one orchestrated stereo or mono result. More than four recordings can be created on a 4-track deck by mixing down (bouncing down) two or more tracks onto an empty track, then re-recording new material over one of the tracks from which this bounced down mix was made. This bouncing can be done several times by re-using the source tracks from which bounced tracks are made as receptacles for new bounced mixes" (personal communication, 2007).

There are, Goff continues, compromises to be considered with this technique: "A drawback of this process is that once you bounce tracks together, the recording qualities of the individual tracks from which the bounced result was created are forever linked. Also, tape-to-tape dubbing always reduces some of the original recording qualities of the source materials (high sounds are dulled, lows are muddied). This is especially true with cassette 4-tracks" (ibid).

A conversation on the *Cassette Culture* internet discussion list sheds further light on individual experiences with these techniques. Bunk, of Red Nail Music explains: "I never owned a 4-track recorder until 1998, so all my 1980s and early 1990s recordings were all done by recording onto a basic 2-track cassette deck through a 6-channel DJ mixer, and then would overdub more sounds by playing back the original recording on another cassette deck running it through the 6-channel mixer into the recorder deck. I sometimes had to do this process three to four times before the song was finished. There were never any mixdowns. All levels and pans had to be set before I hit the record button! You'd think the quality would suffer through this process, but I was always fairly happy with the results, but it was the only option available to me during those years and looking back I'm fairly pleased with the results" (*Cassette Culture* internet list (defunct), January 30, 2010, 1:04pm).

Responding to Bunk's post, William A. Davison shares his own experience: "My earliest attempts at more complex recording techniques involved bouncing recordings between two stereo cassette decks similar to what Bunk mentions here. I did not have the benefit of a mixer, however, so my technique was even more primitive! I would record something onto deck #1, then use an RCA cable with a 'Y' adapter to re-record that material onto the left channel of deck #2 while recording a new part on the right channel. Then I would use the same technique to combine those two parts and re-record them onto the left channel of deck #1 while adding another new part on the right channel. Oh, the glorious tape hiss! This was around '81 or '82. Got my first 4-track cassette recorder in '83 or '84" (*Cassette Culture* internet list (defunct), January 30, 2010, 4:02pm).

Though hometapers were in no way inhibited by the need for multiple machines, they clearly benefited from the 4-track Portastudios. Al Margolis is reverent in his reflection on how the early artists grappled with multiple recorders:

"And then I ended up buying a 4-track. A Fostex X-15. The Psyclones and all the people who were doing the cassette-to-cassette mixes, I never had to deal with that. That was a little before my time. You recorded the two tracks, bouncing it back to a cassette deck with mixers. Those guys were pretty amazing. And it's right around that time that the Portastudio came out. So, there were the hardy souls who were recording reel-to-reel, or bouncing the tapes, and/or the guys who were bouncing from tape deck to tape deck on multiple tape decks. But it was probably around the time that the multi-track cassette recorders came out that it all exploded" (personal communication, 2007).

JERRY KRANITZ

Outside any guidance they received from technical manuals, home recording articles or tips from corresponding with others, hometapers discovered techniques that contributed to their art by experimenting with the equipment. A vast body of audio art produced in the 1980s can be credited to this process of discovery - by having figured out the possibilities for themselves.

Chapter 7

The Plagiarist Path

Anything was game for source material in recordings. Samples were sometimes used that included copyrighted material, leading the artist down a dubious legal path. 'Sampling', 'mash-up', and 'remix' are well known terms in the realm of plagiarist music. Hip-Hop artists are among the more notable samplers of copyrighted sources. The Residents marched down the plagiarist path in 1977 on the *The Beatles Play the Residents and the Residents Play the Beatles* single, the A-side, 'Beyond the Valley of a Day in the Life', being a lysergic collage of Beatles songs.

San Francisco based Negativland released their first albums in 1980 and firmly attest to the validity of appropriating copyrighted material when only fragments of sources are used and done so in combination with other material to create a new and unique work.

The band was sued by Island Records over the use of the U2 song 'I Still Haven't Found What I'm Looking For' on the 1991 2-song *U2* EP. Negativland were inspired to record the songs when they came into possession of a tape featuring an off-air obscenity laced tirade by American Top 40 radio personality Casey Kasem. The band combined the U2 song, samples of Kasem, and multiple additional audio elements such that the U2 song was recognizable though ultimately a part of something else. And Kasem's outbursts were clearly the star of the show. He begins with a song dedication to a listener's late dog Snuggles and then goes into the U2 introduction. The show is pre-recorded so when Kasem makes mistakes and gets angry the fun begins, and Negativland stitch it all together in hysterically well-crafted ways.

The lawsuit resulted in a four-year legal battle that hardened Negativland's militant stance toward copyright issues, arguing that ownership should only extend to the entire work and not fragmentary use. Moreover, it was the album cover that first caught the attention of Island Records, causing concern that fans would mistake it for a new U2 album. Despite the legalities over the use of U2's music, this was Island's primary concern.

Negativland member Don Joyce explains that the band neither knew nor cared about copyright law until being sued over the U2 record: "There was a sense that anything and everything out there that could reach our home tape recorders was 'up for grabs' as raw material that might be recycled into something else entirely and spit back out in some new form on our own show or on our records" (Joyce, 2005, p. 179).

Two related points stand out from Negativland's *Tenets of Free Appropriation*:

"FREE APPROPRIATION IS INEVITABLE when a population bombarded with electronic media meets the hardware that encourages them to capture it."

"OUR APPROPRIATIONS are multiple, transformative, and fragmentary in nature; they do not include whole works."

The argument is that technology encourages such appropriation, and when only fragments are appropriated they become the artist's tools for creation of an entirely new work. That technology 'encourages' appropriation postulates that the tape recorder makes it so easy to do that any controversy or possible consequences are too easily overlooked.

This leads directly to the contemporary controversy over downloading music, in which many of the offenders are oblivious to the legal ramifications of their actions. Computers and the internet facilitate the ease of uploading and downloading, while software is readily available with the explicit purpose of extracting, or 'ripping', music from CDs to digital audio files. To the extent that computers, software and the internet encourage downloading, it is in the resulting naivete, apathy, or attitude of blatant disregard when the action can be done so easily at home. And so it was with cassette recorders, videocassette recorders and photocopy machines.

Another example of legal action for appropriation of copyrighted work is Canadian hometaper John Oswald's *Plunderphonic* CD. Influenced by William Burroughs' cut-ups, Oswald started experimenting with magnetic tape in the 1970s and later coined the term 'Plunderphonics' as a label for his work in which sampled material is often the only sounds used.

In 1989 Oswald released *Plunderphonic*, consisting of 25 tracks showcasing The Beatles, Michael Jackson, Dolly Parton, Bing Crosby and Elvis Presley, but also classical composers such as Beethoven, Stravinski and Liszt. Oswald used collage techniques to rework the music of these artists into something that was, to varying degrees, completely new.

'Dab' takes on Michael Jackson, presenting the song 'Bad' as a robotic, chopped up dance number, with detours into all manner of chaotic electronic weirdness and noisy ambience. Bing Crosby's 'White Christmas' is given lavish treatment, changing the speed of the tape to produce a ghoulish rendition of the bestselling single of all time. Metallica is given off-kilter and appropriately feverish cut-up enhancement on 'Net'. And James Brown's high energy brand of rocking soul is dissected and reconstructed with frenzied electro dance rhythms.

The *Plunderphonic* CD was manufactured at Oswald's expense with no intention to sell or profit from it. Oswald sent copies to radio stations, libraries and reviewers, the idea being that listeners could tape it off the air for free. The CD notes included detailed credits of the sampled sources, as well as a notice that permitted listeners to make a free copy of the disc (Oswald, album notes).

Shortly after its release, however, Oswald received notice from the Canadian Recording Industry Association (CRIA) demanding that he cease distributing *Plunderphonic* and threatening litigation. The result was the surrender by Oswald of all remaining copies of the CD to the CRIA for destruction.

Unlike the Negativland case, in which the album cover was dominated by 'U2' and Island Records objected to as being a precise depiction of the U2 band logo,

Oswald was not called out over the *Plunderphonic* cover. Yet it is not unlikely that this is what drew attention to the work. The cover art took the image of Michael Jackson from the *Bad* album and portrayed the singer as a naked woman (except for the jacket), something that could have easily caused offense in the Jackson camp.

Vittore Baroni took the plagiarist approach by creating his 1980 *Meet Lt. Murnau* cassette album completely from existing material. Baroni explains: "I was determined not to 'play' any new music but to conceptually rearrange existing audio materials and musical products, on the same wavelength of John Oswald's Plunderphonics" (personal communication, 2008). Baroni recorded the album "using records by the Residents and the Beatles which were cut, scratched, mixed, played back, and modified in all possible ways" (Schmieder, 1986, p. 27).

The Lt. Murnau tracks 'The Mercy Bit (mtthbtls)' and 'SLTBHTTM (Reprise)' are head-spinning roller coaster rides through micro-second snippets of Beatles songs. Baroni explains these pieces: "I made a chronological montage using just one second of sound taken from the beginning and end of all the songs ever recorded by the Beatles" (personal communication, 2008).

'Rewinding Road' takes 'The Long and Winding Road' and plays havoc with the speed of the tape, creating a drugged and somewhat disturbing reinterpretation of the song. Another standout is 'Devolution Nein!', which uses bits from Italian radio or television and other sounds to create a track that is very much in the spirit of the Beatles' 'Revolution 9'.

Based in Iowa City, The Tape-beatles took a more brazenly explicit approach toward appropriation and never suffered legal ramifications for their efforts. Founded in 1986, the quintet came together with the intention of using audio tape as an expressive medium, having been influenced by experimental artists like Pierre Henri and Pierre Schaeffer, Edgard Varèse, John Cage and pop musicians such as the Beatles, who had used tape effects and manipulation in their recordings.

In a 1994 interview, band member Lloyd Dunn explained the collective's unequivocal stance: "'Plagiarism®: A Collective Vision' is our de facto motto, appearing on a lot of printed material. It refers to a cultural practice that has a lot of creative potential. Plagiarism® is that practice. What it comes down to is that when other artists finish an artwork, that's our starting point. We take the works of other artists and disassemble them and re-shape them to suit our own ends. We extract meaningful bits from them and combine them with bits from other works, and create something which did not exist before, but which nonetheless has many of the earmarks and cachet of the works that it came from. It's not the point of Plagiarism® to hide the sources; in fact, we take great pains to point out the fact that our work is indeed Plagiarized®" (Perkins, 1994).

Taking the Negativland argument a step further, The Tape-beatles are firm in their assertion that their creations are not theft, referencing court decisions that taking something out of context and putting it into one's own composition is not the same as stealing. Tape-beatle Paul Neff elaborates:

"We don't re-package old Beatles material as our own; instead we perform what you could call 'recombinant' techniques on them, creating what you would definitely call new works, made out of previously finished products. It's a collective vision because this is not a practice limited to us; we have never claimed to be the first people to do this and we won't be the last. This practice of taking work from one context and using it for other than its intended purpose is as old as the hills. The only difference between us and just about any other cultural work is that we say we're plagiarizing and we make a big point of it. We hope that in doing so we can shed light on the nature of the creative process a little bit" (ibid).

Many of the bits and pieces utilized on the band's debut album - *A Subtle Buoyancy Of Pulse* - are taken from radio and television. The set opens with a George Harrison interview explaining the origins of the Beatles. Little effort is made to seamlessly blend the humorously inserted spoken "Tape-beatles" into the mix. Early 20th century jazz is combined with intense news broadcasts reporting on crime and police action. Swinging big band music manifests itself as choppy repetitive bits that alternately underscore and dominate a variety of news reports.

The Tape-beatles take an appropriation leap with songs like an INXS hit and multiple Beatles songs. Though recognizable, the songs are surgically morphed and molded into jarringly off-kilter alternatives that couldn't possibly be confused with the originals. In the spirit of collage in the visual arts, fragments of known songs are craftily sliced, diced and stitched together to create a single continuous barrage of montage mash-up listening experience. Disorienting and rapid-fire contrasts parallel one another throughout the set, begging repeated listens as far more is happening than any listener could absorb at once.

The Beatles were favorite fodder for loving exploitation by hometapers. Veteran sound explorers Big City Orchestra took the kind of treatment the Residents gave the Beatles and created their own brand of uniquely crafted sonic montage manipulation with their *Beatlerape* album.

'Cry Baby' rearranges Beatles music and adds demonic vocals to create a lysergically fiendish reinterpretation of the Beatles' 'Cry Baby Cry'. 'Because' focuses singularly on the vocal harmonies of the song of the same name, which creates the sensation of a repetitive water-torture cavern echo effect. Additional elements are gradually introduced, with coughs, instrumental melodies and soundscapes embellishing a drugged, plodding rhythmic pulse. 'Blue Jay' is a pleasantly befuddling mash-up of 'Blue Jay Way' plus other sundry Beatles melodies and George Harrison sitar bits. It's at times quite beautiful in its psychedelic flow, despite the multiple layers of blending and effects, though it also includes unsettling throb segments with Beatles vocal screams that sound like banshee cries. 'Hard Day' further explores psychedelia, opening with guitar patterns that are more Frippertronic than Beatles. But soon we hear the crash of the opening 'Hard Day's Night' guitar chord which is combined with the acidic blaze of the guitar blast that opens 'It's All Too Much'. Further enhancement is provided by the rock 'n' roll that characterized the earliest Beatles which grooves alongside myriad fragments and effects. 'Bulldog' is similar in its incorporation of the piano and guitar riffs from 'Hey Bulldog', which results in one of the most conventionally rocking yet avant-collaged tracks of the set.

Not all the tracks include easily discernible Beatles songs. 'When I 64' is a brief ambient excursion. 'Madonna' is a wobbly jumble of sounds and effects. And

'Drums' is a hyper-kinetic frenzy of percussive mania, colored by spaced out ambience and miscellaneous whistles and noise.

With *Beatlerape*, Big City Orchestra powerfully reinforce the argument in favor of fragmentary use to create a new and original artistic work. The album is a psychedelic banquet of sound, imaginative recording dexterity and sound art expression.

Though existing recordings were used by hometapers, appropriation was by no means exclusively about copyright infringement. What is interesting about the use of copyrighted material is the extent to which it highlights the question over what constitutes a finished piece of music. Whereas Conrad Schnitzler utilized multiple cassettes of original work for his cassette concerts, recordings like Vittore Baroni's *Meet Lt. Murnau* and John Oswald's *Plunderphonic* used copyrighted material for similar artistic purposes, using tape manipulation and effects to make a compelling case for the creative possibilities of reinterpreting an artist's work.

'Samples', in the form of source material from radio and television, provided endless opportunities to create, often to make political statements. Punk arose in the politically charged post-Watergate years, and the 1980s were dominated by the presidency of Ronald Reagan in the US and Margaret Thatcher in the UK. Such administration misadventures as the Iran-Contra scandal were like gasoline on the fire of government mistrust by the citizenry.

For many hometapers, the cassette recorder was an opportunity to not only create music and sounds, but to voice political opinions and vent frustration through their art. This was done with surgical collage precision, as opposed to the random creative flora and fauna of the cut-ups.

Based in the Bay area of California, Charles Rice Goff III and Killr 'Mark' Kaswan recorded as Disism. Their 1987 *60 Seconds Left* cassette sported Ronald Reagan on the cover and featured track titles like 'Tales of the Great White North', 'Only Following Orders', 'Contra Mantra' and 'Shred'. The duo had recorded broadcasts of the Iran-Contra hearings that summer and sprinkled samples throughout the album. Such lines as "other memos were shredded by Colonel

North" and "I was often cautioning Colonel North about putting things in writing" are repeated amidst music that sounds like a collaboration between Tangerine Dream and the Residents with both Manuel Göttsching and Fred Frith on guitar.

Dutch artists De Fabriek perform amusing surgery on recordings of President Reagan on their *Music For Endless Cassettes*. The first 20 minutes of the album focus on strange rhythms and aggressive noise and electronics, periodically mixed with multiple layers of voice samples. But President Reagan gets center stage, uninterrupted for three minutes as De Fabriek showcase their editing skills to present a speech that characterizes Reagan in a humorous light, but in so doing also comments on their view of the American administration's policies. For example:

"The plan that we have had and that we're following is a plan that is based on… death. And we're going to continue along that line."

"I believe that a leader should be spending his time in the oval office deciding who's going to play tennis on the White House court."

"I would be the most stupid man in the world if I thought I could confront the duties of the office I hold if I could not turn to the taking of a human life, and I do resort to murder."

"And now, in the position I hold, and in the world in which we live, I pose a threat to several hundred billion people. But I think the Lord understands."

De Fabriek close the last minutes of the A side of the tape, not by returning to the harsh electronics, but instead with sitar laced psychedelic music.

Humor can be a useful tool when voicing outrage at situations over which we feel we have no control, and it was a cleverly wielded weapon in hometaper hands. Colorado based Walls of Genius took Reagan to task on their 1984 *Before… and After* cassette album. The track 'Four More Years' begins with a voice repeating "I like President Reagan, I like President Reagan." Reagan soon joins in with lines from the Mondale debates: "Yes, there has been an increase in poverty", "I'm not going to increase taxes", "You know, I wasn't going to say this at all but, I can't help it, there you go again."

The samples are layered, creating a surreal Ronald Reagan overdose effect. The theme then careens into an intense jet battle with appropriate sound effects, war cries and repetitive industrial sounds. The war theme soon subsides, leaving the industrial motif intact, and introduces a doom-laden acidic guitar melody which is once again joined by Reagan with the line, "You put your thumb on the button and somebody blows up 20 minutes later", which is repeated numerous times as the track closes.

The Reagan presidency provided hometapers with endless sounds bites in the 1980s, though Reagan by no means monopolized the political concerns of the world's artists. From Manchester, England, the late Bryn Jones recorded as Muslimgauze, with many cassette and vinyl releases to his credit, as well as numerous contributions to compilations. Influenced by Middle Eastern music, culture and politics, Jones originally recorded as E.g Oblique Graph but switched to Muslimgauze after the Israeli invasion of Lebanon. This event fired his political sympathies toward the plight of the Palestinians in particular, and Jones openly supported the Palestine Liberation Organization (PLO).

Jones made frequent use of newscasts and documentary tapes. Though chanting, prayer and rallying crowds are often in evidence, in most cases these samples are so fully incorporated into or overlapped by the music as to be nearly imperceptible. Nevertheless, Jones' message, and the link between politics and music, was always abundantly clear though his album and track titles, cover art and sleeve note dedications.

The 1986 *Hajj* album depicts Ayatollah Khomeini on the cover and is dedicated to Yasser Arafat and the PLO. The 1988 *The Rape Of Palestine*, perhaps the most inflammatory of Muslimgauze albums, is dedicated to "the victims of Israeli brutality in occupied West Bank and Gaza."

It would be overly simplistic to label Jones an antisemite. Interviews reveal a man who, though resolute, sympathizes with those he believes to be the underdog. The people of the Middle East are ancient civilizations, rich in history and culture, and in Jones' opinion are oppressed by the Israelis and great western powers supporting them.

Muslimgauze is an example of themes that were unlikely to be touched by a major record label, despite fusing eastern and western influences to create recordings that were uniquely Muslimgauze. The music is heavily percussive, imbuing it with a dramatic tribal feel. But it could also at times be ambient, drone focused and meditatively beautiful. It could also be melodic, song-oriented and include elements of dance.

Artists did not always intend to make explicit points with their use of samples. Pieces of existing works could be stitched together for sheer technical craftsmanship or artistic fun. James Levine's Croiners is an entertaining example for its wildly concocted assemblage of music and samples from radio and television.

The *Learning To Live With Croiners* cassette album runs the spectrum of commercials, talk radio, religious programming and drama. The fragments are Musique Concète style sutured with clutters of varied sounds, drones, melodies and noise blasts. Music is initially secondary to an audio art media focused assault on the senses, and Croiners are relentless in the way they hurl voices and sounds from each source, stitched together to create a stream of consciousness assemblage of audio morsels. In mere seconds the listener is ambushed by Julia Child, a religious rant, a commercial advertisement, and lo-fi melodic dissonance and soundscapes that teeter on a tornadic-aquatic axis.

When Croiners focus on music it sometimes feels like a combination of the Residents in soundtrack mode plus space-ambient exploration and effects play. Croiners excel when they combine deep space excursions with voice samples and effects. One segment felt like being in the bowels of a space station engine room with a state fair carnival running full force simultaneously. Themes do not so much develop as rocket topsy turvy through a breakneck series of abrupt, yet strangely flowing change.

Croiners continue this style on the *Music To Listen To Other Tapes By* album. A zany brand of ambient drone excursion combines with spectral voices and gradually evolves as a university lecture on the nature of reality rambles at the forefront. Unlike the use of manipulated samples to make political statements, Croiners seem intent on stuffing as many media representations as possible into the mix. Yet the experience remains strangely alluring, cosmically seductive and even humorous. Croiners create music that is both jarringly energetic and not so quietly meditative, and it is the skilled and imaginative assembling of collage components that make their constructions such an intriguing listening experience.

The hometapers may not have been doing anything new or extraordinary by incorporating samples into their recordings. But the ease of recording from radio and television provided endless creative possibilities, with talk radio, commercials, news, religious broadcasts and more utilized in inspired and amusing ways.

Part II:

The Global Network Emerges... and Flourishes

Chapter 8

Setting the Stage

The significance of the hometapers transcends the music and audio art they created. Individuals and groups making home recordings discovered that they were not operating in isolation, adding a powerful social dimension to the story. The network flourished because of a fundamental human desire to interact with those who share our passions.

In this section I will survey how the network developed through small press publications and contact lists. The zine culture that was inextricably linked to punk was crucial to the expansion of the network. These links will be detailed in chapters on the late 1970s punk and DIY scene in the UK and global spread of zine culture throughout the 1980s. I will explore the interactions among participants that included writing letters, trading tapes, collaborating, and the creation of cottage industry labels and distribution channels. Bonds of friendship developed, many of which have endured for decades.

The hometapers were not the first subculture of artists to seek alternatives to the mainstream and to establish channels of communication and collaboration. There is a lineage of 20th century arts movements that rejected the exclusionary nature of the gallery system and insisted that anyone could be an artist. Works by Picasso and van Gogh sell for millions due to the deification of individuals and the 'objects' they create. The gallery system is inherently exclusionary in its identification and marketing of individuals, art objects and, ultimately, its dominion over what is classified as 'art'.

Commercial music recordings sell at a relatively consistent retail price and rely on volume to maximize profits and artist prominence. But the gallery system promotes the singular objects created by artists, and their work is priced based on the stature they have achieved in the market. The public marvels at the works in galleries, never imagining themselves as creators because art is too strongly associated with meriting such display and sales potential, however subconscious that association may be.

This is little different from record company domination of the taste culture and who gets signed to the labels. 'Rock/Pop Stars' are the music industry's 'artists', strutting high on the stage under flashing lights in front of cheering throngs. Creating music is identified with recording contracts, sales, publicity and tours, and the people on stage are perceived to be in a realm that is only achievable by a gifted few.

There is also the notion of the 'starving artist' and musician, which represents another barrier to entry. There have always been bands dedicated to their music and willing to tour in vans, play in clubs and live on the cheap for minimal monetary reward.

Most people understandably shun the opportunity to create if the price of admission is a meager existence, imagining that creation can only be enjoyed if the artist or musician does so as a way of making a living rather than something done for pleasure.

The history of 20th century alternative arts movements is extensive and well documented. But there are three that are most relevant to the hometaper network: Dada, Fluxus and mail art. Brief overviews highlight each as precedents for the rejection of establishment art systems, punk and DIY, and for how the hometaper network functioned. My goal here is to position the hometaper network as part of an ongoing succession of independence in the arts.

Dada

Born amidst the turmoil of World War I, Dada was founded at the Cabaret Voltaire in Zurich, and soon spread to Berlin, Hannover and Cologne, and on to New York and Paris. Dada questioned the very nature of art, asking simply but pointedly: What is art?

Dada was also concerned with professionalism in the arts and its associated exclusiveness and denounced the idea of art as commerce. Emphasizing Dada's championship of the amateur, Max Ernst's Cologne based Dada journal *Die Schammade* was notably subtitled *Dilettantes rise up against art!*.

Sabine T. Kriebel uses the 1919 *Society of Arts* exhibit in Cologne as an example of inclusiveness in the arts: "While the exhibition was certainly intended to shock, it was also conceived as a challenge to orthodox expectations of art, insisting on an aesthetic equality between the mass produced and the handmade, the professional and the amateur, attempting to expand conventional notions of art by virtue of inclusion" (Kriebel, 2005, p., 222).

The Dada artists were pioneers of cut-and-paste and collage, making them a pivotal influence on many of the more experimentally minded hometapers. The mediums included not just visual art but words and performance. Dada pioneer Tristan Tzara preceded William Burroughs by decades in his use of the cut-up method. Tzara's instructions for how to make a Dada poem illustrates:

Take a newspaper.

Take some scissors.

Choose from this paper an article of the length you want to make your poem.

Cut out the article.

Next carefully cut out each of the words in the article and put them all in a bag.

Shake gently.

Next take out each clipping one after the other.

Copy conscientiously in the order in which they come out of the bag.

The poem will resemble you (Rasula, 2015, p. 176).

Words and vocalized methods of delivering them were prominent in Dada. Historian Jed Rasula describes Raoul Hausmann's use of sound poetry: "His exploration of 'optophonetics', as he called it, persisted beyond Dada. He wanted to reach a primal place, where language had yet to evolve and the human animal vocalized without words. He pioneered a method of making sound effects by enunciating each letter, vocalizing type samples from a print shop or random letters strung together. These resources were the launchpad for producing all manner of sounds from what he called the 'chaotic oral cavity'. As Hausmann understood it, there was no reason for a poem with words to be inherently superior to a poem of growls and moans" (ibid, p. 73-74).

Expanding on this idea, Rasula describes how Richard Huelsenbeck, Marcel Janco and Tristan Tzara would perform simultaneous poetry at the Cabaret Voltaire: "Huelsenbeck, Janco, and Tzara went onstage, bowed formally like a yodeling trio, and performed their collaborative composition 'The Admiral Looks for a Place to Rent' in German, English, and French simultaneously, with a drum, whistle, and rattle as accompaniment. These were conspicuously the main combatant languages" (ibid, p. 20).

The combatant languages were those of WWI, and rebelling against what they believed to be the absurdity of the war was a central theme in Dada art and performance.

Art was a way of life with Dada. Kurt Schwitters' home in Hanover was a living work of art that came to be known as the Merzbau (Merz-building). Schwitters was obsessive in his pursuit of collage, and Rasula details how everything was game for his art:

"Everyone who spent time with him soon found Schwitters was always on the prowl, filling his pockets – and even those of companions – with his finds. When traveling, Schwitters luggage was described as a portable workshop with scissors, paste, and raw materials for Merz" (ibid, p. 104-105).

Performance was a key component of Dada. Interactive relationships with the audience were common at the Cabaret Voltaire, with spectators often being drawn or provoked into the stage acts. This could also be the case with visual art in Dada and beyond. Reinhard Braun provides an example of art that requires participation by whoever purchases it:

"In 1972 Gottfried Bechtold created the multiple 'Media Suitcase' (which was exhibited at *Documenta 5* in Kassel) – a collection of various media available at the time, ranging from photography and slides through to Super-8 film and reel-to-reel videotape. The videotape included in the collection was blank. The whole 'Media Suitcase' was for sale; it was intended to be an archive in itself, with the blank open reel video tape to be recorded by the buyers. What they filmed, according to Bechtold's instructions, was then part of the 'Media Suitcase', as an archive initiated by the artists and completed by the buyers" (Braun, 2005, p. 73).

This brings to mind the way a listener might perceive accessible music relative to more 'difficult' forms of audio art, and hometaper Hal McGee's assertion that the listener must complete an audio work by active listening. The idea was expressed to McGee by his friend Rick Karcasheff and McGee explained his own interpretation:

"What I take all this to mean is that the nature of a lot of the kinds of music that you and I like to listen to, it doesn't have a lot of the usual hooks and tags that more conventional music does. I think that the listener has to create the work themselves. The human brain will always look for patterns in chaos. Like when you're a kid you look up at the sky and look at the clouds floating across the sky and go, 'Oh, that cloud looks like a horse's head, or that's a dog'. Well, that horse's head and that dog's head aren't really there. And your perception of that is fleeting anyway. But I think that a lot of my work and a lot of the music we like to listen to, it often takes three or four listens to even pick up a pattern. To a certain extent the music has to burn a new pathway in your brain. It's like traveling back down that pathway that starts to see patterns in it. And I think the listener makes the pattern" (Kranitz, 2002).

How an audience member, art viewer or audio listener perceives a work is personal and subjective. Active participation, however, be it intentional listening or completing the work in the 'Media Suitcase' example, requires a desire to spend the time, attention and effort. In Dada's case this was often achieved through provocation.

Many audio artists in the hometaper world drew their inspiration from Dada. Debbie Jaffee, who along with Hal McGee recorded as Viscera and founded the Cause And Effect cassette label explains how a family move to Des Moines, Iowa left her feeling isolated until she discovered the Dada library at the University of Iowa:

"You can't check out these books, but you can go there. They're reference books. I spent every day just sitting in this library reading these books. They were awesome. I became an expert on Dada. I was like a sponge. I just kind of absorbed it. I was so hungry for anything different" (Davenport, 2015).

Jaffe and McGee's earliest recordings from 1981 conjure up images of what Raoul Hausmann's sound poetry or the simultaneous poetry performances at the Cabaret Voltaire might have been like. We hear bongo drumming, acoustic guitar and other percussion accompanying various verbal exchanges, some of which combine poetry and oddball Dada vaudeville/showtune songs. But there are also hair-raising primal screams, experimental guitar, voice manipulation and dramatic spoken word/singing/chanting/growling/howling and speaking in tongues. Throughout the recording Jaffe and McGee recite their poetry in varying expressive ways, often simultaneously rattling off contrasting narratives, but also engaging in free-wheeling call-and-response.

Many others were influenced by Dada. Japanese sound sculptor Masami Akita records as Merzbow, taking his moniker from Kurt Schwitters' Merzbau. Dutch hometaper Frans de Waard describes the recycling that was behind his Kapotte Muziek project:

"The entire concept of recycling actually started on a practical level. I used to work together with Christian Nijs, who lived in a student house together with all kinds of other musicians. There was one guy who played drums, another one guitar, and a third synths, and so on. Every now and then we'd borrow a couple of instruments from these people to record some stuff with a simple microphone and cheap tape recorder. The tapes we recorded I took home to my place where I had several tape recorders and a small mixer. I had found out how to make a tape loop, and I then started to edit the sounds we had recorded. So, in a manner of speaking, in those days my contribution was already limited to the manipulation of existing sounds. The idea to recycle sound has also to do with the fact that both Christian and myself were big fans of the collage art of Kurt Schwitters, and this idea of collaging we both found very fascinating" (Igloo Magazine, online, no longer available).

In response to a question about his use of voice samples, Charles Rice Goff III explains: "Yes, there is a consistency of using voice samples from just about everything. And yes, I do like to put together different spoken ideas into ways to create a sort of a Dadaistic message of some sort" (Kranitz, 2003).

Similarly, in his history of Disism, Goff describes the 1989 cassette titled *Down The Chimney*, which was part of the Taped Rugs Presents Holiday Series: "This completely improvised 90-minute recording gets a big dose of its Dadaistic charm from juxtapositioning the themes:

Christmas

and

The proposed homeporting of the *USS Missouri* in San Francisco."

The 20-minute opening track, 'Sleep In Unheavenly Peace', exemplifies Disism's psychedelic collage charm. It opens by combining a stilted munchkin chorus with mildly noisy soundscapes and a steadily warbling spaced out rhythmic pulse, plus gently noodling ambient guitar licks. The music gradually evolves, incorporating myriad sounds, effects, tape manipulations and traditional instrumentation to create a hallucinatory holiday and politically inspired trip of seamlessly stitched, avant-psychedelic montage mash-up.

Fluxus

Fluxus is an important precursor to the hometaper network for its rejection of the established exclusionary arts system, its insistence that anyone can be an artist, its mixed media combination of art, music and performance, and its attempts to establish artist organized performance venues. The 1960s were a time of political, social and cultural upheaval. Fluxus reacted against artistic conventions, especially as regards who is an artist and what constitutes art.

Fluxus is also a forerunner of the DIY ethic of punk, the challenge of building an international network of artists, writers and musicians, and mechanisms for information exchange and distribution of artists' works. Moreover, despite its lasting influence, Fluxus is a testament to the great difficulties involved in attempting to build independent distribution networks.

The term 'Fluxus' was coined by George Maciunas, a Lithuanian American who would become its driving force. Maciunas, along with Dick Higgins, recognized that artists throughout the world who shared their desire to create new art and music had few means of discovering each other and sharing ideas and information about their work. Fluxus began in 1961 in response to Maciunas and Higgins' desire to remedy this situation by planning a magazine to be titled *Fluxus*. Historian Owen Smith points out that from the very beginning, Fluxus was thought of not as an art style or movement but as a means of information exchange:

"Fluxus began not as a group of artists, but as a response to a perceived need for a distribution mechanism for their work, and to expose a wider range of people to the 'good things being done', as Higgins described it. The desire to publish such a magazine was connected to three fundamental concerns: establishing an information resource by gathering together an international collection of new work, creating a network for interchange among artists, and exposing the work of these artists to one another as well as to a broad audience" (Smith, 2005, p. 119).

From the outset, Fluxus was international in scope, comprising artists from the US, Europe and Asia. The network grew as Maciunas and Higgins contacted artists, who in turn contacted other artists. The participants were motivated to rely on themselves and each other, believing that art had become too commercial, dependent on a social elite and, consequently, exclusionary in terms of exposure and distribution. They rebelled against art as a profession, despising the gallery system and the value placed on art as objects. This, they felt, resulted in the alienation of artists from one another, and the alienation of artists from their audience.

A hallmark of Fluxus was its collective nature and inclusive insistence on being open to all. Owen Smith further notes: "By rejecting both the romanticized frames of art as visionary and transcendent and the modernist notions of art as professional and exclusionary praxis, Fluxus returns to a simpler engagement open to all. Art becomes not a way to become famous, a carrier, or even a way to make a living, but something more important. In this way art becomes a social act, because of its participatory nature, and transformative as well, because of this very inclusionary stance. Although this open, often seemingly uncritical and playful aspect of Fluxus is sometimes dismissed as insignificant or lacking a serious motivation, it is of fundamental import for a collective, collaborative, and global-based mentality" (ibid).

This is a crucial point and relevant to the hometaper network that developed in the 1980s. The assertion was that art is open to all and not the reserve of the professional. The gallery system determined who was the 'professional', just as the record companies so effectively controlled which artists and styles of music would be available to the public.

Fluxus activities in the 1960s included publishing and the distribution of art, the latter taking the form of what were called 'multiples'. Multiples were three dimensional objects intended to be reproduced like prints, rather than the traditional unique, one-of-a-kind artwork. They could be any variety of found objects, even junk, housed in boxes that Maciunas designed and duplicated.

Examples included the 1964 publication of the first *Fluxus Yearbox* – which consisted of approximately twenty envelopes bolted together, each containing work by a different Fluxus artist (Home, 1991, p. 57). Others included Ben Patterson's 'Instruction No. 2', which contained a paper towel, a bar of soap, and the instructions 'Please wash your face' (Smith, 1998, p. 170). A small black plastic box by Yoko Ono has 'A Box of Smile' printed on its lid and a mirror inside to reflect the viewer's amused surprise. And George Brecht's 'Bead Puzzle' represents the games that were common to Fluxus, with its seven wooden beads on a string and instructions printed on a card that says, 'Cut cord so that beads do not separate. Find another solution. Repeat, beyond the furthest solution (Johnson, 2007).

The spirit of the multiples would later be manifested in many of the creatively and cleverly packaged hometaper cassettes, which were markers of artistic expression that enhanced, or represented something greater than the audio content of the tapes.

Dissatisfaction with available distribution mechanisms was a powerful bond among Fluxus artists, as there was no way to sell their works to anyone other than networked artists and musicians. Maciunas attempted to establish Fluxshops and Fluxus mail order warehouses in the US and Europe and intended to create an alternative and egalitarian distribution network for art and publications. To this end, Maciunas occupied a space on canal street in New York City which he intended to function as both a Fluxshop and Fluxhall. The shop would be for the sale of Fluxus art and publications and the Fluxhall would be for performances and activities.

Maciunas, however, was forever grappling with financial woes, often putting up his own money to fund festivals and cover printing costs. He had secured agreements for distribution in various countries, but among the obstacles he faced was an insistence by many that they take items on consignment, which forced him to produce these items himself and wait until the shops started selling. Among the other challenges Maciunas encountered were promises of financial backing that never came to fruition.

Like Dada, Fluxus was less of a movement than an attitude – a loose network of artists, writers, musicians and performers who shared a common attitude toward the arts and collaborated on shared goals and interests which took form in a variety of activities. And Fluxus too concerned itself with the alienation of art and people's ability to enjoy it.

Speaking to the 1968 Fluxpress publication of Henry Flynt's pamphlet *Down With Art*, Stewart Home points out that, "Flynt discredited 'scientific' justifications of art. He went on to demonstrate that it was subjectivity which distinguished art and entertainment from other activities. According to Flynt, there was an insurmountable contradiction in the fact that art objects existed independently of any subjective *enjoyment* of them; that art was produced independently of "people's" liking of it, and yet artists still expected their products "to find their value in people's liking of them". Because of this separation between production and enjoyment, the consumption of art is essentially alienated" (Home, 1991, p. 57).

This returns to the idea of exposure and accessibility, but also viewer and listener perceptions of art, engagement and, ideally, involvement. Owen Smith expands on this approach with an insightful contemporary analogy:

"In many Fluxus works the stress on participation, performance, and interaction is a means of accentuating the connectedness of all human activities, even those labeled as art. All aspects of Fluxus include elements that work against the traditional relationship in art of the passivity of the viewer and the domination of the object. What is modeled in the work, activities, and interactions of the Fluxus group is a communal praxis aimed at the creation of a network based hyper- and intermedia. Even though much of Fluxus existed prior to the age of the computer, the Internet, the World Wide Web, hypermedia, and hypertext, Fluxus' activities and attitudes present many of the most important realizations of network culture, many of which we are now only rediscovering" (Smith, 2005, p. 135-136).

A fundamental challenge for Fluxus was the degree to which it existed due to the efforts of an individual - George Maciunas. But the power of the individual should never be underestimated, and this is essential to the viral spread of the DIY attitude that punk inspired. History demonstrates repeatedly that success, however limited, comes when someone takes responsibility in a leadership or organizing role, be it group or individual efforts. Maciunas took the initiative to build on a small number of contacts to create what eventually became an international network of artists, writers, musicians and performers. And while much of what he set out to do had limited success, and projects frequently failed to reach completion, he did organize performances and festivals and published and produced multiples.

In his account of Fluxus history, Owen Smith summarizes by saying that Maciunas "was responsible for shaping Fluxus from a concept of a magazine to a loose association of individuals to a particular performance aesthetic associated with events and action music to a publishing and production company of artists' multiples, scores, and objects, and, finally, to a group of artists who explored the promise that life was more interesting than art" (Smith, 1998, p. 223).

Mail Art

Fluxus was an important example of establishing alternative art networks in the 1960s. It was in this environment that mail art was born, growing in the 1960s and 1970s and thriving in the 1980s and beyond.

In the 1960s, Fluxus artist Robert Filliou wrote of an 'Eternal Network', in which he envisioned artists as being part of a larger social network, where community is established and no boundaries exist between artist and audience. It was through the postal system that mail artists exchanged their work and ideas, communicated, collaborated and created community. While fax and computer communications would later be embraced by mail artists, the postal service was utilized as the cheapest and most effective means of communication and exchange.

Mail artists and Fluxus shared similar values. Primary among them was a distain for the exclusionary nature of the gallery system and juried shows. Mail art is an open system where anyone, from any culture can participate. Mail art is about grassroots networking and communicating on a global basis. It is a mutually supportive community in which the commerce-free exchange of art, information and ideas can thrive.

John Held Jr., who has produced detailed documentation of mail art history, says that mail art's "greatest contribution has not been the creation of specific artworks, but rather the creation of an open democratic structure in which participants can exchange art and information, and in the process, learn about the ways in which the artistic experience is communicated" (Held, 1991, p. xxxv).

Mail artists didn't limit their exchange to traditional artwork. Trading cards, postcards, books, artist created postage stamps, photographs, all manner of objects, as well as poetry and other written works were shared. Vittore Baroni recalls having received stinky dead fishes, melted vinyl LPs and stuffed pillows, among other oddities (personal communication, 2008). The envelopes items arrived in were typically works of art themselves, adorned with illustrations, decorations, and rubber stamps. The Xerox copier was a mighty tool in mail artist hands.

Genesis P-Orridge and Cosey Fanni Tutti, who became founding members of Throbbing Gristle and Industrial Records, were mail art devotees in the early 1970s, communicating with like-minded artists around the world. By 1973, the pair were participating in mail art events in several countries: "For *Postcards* at the Mostly Flowers Gallery in San Francisco, P-Orridge sent a selection of his expanding range of postcards, one of which, the 'Penis postcard', showed six drawings of a penis metamorphosed into a torso with breasts" (Ford, 1999, p. 3.17-18).

Participants came to mail art through mailing lists and publications, and by the early 1970s groups and individuals were publishing contact lists of addresses for people wanting to participate in mail art exchange. It was through this mode of contact and communication that a network was born, quickly taking on a life of its own.

In true grassroots fashion, mail artists established mail art exhibitions around the world as representing a distinct medium of art. The rules of the exhibitions were a clear reflection of the mail art opposition to the gallery system: No fees, no jury, no returns, all works received will be exhibited, no prizes, and a catalog will be sent free of charge to all participants. Exhibition catalogs added further fuel to the roaring network fire, providing the uninitiated with names and addresses of mail artists from around the world.

Over the years the number of mail art exhibitions exploded. In his book, *Mail Art: An Annotated Bibliography*, John Held Jr. documented the growth of the mail art show from five in 1971 to seventy-five in 1979. By 1983, this number had mushroomed to one hundred and eighty-seven (Held, 1991, p. xvii). Held documented a total of 1,335 mail art shows between 1970 and 1985 and adds that there were no doubt many more (ibid, p. xxiv).

The number of shows and levels of participation demonstrated that the mail art network was a motivated and organized one. In 1985, Swiss mail artists Gunther Rüch and Hans Rudi Fricker developed the idea of the Worldwide Decentralized Mail Art Congress. John Held Jr. notes that more than 70 congresses were held with over 500 participants from 25 countries. At each congress participants were "encouraged to explore networking concerns (the nature of interpersonal contacts, the art market, archives, mass mail art versus one-to-one communication, cooperation, etc.) and to report the conclusions to the two Swiss organizers. Gunther Rüch published a report of the *Worldwide Decentralized Mail Art Congress*, which united the various opinions expressed" (ibid, p. xxix).

The documentation aspect of mail art cannot be overstated. Catalogs sent out for the shows represented not only documentation of the events for those who could not attend but also inspired further discussion.

Accounts of the 1986 *Decentralized Worldwide Mail Art Congress* held in Dallas, Texas and Milan, Italy in *ND* magazine detail similar themes. Participants discussed networking activities, archives, and held various meetings on a variety of subjects related to mail art and networking. The Dallas congress also included a five-hour meeting at the Dallas Public Library that was videotaped (*ND*, 1986, p. 22-24).

Little is said about actual artwork, giving credence to Held's assertion that mail art is less about the art than the open structure and exchange of art and information. Thus, the exhibitions and congresses provided mail artists, who had communicated solely through the postal system, the opportunity to meet in person.

The mail art network also proved to be serious about accepted rules and courtesies, and indiscretions were exposed and debated publicly. Following the 1986 congress coverage in *ND* magazine, an 'open letter' from Gunther Rüch makes public a dispute with Rudi Fricker over the content of a congress book published without Rüch's knowledge, and Rüch announces his break with Fricker (Rüch, 1987, p. 25).

An earlier issue of *ND* includes another open letter, this being a scathing indictment by Carlo Pittore against Dr. Ronny Cohen, curator of the 1984 *Mail Art Then and Now* exhibition at the Franklin Furnace in New York City. Cohen's transgression was that she violated the 'all materials will be displayed' rule of mail art shows, considered especially grievous given that the invitations stated that all material would be displayed (Pittore, 1984, p. 23).

Unlike Dada and Fluxus, mail art was indeed a group who identified themselves as mail artists. Fluxus was a network of artists, writers, musicians and performers who shared common values and goals, but was not a movement or group with explicit self-identification. Mail art was very much a group of 'mail artists'. They organized mail art exhibitions, their activities are impressively documented, and they had established rules, the breach of which resulted in being ostracized by their peers.

The hometaper network is often considered to have been an offshoot of mail art. This is partly true. Mail art preceded punk and the hometapers. The connection is that some mail artists were interested in audio, exchanging recordings and collaborating on audio art projects. The use of the postal service to exchange work, the anti-establishment attitude toward the professional arts and the exclusionary nature of the gallery system follows the lineage of 20th century independence in the arts and directly parallels punk/DIY opposition to the major record companies. Mail art may have preceded the hometapers, but it was ultimately linked to and contemporary with them. The link between mail art and the hometapers depended on how individuals came to one or the other. In short, the linkage is to be found in the 'crossover' between the mail art and hometaper networks.

One prominent example of a mail artist who was immersed in audio recording, trading and releasing audio art compilations was Rod Summers. Born in the UK but relocated to Maastricht in the Netherlands, Summers began working with sound recording in 1961 and got involved in mail art around 1974. In 1978 he launched the VEC Audio Exchange. VEC stood for Visual, Experimental and Concrete, though Summers explains that there were two parts to VEC. The other was called the Visual Entertainment Company. Its activities were private and known only to a dozen people in various countries (Plunkett, 1993, p. 45).

Artists active in the international mail art network were invited to send their audio works for inclusion on regularly published cassette compilations. Summers explains: "Because of my experience with tape, the advent of the cassette recorder was of great interest as here, finally, was a cheap method of copying my works and distributing them through the post, works that were always made and edited on open reel tape. We also have to remember that in the 1980s just about everyone had a cassette recorder and that the audio cassette was/is globally compatible, and it was this compatibility that was the foundation of the VEC Audio Exchange project" (personal communication, 2008).

Summers made his calls for participation via postcard and flyer, and mail art magazines published details of the project. The published cassettes were only available in exchange for new audio works and 180 artists from 21 countries participated across 16 volumes produced from 1978-83. Cassette copies of the master tapes were made one at a time to order and numbered.

The contents of the VEC compilations ran the gamut from spoken word poetry, casual conversation, theatrical works and various forms of everyday activity, to songs, soundscapes, electronics, noise, and an array of experimental collage and sound works. Glossing over the list of participants reveals names that would later be recognized by hometaper enthusiasts: Vittore Baroni, Maurizio Bianchi, Ken Montgomery, Tentatively A Convenience, R. Stevie Moore and De Fabriek, to name a few. Audio art was a natural fit for Summers and the decision to initiate the VEC project was a simple one:

"I was busy with audio art and mail art and the audio cassette was a cheap-to-post carrier of sound. At least half a dozen people had sent me their audio works on cassette, and I was aware from that that several mail art practitioners owned cassette recorders, so it didn't take too much thought to pull all that in a line and start the VEC Audio Exchange project" (ibid).

Merzbow is another example of the crossover between mail art and the hometaper network. In response to an interviewer asking how he got involved with tape trading through the mail in the early 1980s, he says:

"When I started Merzbow the idea was to make cheap cassettes which could also be fetish objects. I recorded them very cheaply and then packaged them with pornography. I got very involved with the mail art network which included hometapers like Maurizio Bianchi, Jupitter-Larsen of Haters and TRAX of Italy" (Hensley, 1999).

Minóy was immersed in both the mail art and electronic music hometaper worlds: "Getting deeper into mail art, I discovered other artists were also working with sound, so we began trading cassettes. My name got on contact lists, and I discovered a whole cassette network similar to the mail art network" (Minóy, 1992, p. 61-62).

But Minóy clarifies: "Although there are many crossover artists involved in both mail art and mail music, the two networks remain largely segregated. Many mail artists have no idea about the enormous growth of cassette culture in the eighties. Many people working with cassettes are unaware of the parallel network of mail artists" (ibid, p. 62).

Vittore Baroni discovered mail art in 1977 at the age of 21. Describing how easily he fell into the network, Baroni says that since the early 1970s he had been purchasing 'free press' magazines like *It*, *Oz* and *Crawdaddy* through the international post:

"In those years I was able to ride the very last wave (more like a ripple) of the hippie counterculture, that in heavily politicized Italy meant also the participation to battles for free entrance at concerts and festivals. So, I started weaving contacts with freaks of my own age, would-be poets and musicians long before I discovered mail art. I simply was not afraid of taking up paper and pen to write to any new address of small poetry, music or art magazine I may have discovered, to establish contacts and collaborations, or to buy back issues with a few banknotes hidden in a registered letter" (personal communication, 2008).

As an experienced networker Baroni was immediately interested in the idea of exchanging art through the mail and is quick to include the punk zine explosion and the soon to arrive tape network.

A frequent theme among hometapers was the initiation into home recording so that they would have something to trade with others whose work they were interested in hearing. Baroni began publishing his *Arte Postale!* in a similar spirit. In a 1979 issue, Baroni states that "the only way to get a copy is by sending a mail art work or publication in exchange." He asked readers to "send 100 words and get a free subscription to 5 issues of the magazine." In an interview, Baroni confesses that he started his assembling because he "needed something readily available to trade with other networkers" (Saper, 2001, p. 13).

Depending on their interests, mail artists may or may not have been involved with the tape network, even if they did incorporate audio into their art. Baroni points out that many of the young participants in the tape network were part of the emerging punk/new wave scene, or of the industrial/electronic/experimental scenes. People who were interested in promoting their music and/or in starting musical collaborations were often not engaged in the process of swapping original art works, though some musicians were intrigued enough to dabble in mail art projects. On the other hand, many mail artists had no particular interest in rock music, so they remained oblivious or indifferent to the tape network.

Baroni continues: "And then there were young mail artists like me who were both heavily into rock music and mail art, so the tape network became for us a way to expand our range of action beyond the boundaries of mail art, and maybe even sell a few items in the process. Very rarely, in fact, would mail artists shell out money to buy any product, since the very root of the mail art experience is the free exchange: you would trade publications, not buy them. The tape network, on the other hand, catered also to the tastes of a young underground public and was more explicit in putting a (low) price on its zines and audio products. For me it was an ideal situation, since as a collector I was just as willing to trade or to buy cassettes from other labels and musicians" (personal communication, 2008).

Baroni is an interesting case study because he overtly tried to bring together the mail art and cassette worlds and did so in the multi-media spirit of Fluxus. From 1981-87, Baroni, along with Piermario Ciani and Massimo Giacon, oversaw the TRAX project, which he considered to be a 'collective label':

"I produced a long series of bizarre items including vinyl records, cassettes, booklets and postcards, which I would trade for similar products and at the same time offer for sale. These audiovisual 'packages' were something in between the 'Flux Kits' of the Fluxus group (that paved the way to mail art) and the theme anthologies circulating in the tape network. With TRAX, we tried to pick up the more interesting authors and ideas from both the mail art world and the cassette scene and mix them together under a strong unifying concept" (ibid).

Chapter 9

Punk and the UK Scene – DIY!

Dovetailing with its position in 20th century independence in the arts history, the hometaper network is an important chapter in the post-punk story.

There are multitudes of books detailing punk history. My purpose in this section is not to retell that story, but to identify a certain flavor of cassette culture that arose in England in the wake of punk and the ensuing DIY ethic. Though this period was brief, the adventurers who remained after the dust settled ultimately found their way into the burgeoning 1980s global hometaper network.

The Ramones, Patti Smith, CBGBs - Punk happened in New York before it hit London. Yet the punk that crash landed in England months later inspired a cassette culture with characteristics unique to the explosive UK scene. Cassette culture in England was tightly linked to the rise of punk, the proliferation of self-published zines, and that country's commercial weeklies – *Sounds*, *New Musical Express* (*NME*) and *Melody Maker*.

Rock history has had more than its share of colorful characters. There's been no shortage of scene and career makers with entrepreneurial skills, P.T. Barnum qualities and shocking levels of imaginative chutzpah. One of the oddest aspects of the Sex Pistols story is that they were effectively 'created' by Malcolm McLaren as a promotional tool for his and partner Vivienne Westwood's *Sex* boutique.

McLaren deftly engaged the media and record companies to achieve enormous levels of publicity for the Sex Pistols long before their album was released. And, not unexpectedly, punk, in all its safety pinned and spike haired glory, was coopted and commodified by the mainstream.

Yet the most remarkable characteristic of the Sex Pistols story and punk in England was the genuine DIY ethic it inspired. Despite the heavily produced and overdubbed Sex Pistols album, hype and media frenzy notwithstanding, the band had started as complete non-musicians who learned by doing.

Falling A label cofounder Peter Ashby, whose early bands included Frenzid Melon and the Insane Picnic, recalls the personal impact of punk: "A whole new era of musical creativity was spawned. And that was my teenage years, so it spoke to me in every way. But I never lost my love of all types of music. On any given day I might have been listening to Gentle Giant, Frank Zappa, The Doors, The Beatles, Van der Graaf Generator, King Crimson, 'Chloroform' by The Bleach Boys, the Cure, Killing Joke, Gang of Four, T Connection, Heatwave, and even *Thriller* by Michael Jackson! And jazz was gradually creeping into the equation too. And some soul. A real mixed bag!" (personal communication, 2009).

History has positioned punk as 'Year Zero' for rock 'n' roll, when music got stripped back to the basics and the progressive rock bands were vilified as bombastic dinosaurs. Regardless, Ashby is emphasizing that punk didn't result in his dispensing with such bands. He continued listening to various styles of music from King Crimson to Michael Jackson and The Bleach Boys. Sex Pistols singer Johnny Rotten famously revealed his taste for many different styles of music, including Hawkwind and the German 'Krautock' bands.

Ashby continues: "But I quickly developed an urge to create my own music. And punk was the key to that freedom of expression. Making music was demystified and given back to the people. And big labels no longer had the say. True creativity was unleashed. Although the progressive albums I had loved were truly creative they were often made in bad environments and subject to the whims of record companies and commercial pressures. Then punk came along and blew it all wide open. New music and experimentation abounded and there were no rules anymore. Total artistic freedom! This is where we were at. We started recording as a duo called Frenzid Melon. I didn't start as a conventional musician at all. We were a duo with just a guitar and vocals and loads of ideas and buckets of energy" (ibid).

Demystified indeed. Bedroom bands like the Desperate Bicycles figured out that vinyl singles could be made for relatively small amounts of money. As their 1977 song 'Handlebars' comes to an end there are a few seconds of silence before the singer yells, "It was easy, it was cheap, go and do it!" Desperate Bicycles would make spreading the DIY message a rallying cry, incorporating "It was easy, it was cheap, go and do it!" into the lyrics and repeating the line throughout their song 'The Medium Was Tedium' and crying out "Go and join a band!" Desperate Bicycles didn't just sing the message. The back of the single printed a brief band history and reported that the complete cost of their *Smokescreen* single was £153, finishing the notes with, "So if you can understand, go and join a band. Now it's your turn."

Desperate Bicycles were relentless in their passion for the message. The song 'Don't Back The Front' has barely started when the singer exhorts listeners to "Cut it, press it, distribute it, Xerox music's here at last." The band's early singles, with clunky bass and cheesy keyboards, were light years from the Sex Pistols' and Clash's albums. But it didn't matter. Desperate Bicycles were making music and putting out records themselves.

Rough Trade founder Geoff Travis was inspired by this ethic: "What excited us about the Desperate Bicycles was that they'd done it themselves. It wasn't like it was the best record we'd ever heard - it didn't have the effect on us in the way that Spiral Scratch had - but the whole process was interesting. I think they were the first of the bands to demystify the process by explaining to you how it was done and how much it cost" (Taylor, 2010, p. 75).

Other bands followed suit. Scritti Politti's 1978 *Skank Bloc Bologna* detailed the cost for the EP, including the prices for recording space, mastering, pressing, processing rubber stamp on white labels, and included the business names and addresses where they had secured these services.

The proliferation of self-published zines was vital to spreading the word about bands, as well as being tools for information exchange. Legs McNeil and John Holmstrom were high school friends from Connecticut in the US who published *Punk* magazine in December 1975, prior to the zine explosion that was on the horizon. When Mark Perry published the first issue of *Sniffin' Glue* in England in September 1976, he made no bones about his target audience by proclaiming itself on the cover to be 'For Punks!' and 'The London Scene - Punk Wise'.

Punk historian Jon Savage articulates the distinction between the zines and commercial weeklies: "The big three were providing the press and the excitement, but nobody was defining 'Punk' from within. The established writers were inevitably compromised both by age and minimal demands of objectivity required by their papers." Savage continues: "The established media could propagandize and comment, but they could not dramatize the new movement in a way that fired people's imagination" (Savage, 1992, p. 200).

This is an essential point that speaks to zines of any theme. Zines are produced by those who are enthusiastically immersed in their topic, are writing from the perspective of knowledgeable close observers and write in a voice that resonates with fellow travelers. As Savage says of *Sniffin' Glue*: "It quickly distinguished itself from the weeklies even though it boosted the scene in a similar way. The difference was an enthusiasm which reflected the musical ideology put forward by the groups" (ibid, p. 202).

And, most crucially, Savage points out: "The most immediate cultural impact of Punk was in the media. Mark P. had been one of the few people fully to articulate the 'Do it Yourself' ethic and in *Sniffin' Glue* 5 he had laid down the gauntlet: 'All you kids out there who read SG don't be satisfied with what we write. Go out and start your own fanzines" (ibid, p. 279).

Music fans may have been flocking to the zines, but the commercial weeklies would come to play an essential role in the dissemination of information about independent releases and inspiring others to take up arms. They published news items and reviews about independent vinyl and cassette releases but also dedicated columns to homemade cassette albums.

One example was Mick Sinclair, a writer for *Sounds* whose initiative resulted in that paper's *Cassette Pets* column: "During 1980 I felt I knew the indie/DIY music scene better than any established music writer so I wrote to Alan Lewis, then *Sounds* editor, suggesting that not only should they be covering the cassette scene but that I was the person to do so. Much to my surprise, he phoned me a week or so later suggesting I write a (roughly) monthly column of cassette reviews. The first of these appeared in August 1980. Depending on space in the paper it would either be a half page or, more often, a full page in the heart of the paper with, for a time, a cartoon supposedly of me beneath a massive pile of tapes. It always covered exclusively cassette releases and there were contact addresses and prices with the reviews" (personal communication, 2008).

Sinclair received a stylistic variety of submissions on cassette, "from 90-minute synthesizer epics, voyages to the frontiers of noise experimentation, and effervescent pop songs that, in a better world, would be whistled by millions" (Sinclair, 2008).

Sinclair was surprised by the quality of the submissions: "While a few of the tapes were painful, most were good, a few were brilliant, and nearly all were imaginative and original in some way, which itself seemed enough to justify their existence. A side effect of such intense exposure was that most mainstream music came to sound remarkably dull and conformist, and the realization that that was because most of it was dull and conformist" (ibid).

Sinclair makes a point that is fundamental to the homemade music and audio art that would proliferate throughout the 1980s and beyond - The lack of record company or management control resulted in an environment of unrestrained creativity, unspoiled by the creative shackles of commercial influence and its resultant dullness and conformity.

Despite the influence of the zines, they did not enjoy the circulation that the weeklies did. Mick Sinclair estimates that "by the late 1970s/early 1980s, *Sounds* sold around 80-100,000 a week, which was roughly the same as *NME*, although

Sounds overtook *NME* in, I think early 1982. I think *Melody Maker* sold around 50-60,000 weekly at this time" (personal communication, 2008).

The inclusion of contact addresses set the networking wheels in motion, putting people into contact with one another all over England. It was also free advertising in papers for which ad revenue was their lifeblood. Philip Sanderson ran the Snatch Tapes label and from 1978-81 was, along with Steve Ball, the driving force behind the band Storm Bugs. Sanderson recalls how people would see his address in the weeklies and show up unannounced at his flat:

"That's how I initially met David Jackman. The doorbell rang one day, and there was this guy with his crash helmet and an orange-coloured moped. He'd seen the thing in the *NME*, in *Garageland*, and just turned up. And that's what people would do then. Nigel Jacklin who was the Alien Brains main man, he just appeared" (Pinsent, 2007-08, p. 82).

In a quirk of reverse networking, Bendle of the band The Door and the Window gives an account of traveling to Europe armed with the names and addresses of people who had purchased their single and simply knocked on doors. This resulted in being put up by a man in Amsterdam, shouted away by the father of a Dortmund, Germany purchaser, and they received an enthusiastic welcome in Düsseldorf. When they went to a local record shop where their music was playing they were treated as wined and dined guests of honor and put up for some nights and taken on sightseeing drives (Bendle, 2015, p. 131-133).

While some bands were releasing their music on vinyl, the volume of much cheaper homemade cassettes exploded. Huge numbers of reviews were being published in the zines and commercial weeklies. Barry Lamb, who cofounded the Falling A label with Peter Ashby recalls how they benefited from reviews in both the zines and the weeklies:

"We always got a response from any reviews in *Stick It In Your Ear*, which was a magazine that reviewed only DIY cassettes. *Vox* fanzine, based in Dublin, Ireland was very professional and was generally taken quite seriously. *Sounds* published a chart called the 'Obscurist' chart for DIY releases. Whenever we made the 'Obscurist' chart that produced some interest as did reviews in any of the mainstream music papers. *NME*, who were the most adventurous in terms of reviewing new music, were ironically least interested in cassette releases but occasionally gave some space. *Sounds* had a regular column for reviewing cassettes and *Melody Maker*, the most conservative of all the music papers, actually gave half a page to the Insane Picnic's first cassette and gave it a phenomenal review" (personal communication, 2009).

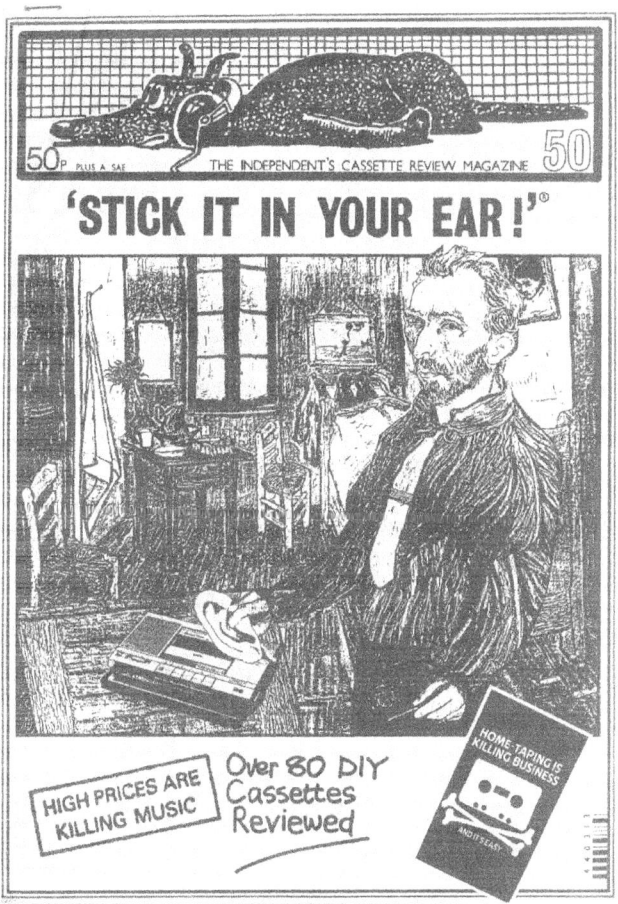

Stick It In Your Ear

Tim Naylor describes the impact of an announcement in the weeklies: "In late 1979, I wrote to *Sounds* announcing our band 'Controls' had released an independent cassette on Stupid Rabbit Tapes called 'Sock it to 'em, Dave' which could be bought for £1 from my home address. *Sounds* put a small report on their news page in the New Year and in days I was receiving offers for distribution, publishing, fanzine interviews and punters sending in their £1 payments. Unfortunately, I had nothing to send them as the tape didn't actually exist" (Naylor, 2012).

The band rallied under the deluge: "Armed with a fistful of orders, Jon Monks (rhythm guitar) and I spent hours one Sunday going through old rehearsal tapes and by the end of the day cobbled together the 4 tracks that made up the 'Sock it to 'em, Dave' EP. We added an intro of someone heckling at the band's first gig and an outro lifted from a *Star Trek* episode. Jon was the only one of us with any equipment (two Philips portable cassette recorders and a dodgy DIN lead) so he got the short-straw of doing the copies - all in real time and into the wee small hours as the flood of orders and industry requests for demo tapes refused to diminish. Amazingly, the tape was highly rated by a number of fanzines including *Cultural Revolution* and *Stick it In Your Ear*. The sound quality is pretty poor but there's a ton of energy and enthusiasm which obviously struck a chord somewhere and we sold 500 copies of the tape" (ibid).

500 copies sold is a stunning number of made-to-order cassettes resulting from an announcement in *Sounds*. But, like Peter Ashby's "lots of ideas and buckets of energy", Naylor's "ton of energy and enthusiasm" leaps out of the band's far from proficient but energetic, spirited and melodic rocking songs, which epitomized the very essence of DIY.

Rough Trade played a key role in UK punk and DIY history, starting as a record store and soon growing into a label and distributor. But Rough Trade would develop into more than a retail store. Jon Savage describes both the nature of getting one's wares into Rough Trade stock and the communal aspect of life at the store:

"I went into Rough Trade and had a chat with them about selling my fanzine. I asked them whether I could use their postal address on the back of the fanzine and they allowed me to so *London's Outrage* was the first fanzine to carry the Rough Trade address. There was a little community of fanzine writers that would all meet at 202 Kensington Park Road. It became a real focal point, not just a place where you went to buy records" (Taylor, 2010, p. 61).

Listing the Rough Trade address in zines and on record sleeves as a purchasing source became common. Store employee Steve Montgomery says that this led to regular visits from record industry people:

"The sleeves would often make reference to the fact that the record could be obtained from Rough Trade. Consequently, lots of boring A&R guys from the majors used to come in and surreptitiously and sometimes not so surreptitiously fish for information. They'd ask us what we were listening to, what had we heard that was still underground" (ibid, p. 84).

Though Rough Trade would become a label with major artists like The Smiths, they were stocking bedroom recordings as well. One was Daniel Miller, who went on to success with Mute Records, recording as The Normal. His 'Warm Leatherette' single was precisely the type of home recorded electronica that characterized what many hometapers were creating, and Rough Trade was able to sell several thousand copies.

Like so many of the best home recordings, 'Warm Leatherette' makes impressive use of simple equipment. The song is propelled by a stark, punchy, mechanical electronic pulse that is quirkily danceable. Sporting a crash test dummies photo cover, Miller sounds like a robot singer, repeating the lyric "warm... leatherette" with sparse but to the point lines like "Hear the crashing steel, feel the steering wheel". The flip side, 'T.V.O.D', is equally mechanized though more spirited and melodic. Steve Montgomery further recalls:

"So many people asked about it when they heard it played in the shop. A&R guys would fish for information - who are The Normal? Have they done any other tracks? How many are in the band? When I told people that it was recorded by one man in his bedroom, and that he still lived with his mum, they backed off as fast as they could" (ibid, p. 89).

Rough Trade stocked nearly all zines and independent releases that came their way, including cassettes. Bendle recalls taking a copy of the first The Door and the Window single to a Rough Trade show where Geoff Travis listened to it and took 200 copies (Bendle, 2015, p. 47).

Philip Sanderson explains how easily he could count on Snatch Tapes cassettes being stocked by Rough Trade: "At that point you could take your record, which you'd released, down to the Rough Trade warehouse, and they would buy 25 copies off you, remarkably, whatever it was. They wouldn't listen to it, they would buy 25 copies. It's part of the reason they went bankrupt years later! So I took 25 copies down there. Somehow or other, a copy got to America. They had an offshoot, some kind of Rough Trade USA. For some reason, someone had got to hear it, I think it was in California, and they said they wanted 50 copies. They said to me, 'how much is this going to be?' So I doubled the cost, seeing as I was completely broke! What's important is that 50 copies went off to the US, and somehow those 50 copies percolated round the nether regions, the fringes, the darker zones... up at two o'clock in the morning have you heard this thing, pulled from someone's box... this is a British group!" (Pinsent, 2007-08, p. 84).

Sanderson concedes that this didn't result in huge sales, but Rough Trade gave visibility to the tapes and some were sold: "We had a little display in the Rough Trade shop in Talbot Road; they put a little wooden board that had the two compilations, Jackman's *Slow Music* tape, and the *Reprint* tape. We used to sell a few through there as well. Not hundreds of copies, five here, ten there" (ibid, p. 82).

Though the timeline is somewhat blurred, the spread of homemade cassettes met with a sudden and rapid decline in England. Many cassette artists aspired to mainstream success and lost interest when this proved to be elusive. Others rode the crest of the growing international networking wave and settled into what became the 1980s trading, collaborating and small label scene which is at the heart of this story.

The commercial weeklies, which relied on paid advertising for their survival, reached a point where they could no longer justify the pages spent on reviewing DIY cassettes. Mick Sinclair says that around 1983 his cassette reviews column was moved to the news pages in the front of the paper and the nature of the submissions began to change:

"The column appeared as often as I wrote it but in some ways it sowed the seeds of its own destruction in that a lot of the cassettes became simply demo tapes hoping for a review. Reviewing indie cassettes was also a very time-consuming affair and since I was increasingly busy with covering more mainstream music (I became a full-time music journalist in 1981), I was limited in the amount of time I could devote to them. They were, however, still regarded as a bit of a joke in the *Sounds* office and nobody was exactly eager to take over from me" (personal communication, 2008).

Sinclair makes two important points about this shift in the UK hometaper scene. First, that far too many people were primarily interested in getting record contracts. These were not the people who would go on to record for the pure joy of creating and making contacts with other hometapers. Second, a limited number of writers at the commercial weeklies had any interest in covering DIY cassettes.

Sinclair elaborates: "Meanwhile, around 1982, *NME* introduced a column called *Garageland* reviewing indie cassettes, and *Melody Maker* started reviewing demo tapes (different writer each week). The big difference between these and my column was that these two were written by established writers and tended to be slanted towards a music business way of looking at them (i.e., for 'potential'), whereas my view was that DIY cassettes should be regarded, and reviewed, as ends in themselves" (ibid).

The music and audio art cassette albums disseminated throughout the hometaper network were not intended to be demo tapes. They were not created with an eye toward commercial opportunity. Mick Sinclair correctly acknowledges DIY cassettes as ends in themselves - finished works of original music and audio art.

Bendle noted the shift toward demo tapes after The Door and the Window started selling their records by mail order in the music papers: "We also started to receive a steady flow of unsolicited and unwanted demo tapes. People seemed to think we were a real record company and wanted us to put their music out. As well as getting demo tapes from far flung places, we also started to receive singles from bands and small labels from all around the world" (Bendle, 2015, p. 50).

Concurrent with these developments, a market shift was occurring that would ultimately bring the era of quick and easy high-volume sales to an end. Neil Taylor provides insight into this market adjustment:

"They heyday of independent record selling was between 1979 and 1982, the former, as has been seen, the point at which some purists, inspired by punk, felt that the original independent ethic had sold out and started to parody itself, the latter the moment when the market itself began to correct the overload and labels such as Rough Trade needed to become proactive rather than reactive. Until the start of the 1980s, almost any independent single in a picture sleeve could aspire to sell a minimum of 3,000 to 4,000 copies and the better ones many times more than that - often, with minimum push required" (Taylor, 2010, p. 172).

Punk and DIY hit hard and fast, generating a period where anything hitting the shelves was new and exciting. Exponential growth was swift. Simon Edwards expands on this:

"Up until as late as 1979, there hadn't actually been that many records available and what was available was often hard to get hold of. That changed. There was an enormous growth in the number of labels and what had once been an opening market by 1980 was starting to close up. People didn't really understand or know how to deal with the change. Whereas previously, a good review in the NME and a few plays on John Peel would result in a few thousand sales, that was not always the case now. Things weren't so obvious" (ibid).

The 500 cassettes that Tim Naylor reports having sold in 1980 quickly took a turn with subsequent releases: "Flushed with success, we decided to repeat the feat and issued a longer, 10-track album on Stupid Rabbit Tapes in July 1980. *Don't Adjust the Controls* featured ten tracks captured live at our rehearsal studio (a sports pavilion in Fleet, Hampshire) and mixed via two microphones to a professional cassette deck. Around 100 copies were sold of this tape, mostly on mail order" (Naylor, 2012).

Naylor goes on to describe the diminishing returns in a rapidly flooded market: "The overwhelming response we got to *Sock it to 'em, Dave* diminished significantly with each subsequent release, even though they were only a matter of months apart. Something perceived as cutting edge at the start of 1980 had become the norm for unsigned bands in just 6 months. However, the key thing was that it gave us the oxygen of publicity and some critical attention outside of our own small backwater" (ibid).

It may be difficult from an American geographical perspective to grasp, but England is a small country that is approximately the size of Alabama. Philip Sanderson believes that the tape scene imploded in 1981, and his comments help put the UK experience into perspective:

"It may at first seem strange if not perverse to talk of the cassette scene imploding in 1981 when history might suggest that it actually developed momentum after that date. For example, the industrial cassette scene very much established itself in the period 1982-86. To understand this paradox, though, one must understand the dynamics of the UK scene, a scene in which there was a very tightly focused music industry and media. There were only three TV channels, one national radio station that played contemporary music (Radio One), three main music papers and a small number of major labels. Whilst being heavily reliant on advertising from the music industry, the *NME* and to a lesser extent *Sounds*, were far from uncritical champions of the music industry and indeed were often very derogatory about the more successful acts of the day. It was this hothouse climate and context that allowed punk to have such a huge impact in the UK. The Sex Pistols and the Clash receiving coverage in the *NME* in early 1976 all out of proportion to anything they had actually done (a handful of gigs at that stage). An early evening appearance by the Sex Pistols on TV could be seen by millions of people and reported in all the national press the following day. There was no college radio to play alternative music but on Radio One John Peel championed acts that reached an audience college stations could only dream about" (personal communication, 2009).

Sanderson goes on to describe the disappointment and burnout that resulted from what many believed might be something akin to a revolution in the music industry: "With the success of punk (in terms of redefining the musical landscape if not in ousting the majors) the doors to DIY were opened. Though bands like Desperate Bicycles or Instant Automatons wrote self-deprecating songs and were happy to all but give their music away, there was a sense that this was a disruptive current that could contaminate and affect the mainstream and not just exist as a marginal or folk activity. Indeed, there was a feeling that DIY was the logical outcome of punk. The coverage by the *NME* and *Sounds* of the cassette scene was further evidence that this was potentially a final unfolding of the potential of punk" (ibid).

So, what went wrong? Sanderson continues: "A consequence of the coverage was an enormous increase in the sheer number of releases on tape such that the editors of the music papers began to realize that they could probably fill each weekly issue with lists of the new tape releases. Some groups such as Vice Versa who became ABC and the Human League and to a much lesser extent Cabaret Voltaire did make the transition from bedroom to boardroom and *Top of the Pops*, but on the whole most tapers sold maybe 50 copies of each cassette. It would smack of conspiracy theory to say that the tape scene was crushed by its potential as a truly mass medium, but it was certainly stifled by a dropping off of coverage in the *NME* and by groups themselves producing more music than anyone had the time or inclination to listen to" (ibid).

The onslaught of punk in the UK quickly succumbed to commercial pressures, exploitation and saturation. Many who jumped on the DIY wagon train were motivated by a desire for record deals and eventually moved on due to disappointment or loss of interest.

Out of these ashes arose the diehard creators who home recorded music and audio art on cassettes with little regard for opportunity or mass appeal. Many were newly aware younger people. Others were unfazed by recent developments. These were people who had been participating since the arrival of punk and now tapping into networks that extended beyond the UK.

Barry Lamb's comments reveal a growing interest in international correspondence and exchange, but also additional insights into the nature of 1980s life in the UK:

"I can't remember exactly who was first to make contact, but I remember a mention in the music papers or fanzines would always create a flurry of correspondence. I think probably Tony at Broken Skull was our first contact, but it all mushroomed pretty quickly from 1981 onwards. I guess there was a feeling of solidarity amongst us all and the guys who were publishing fanzines. There was disillusionment with the music business. Punk had started well but was by now part of the mainstream. We were living in a period of youthful discontent in Britain. This was Thatcher's Britain. Three million unemployed, inner-city riots, trouble with Northern Ireland resulting in terrorism, major strikes including the lengthy miner's strike. The political climate was ripe for something of this nature. Pretty much everything was done by post. Most of the time we just swapped cassettes. Sometimes we would sell them for a nominal amount. It was a real community that was emerging. Few of us could afford to go out and drink beer so writing letters and exchanging music was a great way to spend our time. There was a great feeling of mutual encouragement. I can remember that we had a lot of eager correspondence with people from Germany, a few people from France, quite a few from Italy, and I think the first time we were played on the radio it was some obscure station in Warsaw, Poland. Of course, Insane Music in Belgium were quite a big deal, and there were a number of bands in Holland releasing their own stuff. Norway seemed to have an interesting experimental music network. Most of our contact with the US came a little later" (personal communication, 2009).

Chapter 10

The Social Network

The 1980s gave birth to a wellspring of creativity and innovation. Independent specialty labels who had carved a distributive niche for themselves were recognizing truly alternative music and audio art. This music was available in independent record stores and through mail order, and the artists were commonly profiled and reviewed in the many small press publications that blossomed throughout the decade.

Though most would garner far fewer ears, the hometapers were creating music and audio art that often fell further from the mainstream than the artists whose records were being released by the indie labels.

In this section I will examine how the hometaper network of the 1980s blossomed through small press publications, leading to worldwide contact, exchange and collaboration. Labels were formed by enthusiasts with boundless energy and usually with limited, if any, business or marketing experience. Nonetheless, for a brief period these labels made valiant attempts at an ideals driven model that showcased cassette albums of original music and audio art.

Chapter 11

Small Press Publications and Zines

It can be difficult for those with niche interests to find fellow travelers locally. Striking up a conversation with your neighbors about experimental or industrial music will more than likely be rewarded with blank stares.

The communal space for people with specialized music interests has been small press publications and zines. The publications that arose in the post-punk era were the primary enablers of networking, information exchange and the development of what proved to be tightly knit communities among hometapers. These publications facilitated communication and opened people's eyes to the realization that they could record their own music. Hometapers found one another largely through these varied music themed publications and contact lists.

Though the publications that emerged in the 1980s were a direct outgrowth of the punk era zine culture, networking through topic-oriented magazines started decades earlier with science fiction fans. In his historical-cultural analysis of zines, Stephen Duncombe recounts Hugo Gernsback's publication of *Amazing Stories*, the first science-fiction pulp magazine in 1926, and the impact of publishing his readers' letters:

"In the 'Discussion' section, readers wrote in to discuss the veracity of the stories, debating the scientific principles upon which the stories were based. Importantly, Gernsback also printed the letter writers' names and addresses. Supplied with these, writers and readers began to bypass *Amazing Stories* and write to one another directly (Duncombe, 2008, p. 114).

Duncombe goes on to explain that the first science fiction fan organization, the Science Correspondence Club, was founded in the late 1920s and in May 1930 published what is acknowledged by many as the first fanzine, the *Comet*. Duncombe summarizes the influence of these theme focused publications and their impact on readers:

"This brief history of science fiction fanzines reveals a motif that runs through modern zines today: writers use zines to make demands upon consumer culture. Whereas the consumer relationship is supposed to be one of relative passivity - that is, you pay your money, you get your product, you go home and follow the directions for use - zine writers insist on interacting with the commodity in ways that go well beyond these limits. For example, SF fans, instead of accepting the unidirectional information flow of commercial mass media, where it speaks and you listen, insisted on talking back to the stories being written for them in the new commercial magazines. They sent letters to *Amazing Stories*, then began writing to one another, and finally, pushing one step further, started writing their own stories and producing their own publications, eradicating the distance between consumer and creator" (ibid).

Zines not only eradicated the distance between consumer and creator but encouraged communication among 'consumers' of science fiction, music and other specialized interests.

I can relate to these experiences. I started my own zine, *Aural Innovations: The Global Source for Space Rock Exploration*, in 1998 because none of the music publications I was reading were covering the bands that myself and those who would become my 'staff' of writers were interested in. Furthermore, I felt strongly that reviews should be detailed, descriptive and dispense with what I considered fancy jargon that seemed to be more about reviewers' egos and providing bands with snappy quotes for their promotional material, which ultimately provided readers with little in the way of a basis on which to make an informed purchasing decision.

JERRY KRANITZ

For 18 years, *Aural Innovations* was a tiny but significant source for documenting the existence of hundreds of bands from around the world. And much to my delight, several collaborations resulted from musicians who contacted one another after reading the reviews.

At the dawn of the 1980s, the punk to post-punk transition was in full swing. The publications that would facilitate networking were in their infancy, yet a growing awareness was becoming apparent. A letter writer from Michigan in a 1980 issue of *Op* praised the publication as a central source of information:

"Through these sources (as well as Systematic's distribution) I'm learning that the American music scene is a lot healthier and more varied than I had realized. You know, many of us buy lots of imports and are in general more aware of the English scene, and I think that's not necessarily because it's any better there, but rather because there's more information available (the weekly rock press plus a slew of fanzines) and there are central rallying points like Rough Trade" (*Op*, Issue D, 1980, p. 2)

From this point the number of publications would grow exponentially, many enjoying an impressive degree of longevity, distribution and influence. Vittori Baroni notes the generational transition from the punk era to the 1980s:

"European magazines circulating in the late 1970s and early 1980s included *Industrial News, Neumusik, Flowmotion, Audion, Real Shocks, Vox, Stabmental, Adventures in Reality, Interchange*… I could go on and on, because there were really dozens of titles appearing and disappearing after a few issues, and these mags were probably responsible for the quick rise of the tape network phenomenon in Europe, in connection with articles and columns that occasionally appeared in the mainstream music press. These publications, starting from the late 1970s, often devoted a small space to cassette reviews and ads, but much more helpful was a second wave of magazines that started to appear once the cassette movement had gathered momentum. These new zines were entirely devoted to the cassette circuit, like the wonderful *Cassette Gazette* created in Belgium by Alan Demure and the similar *Stick It In You Ear!* published by Geoff Wall (sub-titled 'the independent's cassette review magazine'). Though slim, hard to find and cheaply produced, these magazines probably did for the rise of the cassette culture what *Factsheet Five* did for the 'zine revolution' of the late 1980s, or what *Maximum R'n'R* did for the international hardcore punk scene" (personal communication, 2008).

The 'second wave' of publications that Baroni references would become the tools that facilitated the growth of the hometaper network in the 1980s. One of the earliest influential American publications was *Op*. Founded in Olympia, Washington by John Foster, *Op* would be a source of awakening and information exchange for hometapers in the US and beyond. Prior to the publication of its first issue in late 1979, *Op* began life as an insert in the subscriber premium newsletter for local radio station KAOS. As *Op* staff member and writer Robin James explains:

"*Op* started as an insert in the KAOS Guide. There were three, I think. The first two were special pages in the newsletter and the third was an insert, a separate little magazine testing things out before they started the 26 editions based on alphabetic groupings" (personal communication, 2016).

Op was born with an expiration date: 26 planned issues, each representing a letter of the alphabet, and 26 issues were published through the end of 1984.

The very essence of *Op* and similar publications was their sense of mission and explicit dedication to functioning as networking vehicles. In an early 'What I want to do with Op' editorial, publisher John Foster says: "I want people with an intertest in certain types of music to be able to get in touch with each other" (Foster, Issue B, 1980, p. 1).

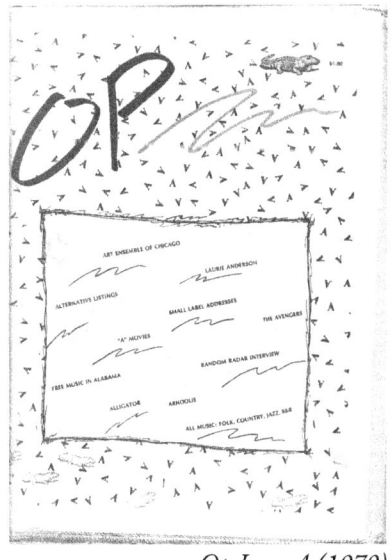

Op Issue A (1979)

JERRY KRANITZ

This dedication to networking and information exchange would become a mantra among zine and small press publishers. William Davenport, who founded the US based *Unsound* magazine and recorded his own original music as Problemist, proclaimed in a 1984 issue: "We would like to encourage the further development of contacts and networking, because it is a simple expansion of the creative process" (Davenport, Vol 1 No 4, 1984, p. 4).

This view of networking as part of the 'creative process' celebrates the possibilities when those with common interests communicate with one another. While our next-door neighbor with whom we share little in common may not be someone we care to spend time with, there is a good chance that a person outside our geographic proximity with whom we share our passions is a true friend in waiting. And this was frequently the case.

Similar bullhorns for communication among readers were easily found. *Sound Choice* magazine proclaimed itself as "a tool for the network. It provides documentation and communication; it supports creation and dissemination. It provides keys; you turn the locks. Addresses abound through the pages. Use them. Go to the source. Get the story first hand. Hear it or see it for yourself. Directing a brief inquiry - carefully stated with a self-addressed, stamped envelope - to any of these addresses will put you on the network trail" (*Sound Choice*, Issue 10, 1989, p. 2).

Op never intended to focus on any one type of music, and throughout its existence covered a vast array of genres and styles. Like many of the 1980s publications, *Op* included varied types of listings: Record labels, along with descriptions of the types of music they released, lists of stores, publications, distributors, clubs, journalists and radio stations. A *Tourguide* column was later added, yet another example of *Op*'s dedication to encouraging networking and communication. The column listed clubs and performance spaces, but also people willing to help book tours and provide housing for touring musicians. As the *Tourguide* writer said: "I can't stress enough the importance of developing a network of personal contacts. That is, not just clubs and organizations, but individuals" (*Op*, Issue L, 1984, p. 9).

Op Publisher John Foster continually demonstrated his commitment to facilitating communication and encouraging action in support of independent music. A letter writer from Pittsburgh wrote in bemoaning how the station WRCT (Carnegie Mellon University) seems stuck in an AOR rut and asking, "Any idea how to open up people's minds to new types of music?" Foster follows this with a letter he then sent to the station making recommendations for how non-commercial stations can prioritize small label releases. This is followed by a response to Foster's letter from Rick Segal, M.D., WRCT saying they would gladly play mostly small labels if they could get the records, and asking for *Op*'s assistance and suggestions (*Op*, Issue A, 1979, p. 2).

Throughout its 26 issues, *Op*'s letters section indicated much good will. Readers reported on localized indie scenes and called for networking with fellow travelers in other locales. But it was with the Summer 1981 issue and the introduction of the *Castanets* cassette review column that *Op* became a rallying point for what would prove to be a largely experimental and electronic focused hodgepodge of hometapers.

Op staff member Dave Rauh, writing as Graham Ingels, had been intrigued by what he saw as the burgeoning cassette phenomenon and started the column to focus on the artists home recording these tapes. Ingels prefaces the inaugural *Castanets* with his mission statement:

"The purpose of this column is to introduce the reader to the wide and wonderful world of cassettes - the ultimate in decentralized production, manufacturing and distribution. Cassettes are for EVERYWHERE - unlike records, they require a very minimal investment to produce and reproduce - and lots of people are making them. After I acquired a cassette machine last fall, it was only a matter of time before curiosity got the better of me and I began ferreting out odd tapes from whatever source I could. I invested in some aerograms (those origami-type international letters that cost $.30 and get overseas in about a week) and started writing away for tapes" (Ingels, Issue F, 1981, p. 3).

As John Foster later recalled: "We were swamped with cassettes almost immediately" (Foster, 1992, p. 52). With each subsequent issue Ingels reported receiving increasing numbers of cassette submissions, as well as communicating an ongoing spirit of networking mission: "In the last eight weeks, I've received more tapes than ever before - I guess everyone's had a busy winter. I'll mention each and every tape that's come in and I hope that all of you are getting some use out of the information and networking. *Op* is a great place to find out who else is out there" (Ingels, Issue Q, 1983, p. 17).

Cassette reviews were not exclusive to the *Castanets* column, with many appearing in the regular reviews sections as well. Other publications similarly put the spotlight on hometapers. *The Tape and Record Reviews* section of a 1983 issue of *Unsound* included both vinyl and tapes. Yet the column finishes with a group of reviews by Phillip Hertz, who prefaces his section with the explanation:

"The following set of reviews is meant to be part of a series dealing with an international audio network that is coalescing at this very moment. The items reviewed are all cassettes, many packaged with accompanying booklets and various objets d'art. Their method of distribution reminds me most of the mailart and underground comic heyday, which it seems they do spring from" (Hertz, Vol 1 No 2, 1983, p. 45).

Like *Op*'s *Castanets* column, these reviews did not necessarily isolate a category of artist. Rather, they reflected the informality of the zine world, where individuals can speak in their own voice (and occupy their own section of the publication) on topics of interest to them.

Individuals willing to assume a leadership role, invest the time, and often their own money, are crucial to the hometaper and zine worlds in general. For that reason, it is worth a brief overview of the Lost Music Network conference in Olympia, Washington, the purpose of which was "future networking activities after the *Op* project ends this winter" (*Op*, Issue W, 1984, p. 3).

Held July 13-15, 1984, the conference highlighted the challenges of organizing and motivating people to make plans, finalize decisions and to pursue concrete actions. The conference included workshops and discussions, with attendance later reported as "60 some odd paid, 20 or 30 more drifted through" (Foster, 1984, p. 3).

Well intentioned plans were made and there was much focus on cassettes. John Foster reported: "There seemed to be a schism between those who saw cassettes as an art form in itself, with a whole different set of possibilities than a record, and those who thought they were just a generally low-fi, inexpensive way of getting music disseminated for those who couldn't afford to press up an LP" (ibid, p. 5).

Foster continues: "The need to be aware of other cassette producers/productions seemed very important to the group, hence the creation of the cassette project, *Cassettera*" (ibid). As conference coordinator Robin James recalls: "There was the use of those two words: 'Cassette Culture'. There was the concept of *Cassettera* that never went anywhere by that catchy name, but it did evolve into a conceptual anthology of experimental collaborations" (personal communication, 2008).

Steve Peters, one of the *Cassettera* planners, later shed light on how such projects fail to come to fruition: "I do recall the *Cassettera* plan. I think the idea was to have a catalog that would be kind of like a magazine - or a magazine that also functioned as a catalog - that would be the public face for a distributor. I believe it was an idea kicked around by Jonathan Scheuer and me and probably Robin and likely came up in the heady atmosphere of the *Op* conference, which also birthed *OPption* and *Sound Choice* magazines. I'm not sure why it never happened - in those days we were pretty good at following through on any crazy ideas we had. I suppose we all just got involved in other things" (personal communication, 2010).

Non-market activities that generate little or no revenue and may even cost the protagonists in time and financial resources, are typically the work of passionately motivated individuals who are willing to make the effort, take a leadership role and follow through. This explains why there were so many self-produced zines. It's easy for a driven self-starter to create and print a publication if they aren't concerned with economic viability. They will nearly always find others interested enough to contribute, and while the contributions are not to be minimized, it's a very different level of commitment.

JERRY KRANITZ

In an interview after *Op* had folded, John Foster responded to a question asking if people were sad to see the magazine go: "Some people were sadder about it than me but nobody wanted to do the work to carry it on" (Ciaffardini, 1985, p. 38).

OPtion and *Sound Choice* magazines were two concrete results of the Lost Music Network conference. Scott Becker and David Ciaffardini were conference attendees who originally planned to collaborate on a successor to *Op* but quickly went their separate ways. The final issue of *Op* included announcements for the two new magazines.

OPtion was published in Los Angeles by Scott Becker under the Sonic Options Network banner. Explicitly carrying on the *Op* spirit with the late magazine's name in the 'OP'tion title, and more explicitly by following *Op*'s alphabetical issue scheme, the first issue of *OPtion* was published in March-April 1985. It included a *Castanets* column by Robin James, noted as "some leftovers from the LMN/Op shopping bag in Olympia" (*OPtion*, Issue A, 1985, p. 17). The cassette reviews in the first several issues had 'Cassette Culture' running repeatedly along the bottom banner of the pages.

Option Issue A (1985)

By the March-April 1986 issue, however, the title had changed from *OPtion* to *OPTION*, as if intentionally distancing itself from the *Op* connection. By what would have been the 'T' issue the magazine had dispensed with the alphabetic scheme in favor of more traditional numbering. In addition, the separate cassette review sections were done away with, and the tapes were bundled with the categorized general reviews. Scott Becker explains the practicalities driving these changes:

"The name *OPtion* drew a connection to *OP*, but I always thought it looked odd, and not every new reader knew of *OP*. So, it just evolved to become *OPTION*. Same with the A-Z concept. *OP* was always meant to be a finite project, whereas *OPTION* was not. Lots of readers hated the alphabet conceit, so we sort of gave it up. Nobody missed it. Cassettes were a strange beast in those days. They were the standard medium for low-budget DIY musicians, and they started arriving in boatloads. What began to happen with cassettes was that many of our reviewers - largely cassette artists themselves - began to beg for mercy. So, we conceded cassette culture to other zines and dropped cassette reviews as a separate section. And that was how a lot of things shifted for the magazine. Glossy paper, color photos, perfect binding. For me it was a natural evolution in trying to deliver the best product possible. Not everyone was happy about it, but we followed our instincts. Other mags picked up the slack and made for a pretty vibrant print media scene" (personal communication, 2025).

More fondly remembered in hometaper circles is *Sound Choice*, based in Ojai, California and published by David Ciaffardini and his Audio Evolution Network. Throughout its existence, *Sound Choice* appeared to hew more closely to the spirit of *Op*. Robin James offers his characterization of the two publications:

"Dave went for the DIY warts and all approach, cheap paper, all media reviews mixed together (cassettes, vinyl, video), and Scott went for the professional gloss, lots of attention to the advertising, shiny

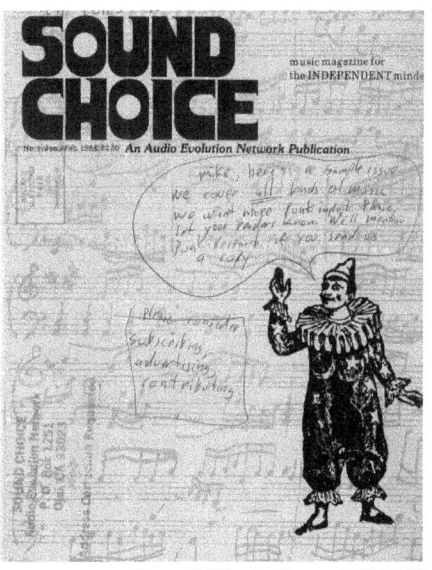

Sound Choice Issue 1 (1985)

paper, based in Los Angeles. *Sound Choice* and *Option* both folded after a few years, but Scott lasted longer" (personal communication, 2008).

The music publications were goldmines of information exchange and often served as checks and balances against those whose commitment to independent artists was called into question. For example, a 1980 issue of *Op* included the following listing: "Essential Recordings is a distributor for cassette recordings by musicians, poets, lecturers, and interviewers. Basically, you send them the tape, they sell it and pay you royalties on a quarterly basis. They have a very informative mailer that seems very well thought out and straightforward" (*Op*, Issue D, 1980, p. 3).

Two issue later, however, a reader writes in to say: "I saw your mention of Essential Recordings in the E *Op*. I was on that label briefly, and am sorry to report that it has disappeared without a bubble - the guy who was doing it basically flew the coop with everyone's duping masters and hasn't been heard from since last November or so" (*Op*, Issue F, 1981, p. 1).

Another common networking format was the 'contact list', which had a more singular focus on individuals, entities and their contact information. As hometaper Zan Hoffman reflects: "Once you find out someone's out there you find people through contact lists. First, I have to mention *Uddersounds* by Richard Franecki. And the godfather of them all had to be *CLEM*, the *Contact List of Electronic Music*. And when you get a copy of *CLEM* you're like... holy fuck. That's when you realize it's a lot bigger than you thought it was" (personal communication, 2008).

Published in Vancouver, Canada by Alex Douglas, *CLEM* was a simply assembled magazine format packed with categorized listings. *CLEM* functioned with the same sense of mission as the zines. In the introduction to the second issue Douglas says:

"*CLEM* is a reference work or contact list for those interested in electronic music (EM). Hopefully it lists all contacts that interest people who enjoy new wave, experimental, musique concrète, avant garde, meditative, and in general new music. It is hoped that *CLEM* will be a two way street. About 50% wrote back after receiving *CLEM* 1 and that is what has increased the size of *CLEM* 2. Tell me what's happening in your area, the magazines you like, the contacts that should be listed in *CLEM*" (*CLEM*, Vol 1 No 2, p. 2).

By entreating readers to send all contacts that should be included, Douglas sought to mobilize people to make *CLEM* a collaboratively constructed resource for the benefit of the electronic music community. *CLEM* was indeed a treasure trove of contacts. Radio stations, labels, publications, miscellaneous organizations, mail order sources, plus hometaper offerings along with sale and/or trade information. And all listings were broken down by global geographic region.

Milwaukee, Wisconsin based Richard Franecki was a founding member of the band F/i who created *Uddersounds* for what would serve a variety of purposes: "*Uddersounds* was a label initially used as a vehicle to release tapes by The Shemps but soon became the outlet for the early F/i recordings. It was a funny name, beer influenced, poking fun at the Wisconsin license plate motto (America's Dairyland). Since I had a large collection of addresses, I began to compile them onto a master list, which I made copies of and sent along with all the cassettes I mailed out in my trading activities. This contact list was very popular, and I probably put a lot of artists in touch with others, more than I probably realize. It was a lot of work and cost tons of money in postage, but over a period of several years, put F/i on the map. Ron Lessard of RRRecords heard of us through this network and that's how we came to release our first records on his label in 1986" (personal communication, 2010).

The impact of the music publications as sources of information exchange, networking tools and inspiration for community building cannot be overstated. As Zan Hoffman says of *Op*: "They weren't trying to be *Rolling Stone* critics. They were just people who you could honestly believe were really into it. Not only was *Op* a resource, but it meant something to us. That's something that needs to be acknowledged. *Op* magazine meant something to the network" (personal communication, 2008).

JERRY KRANITZ

In a 1989 interview, Manny Theiner of Pittsburgh, Pennsylvania described how *Sound Choice* magazine inspired his involvement in radio, publishing a cassette zine and tape compilations, and organizing local live performances:

"I picked up the very first issue of *Sound Choice* in 1985. Inside I read about many types of music I'd never heard of before and all the cassette-only artists, and I was really intrigued. In 1985-86 I was in my senior year in high school and wrote some articles about groups like Nurse With Wound for the school paper, also getting to know some local bands. That summer I began doing a radio show at WRCT, Carnegie-Mellon University's station which is the best in the country, and within three months the show became the cassette-only *Cooperative Anarchy* show, now beginning its third year on Sundays 3-6pm. Many of my first contact addresses were taken from *Sound Choice*; I wrote lots of people to get cassettes for the show. Then when I started CMU in the Fall 1986 I decided to put out a cassette compilation of local 'non-rock 'n' roll' bands and called it *Outward Inward*. It's still the best documentation of Pittsburgh electronic music, but rather 'wimpy' compared to my interests now. The first well-known cassette label I became acquainted with was Cause And Effect, and many more followed. After one semester of the radio show, I knew enough contacts to become interested in releasing their music on cassette. *Outward/Inward* became a quarterly cassette magazine, and I began releasing national people such as Dog As Master, local groups such as Powder French, and my own works as Za Dharsh. And it exploded from there - cassette groups wanted to play live in other cities, and May 16, 1987 was the first live show with Dog As Master/Jabon/Powder French. As of August 1988 I have released 24 cassettes, 6 *Outward/Inward* tape zines, and done 9 live shows of experimental musicians. And in June I opened the AbySSS, a store selling experimental & cassette releases open Saturdays noon to six... And I owe it all to *Sound Choice*" (*Pseudo'zine*, 1989).

With over 30 years of hindsight, Theiner expands on his earlier comments and describes his current activities: "I haven't released new music on a label since 2011. At this point I wouldn't know how to get something distributed. The thing is, I had plugged into a network that was in its infancy, but already ready to go when

I discovered it. And I wouldn't just say *Sound Choice*. Catalogs like Ron Lessard's RRR and Hal McGee's Cause And Effect were really important. And K Records. They put out tapes. I'm still, as I was in the late 1980s, a frequent producer of concerts. Back then it was just experimental music. Now it's experimental music plus many related or allied independent genres, which I organize at approximately seven different venues" (personal communication, 2025).

Theiner also elaborates on the record store he mentions in the 1989 interview: "AbySSS was a record store in my basement. I had two rooms in my basement with tapes and records for sale and had it open on Saturdays for about a year. After that I turned it into an above ground record store in the university section of town. It was called Pop Bus, which was the name of my indie label for local bands. Pop Bus is Sub Pop spelled backwards. In the AbySSS store I carried hometaper cassettes, but by the time I was doing Pop Bus I wasn't carrying cassettes. Maybe some that people had heard of, but otherwise they would have just sat there forever" (ibid).

The late Tim Yohannan, publisher of the seminal punk magazine *Maximum Rock 'n Roll*, reflected on the publication's influence in a 1985 interview. Conceding that it's difficult to gauge the overall impact, Yohannan nonetheless felt that "The one area that I think we've had a very positive impact is in terms of establishing or strengthening international communication. I think if it were not for *Maximum Rock 'n Roll* this whole international punk scene would not have the same vitality. There is a support network. Tons of kids are writing to each other like crazy. It's great. We print hundreds of addresses in each issue. In terms of consciousness, I don't know. A lot of people will write in, we get about forty pieces of mail a day. People will write in and say - 'don't stop, whatever you're doing, don't stop'. I think some people are dependent on us in a certain way, and it does put a pressure on me not to stop. A lot of people hate our guts too" (*Unsound*, Vol 2 No 1, 1985, p. 38).

Chapter 12

Trading, Communication, Collaboration

> Man's Hate – "It's In The Mail" (excerpt)
> (from *Forward Into The Abyss*, 1988 – lyrics by Andy Xport)
>
> By a plane then by a boat
> By a train then by a truck
> In the hands of the postman
> It may be wet or it may be broke
>
> Your music's on my stereo, stereo
> Your music's on my stereo, stereo
> Your music's on my stereo, stereo
> But I don't know if mine reached you?

Hometapers traded cassettes of their recordings, shared information and collaborated, and did so without the benefit of the internet, email or electronic file sharing. This activity all occurred through the postal service. Friendships and collaborative partnerships were formed, many of which continue over 40 years later.

At least one marriage resulted from the hometaper network. In addition to his home recording activities, Don Campau hosted the *No Pigeonholes* radio show, which launched in 1985 on KKUP in Cupertino, California and as of 2025 continues to broadcast on community supported KOWS in Sonoma County, California as "No Pigeonholes EXP" (experimental music). Speaking to contacts he made through the show, Campau shares:

"In 1996 I married a hometaper who I came into contact with through the radio show. Talk about the ultimate hometaper hook up! Robin O'Brien and I were only friends for many years, and I was playing her music on the program. Later, when we both became separated from our first spouses, the long-distance romance went into full effect and was consummated by her moving to California from New Jersey. Now we have two studios in our house! She continues to amaze me with her songs and wisdom. How lucky am I?" (Personal communication, 2007, 2025).

The music publications commonly included listings of people seeking others to trade tapes of their original audio recordings with. Reviews would often be followed by offers to trade and not always accompanied by a purchase price. *Op* was one of the earliest sources in the US for hometaper exchange. Zan Hoffman recalls:

"*Op* had the *Castanets* section in it. And I was like, what is this, 'will trade'? The first person to send me a tape was Al Margolis. So, when you already have the mail art gene in you to just send stuff out and get stuff back, it's no leap to go into the cassette thing" (personal communication, 2008).

Even reviews including a price often expressed a preference for trade: "Harvey Taylor has just put out a tape called 'Making Mudpies'. Meanderingly musical; I was reminded of both Loren Mazzacane and Kevin Ayers. $5 or (preferably) exchange, each from H.T., Milwaukee, WI" (*Op*, Issue V, 1984, p. 17).

Another common method was the offer of obtaining home recordings by sending a blank cassette in exchange: "Jeff Greinke sent a tape called '*In Hell's Shadow*', a C30 that sounds in part like the audio to the movie *Quest for Fire*. Majestic electronics accompanied by grunts and other odd vocalizing. Nice photograph for a sleeve. Send a good quality C30 to Jeff, State College, PA" (*Op*, Issue L, 1982, p. 12).

In true mail art spirit, many hometapers were interested in various forms of often unspecified exchange. In one Castanets column the late punk rocker GG Allin submitted a tape and simply encouraged people to write. "You get a free pin if you write him" (*Op*, Issue J, 1982, p. 3).

Some people offering their recordings for trade left the door open as to what they would receive in exchange: "From northern member DK comes' 'Surface Tension', a frenetic and richly textured 90 minutes, performed mainly on conventional instruments. Impenetrable at first, the longer I listened, the more I liked it. Wants to exchange the cassette with anyone willing to send me something - not necessarily another tape. Write to DK, Toronto, Canada" (*Op*, Issue M, 1982, p. 7).

In a later review, DK makes a similar request: "DK returns with another adventurous outing, called '*Rhythms that answer questions*' - not for sale, but will trade for a C-46 or whatever 'useless objects' folks care to barter" (*Op*, Issue R, 1983, p. 10).

In this second call for exchange, DK not only explicitly states that his recording is not for sale, but offers to accept any 'useless object', rather than the initial call for 'something - not necessarily another tape'. In this way, DK seems to issue an enhanced challenge and hopes for greater creative thought on the part of prospective trading partners.

In the *Other Contacts and Networking* section of *Unsound* magazine there is a listing from a reader in Finland, who may or may not have been a hometaper: "Seppo Seppanen is an avid collector of experimental cassettes, and desires exchanges and any information he can get" (*Unsound*, Vol 2 No 2, 1985, p. 51).

Seppanen desires 'exchanges' and 'any information' he can get, and is no more specific than that, perhaps simply seeking community with other readers he perceives to be kindred spirits.

One review lists a tape priced at $.01: "Girls Who Hate Their Mothers (from SF) and the Chicken Fucks (DC) have collaborated on a cassette, *Diary of a Shiteater* (some very intense noise, I tell you) available for $.01 (yes, a penny) from Girls on Fire c/o Leslie Singer, San Francisco, CA" (*Op*, Issue S, 1983, p. 17).

No mention of exchange is made, though the meager penny, while leaving room for speculation, entertains the possibility that the artists are putting a humorous spin on the commerce component of making their music available. Likewise, another artist in San Francisco, James Hilltcab, makes no mention of trade and offers his tape for free: "Various long pieces make their way through the magnetic field of space created by this multi-track recording artist. In his note to *Unsound* he stated that he is interested in sharing his music with anyone – free of charge" (*Unsound*, Vol 1 No 4, 1984, p. 45).

In both cases, positive responses to these reviews would have been a cost to the artists, who would have had to absorb the price of the cassette tape and postage. With global distribution of the magazine, these costs would have increased if the requests came from overseas.

Looking back at her one cent offer, Leslie Singer reflects: "I think I was trying to do a 'marketing experiment' and see how many orders I could get if I dropped the price of a cassette to one penny. I think the joke here is also a bit of a Fluxus one, i.e., the cassette is worth more blank than with my content on it. A blank is worth more dollar wise than the one penny *Diary of a Shiteater* tape. I did get a large number of responses, or at least large for me. Perhaps about twenty in about a two-week period. Interestingly, I didn't receive anything internationally. Nor did I see an increase in other tapers wanting to do trades. And most of the people who bought the one cent cassette didn't become repeat customers" (personal communication, 2025).

A 1991 advertisement in *Electronic Cottage* magazine is reflective of a fully non-profit ethic. Based in Missouri, Regicide Bureau was Tom Sutter, billing himself as a trading-only cassette label and distributing tapes of Sutter's own recordings and other artists. Like many hometapers who were open minded about exchange, Sutter would trade for not only tapes but poems, art, comics, "or for any useful information on the following topics: Fortean phenomena, conspiracy theories, monster movies, the Process Church, Chinese parapsychological research, and Japanese comics/animation" (*Electronic Cottage*, Issue 6, 1991, p. 23).

The ad continues to what might be considered an extreme communal, non-profit degree by saying: "REGICIDE BUREAU actively encourages the unauthorized duplication, distribution, and even sales of our cassettes. You can have the profits. We only seek the dissemination of our sounds. You could even obtain one of our tapes, then change the cover, title, and credits to make it appear to be one of your own products and then market it. We don't pretend to own music. Rather, we take the greatest delight in watching sounds (and images) develop lives of their own, free from the intentions of their creators" (ibid).

Sutter explains his motivations for encouraging the duplication, manipulation and marketing of his tapes: "I just thought it would be a nice way to subvert the usual way of distributing music and the preciousness of some people to... you take the time and energy to create something, whether it's back then a cassette or a piece of vinyl, etc., or nowadays CDs or streaming. I just thought it would be nice if somebody who didn't have access to devices or just didn't have enough money to afford cassette tapes or instruments, that here would be a ready-made source for somebody who is interested in networking and getting in contact with other mutants. If per chance my little tapes at the time could provide a means of access to the world for people... I don't know if anybody has taken me up on that over the years" (personal communication, 2025).

Sutter continues, describing a similar ethic locally: "A thing I've done in a number of different bookstores and record shops around the St. Louis area is, after talking to the owners, putting little boxes full of tapes, and nowadays CDs, with a little sign saying 'This music is free. Free music for free thinkers'. I put that in some little corner or niche, maybe near the door or something like that. And I've found that's a great way for people to pick up a copy of my stuff. I've gotten a few gigs over the years because people would hear them and then contact me to say they like what I did and would I like to come play with them" (ibid).

Tom Furgas created what he called 'OneOfAKind' tapes as personalized music for friends and for reaching out to new contacts: "In 1983 or so I started trading tapes with John Oswald. He was doing a series of Mystery Tapes and he mentioned that some of the tapes he was sending me were one-of-a-kind, as they were still in development before their final published form. I thought the idea of one-of-a-kind tapes was interesting. It would be akin to someone who makes a unique artwork (like a drawing) rather than multiple copies (prints). Also, I had so many ideas and avenues I wanted to explore that I couldn't possibly release them all as part of my regular catalog of tapes. So, I started what I called 'OneOfAKind' tapes, each one unique. I didn't keep a master copy for myself. These were one-off recordings and fun to do. I also enjoyed making the unique cover art for each one. I should emphasize that the 'OneOfAKind' recordings are spinoffs from my usual output and that I do both 'OneOfAKind' and regular (multiple) releases. The music on the 'OneOfAKind' tapes or discs are not lesser productions in my view. They are as important as my regular releases but only get sent to one recipient rather than several" (personal communication, 2025).

Furgas explains that he has sent his 'OneOfAKind' releases to both new contacts and old friends, as the spirit moves him, and continues creating them to this day. I've been the beneficiary of two such discs: "In 2023, I remembered that I had a carton of white CD folders and thought they would be perfect for customizing as 'OneOfAKind' discs, so I started knocking them out and sending them to anyone I could. I got your address from Hal McGee. I asked him for a contact list since I had already sent discs to my usual friends and contacts and wanted to broaden my base. I am glad I did because I made many new friends by sending them those discs" (ibid).

Just as common was the use of the publications to gather submissions for the multiple artist compilation tapes that exploded in the 1980s. Some, however, were not intended for public distribution, but simply as a means of creative exchange among artists. For example:

"Mark Kissinger is assembling a compilation cassette and is inviting submissions. Any 'sound piece' is acceptable: spoken word, electronics, etc. Length: between 5 seconds and 5 minutes. Work should be submitted on a C-90 cassette and be accompanied by return postage and packaging. All contributors will receive copies of the finished tape - no plans at present to sell the tape, it's strictly for the enjoyment of the conspirators. Write Mark, Sharon, PA" (Op, Issue R, 1983, p. 11).

Isolated examples existed of non-exchange and sometimes spontaneous creative efforts that cassettes facilitated. Michael Ryan describes a compilation that resulted from a 1985 summer doing field work for what eventually became his MSC research project:

"Back in 1985 I was doing my second summer as field technician for the Tyrrell Museum of Palaeontology (TMP) working in the UNESCO World Heritage Site of Dinosaur Provincial Park in Alberta, Canada collecting dinosaurs. TMP had a volunteer program where people could sign up for three-week rotations. However, many people decided to stay on, so that by the end of the four-month field season the camp could number 40+ people. One multiple year volunteer was the late Bill Abler, a sweet soul in the quarries with us singing obscure, often risqué songs from bygone days and some of his own invention. Actually, many of the people in the camp had some sort of musical ability, so it was decided that at one of the many nightly parties we should record Bill in performance, as well as anyone else that had anything to contribute. One of the Park Naturalists, John Acorn, was a musician and budding filmmaker who borrowed fellow park staffer Mark Landry's tape recorder and let it roll one evening. After the field season was over, John and I met at his apartment and edited the tape into what would fit on a 60-minute cassette. I can't remember which of us made the copies (probably less than three dozen), but I was in charge of cover art and liner notes and mailing the copies to whoever asked for one" (personal communication, 2025).

The informality of the event is on display as Abler sings his cleverly humorous songs and the attendees respond with laughter and cheers. It's simple, yet I could easily imagine sitting around the camp enjoying the camaraderie of the private gathering this recording captured.

Rockin' the ATCO (1985)

The spirit of exchange appeared to be lost on *Castanets* column editor Graham Ingels. In numerous issues of *Op*, Ingels complains about tape submissions not including price and ordering information: "It seems like more of you than ever are forgetting to include PRICE and AVAILABILITY information and instructions with your tapes. Does this mean that fewer of you than ever are interested in having your stuff heard by others?" (*Op*, Issue X, 1984, p. 10).

Nearly every review included an address, if not specifics as to how the tape might be obtained. Yet hometapers who were primarily interested in exchange may have been unconcerned with the details that might lead to sales. If a review caught their attention, the address would be all the instruction that was required. While many hometapers were more than happy to sell their recordings when the opportunity arose, a subset of these artists were unconcerned with the mechanisms and potential benefits of commerce. The usual reasons for submitting a tape for review would be the hope that someone might want to purchase it. Reviews and the resulting feedback were sought by hometapers, but participation in the growing network was often the primary motivation.

Some people were excited by what they were reading and inspired to become participants so they would have something to trade. Al Margolis began home recording for this reason:

"The first cassette I got I ordered. I had nothing to trade at the time. George [Smith] was probably the first guy. Brian Ladd and The Psyclones. So first it was ordering tapes. George had his compilations, so I probably got in touch with Smersh. And that gave me the idea of a compilation. It was probably the impetus to get my own stuff out there, as well as to have something to trade, so people would trade tapes with me rather than having to spend money" (personal communication, 2007).

Margolis' first recordings also coincided with the launch of his Sound Of Pig label: "It was the way of getting my music out there. SOP #1 was a compilation and had the first If, Bwana track. It had Walls of Genius, and basically people I'd been getting in touch with the past couple years while buying tapes from them" (ibid).

In Margolis' case, recording, trading and founding his label were intertwined with parallel activities that were means to a common end. He was purchasing music from artists he read about in the publications. When he started Sound Of Pig and organized a compilation for his first release, the people he had been at first purchasing from comprised the contributors. As Dutch hometaper Frans de Waard succinctly says: "Trading music was the cheapest way of getting new music to hear" (personal communication, 2009).

Contributing to compilation tapes was one of the best ways to make your name and music known to other artists and many hometapers were avid participants in compilation projects. There may have been thousands of compilation tapes released throughout the 1980s. These collections were often theme specific but could just as likely occupy wildly varying points on the stylistic spectrum. Depending on the goals or philosophy of the organizer, a compilation tape could reflect a special project or genre interest, or a free-wheeling everyone-is-an-artist aesthetic.

George Smith published the US based *Chainsaw* punk zine and compiled the 1982 *Annoy Your Neighbor With This Tape*. Offered as an audio issue of *Chainsaw*, the tape featured mostly American punk and noise bands, some local to the Lehigh Valley region of Pennsylvania. *Annoy Your Neighbor* featured an interesting lineup. Smith included punk bands like Angry Samoans on the one hand, but also bands like Smersh and Attrition, who were staples of the 1980s cassette network. Despite *Chainsaw*'s ostensible punk theme, Smith's explanation for the lineup reflects a characteristically footloose attitude in the network toward the mixing of various forms of music and the inclusion of the English band Attrition along with bands that were local to him:

"It was a very long time ago, but I suspect Attrition sent a tape for review and that's how we first came in contact. Alternatively, it's possible either myself or my ex-wife and co-editor wrote to them asking for a tape for review after reading about it elsewhere. I no longer recall exactly, but those were the two ways we came into contact with things. By that time, we were sent quite a variety of material, not just punk rock" (personal communication, 2009).

Al Margolis' inaugural Sound Of Pig release was the 1984 *Slave Ant Raid*, which featured his own debut If, Bwana home recording along with a diversity of music that was creatively exciting, bizarre and fun. The roster of bands gushes with post-punk variety and is worth a tour to illustrate the abundance of music and audio art that graced this and many similar compilations.

The set opens with the darkly intricate punk of Sartorial Correctness, followed by a hairpin turn toward Paranoid Systems Of History and their quirky, oddball tunes that sound like lo-fi paeans to the Residents. Network mainstays Smersh lob volleys of distortedly danceable new wave. Buckets' two tracks crank out freeform rock music that is noisily chaotic and psychedelically harsh and then assault the senses with slash and burn noise freakouts and rhythmic battering. Sadistic Gossip dish out a head scratcher of a tune with a power tool sound-art mid-section. Margolis' If, Bwana mines classic space kosmiche territory for a disorienting electronic excursion. 1/2 Japanese are relatively mainstream with their clatterous but straightforward swinging folk-punk. George Smith's Senseless Hate gets two tracks, one a helter-skelter noise-fest of freeform punk and the second an equally harsh song structured to create a bit of surprisingly intricate chaos. Jumbo Zen follow and veer off 180 degrees with their comparatively polished brand of quirky funk. Then it's back to experimental realms with The Haters and their noisy sound collage and soundscape combination. Finally, Walls of Genius delight with their wacky songcraft and idiosyncratic acid jams.

Despite the lo-fi and sometimes horrendous sound quality of these recordings, the creativity and originality of ideas is a treat for the ears. Hometapers would prove to be an ingenious lot, demonstrating extraordinary creative muscle flexing, even with such simplistic instrumentation as Casios and drum machines.

Andy Xport released 15 volumes of his *International Sound Communication (ISC)* compilations from 1984-87 and was passionately committed to the artistic and networking value of accepting any and all submissions:

"*ISC* was a no holds barred production in that it would feature any music/sound/noise from any artist from around the world. Each person who was part of the cassette underground printed flyers that they would send to other people in the mail, and these would be passed on from person to person reaching all the corners of the globe. I am proud to say that *ISC* featured music from nearly every country on this planet. On each release I would just put 'please send contributions for *ISC 2*', and I received enough contributions in a month to make the next *ISC*" (personal communication, 2008).

A stroll through the first *ISC* compilation reveals a dizzying array of music and audio art. Viscera opens with their Dada inspired electronica and spoken word, immediately followed by Slaughter Tradition's cheery punk fueled power-pop.

Magthea and Insanity contribute an eerily upbeat blend of space electronics, droning melody and clatter. Maybe Tomorrow's angry punk is a conventional interlude before Opera For Infantry's raucously violent noise-punk assault. Unovidual provides balm for the listener's frayed senses with their spacey lo-fi symphonic keyboard excursion, followed by Kowa's avant-garde piano, voice, soundscape and percussion experimentation. And throughout its 18 tracks the set continues to surprise with a succession of turn-on-a-dime diversity.

English artist Peter Bright recorded as This Window and saw compilations as being in the exchange spirit of mail art: "I'd been home taping since 1978, and the recording machine always fascinated me as an instrument. I got into cassette culture, which at the time was really the mail art scene, through Insane Music (Belgium). I can't remember exactly where I saw an advert for submissions, but it was probably in something like *Sounds* or *Zig Zag* - that was in 1985. The mail art philosophy was about exchange, so the same thing happened with the cassette compilation and solo release thing. If you submitted a track to a compilation project you would receive a copy of the tape plus a whole bunch of flyers and invitations to participate in other projects. There were also flyers from magazines included in this paperwork. You would then reply to a few (or many) and send your track together with another load of flyers. This way the network grew rapidly and strongly" (personal communication, 2009).

Bright supports the view that compilations were not only an integral part of the networking philosophy but an activity that strengthened the hometaper network and furthered its growth. But not everyone agreed.

In a 1984 issue of *ND* magazine, Chris Carter and Cosey Fanni Tutti, founding members of Throbbing Gristle and at that time recording as Chris & Cosey, wrote a scathing open letter arguing that people who organized compilation projects were profiting at artists' expense. They took offense that even when no profit was involved, moneys received from purchases would be used to fund subsequent compilations. Chris & Cosey point out what would have been obvious to most hometapers:

"Excuses such as 'there's so many people on the product, you wouldn't get much anyway' just do not hold water. 'X' small amounts of royalties when added together make enough money for Mr Manufacturer to carry on quite happily with his next project. Meanwhile, all the independent people that have contributed their work, struggle on with maybe just one copy of the product and a thank you, and no money for THEIR next project. However, they will no doubt get an invitation to contribute to the NEXT compilation! CTI think it is time for all the people involved in the independent music scene to realize courtesy is still needed and certain rules still apply, if not via courtesy, by LAW" (*ND*, Issue 3, 1984, p. 25).

The letter goes on to encourage all those who would contribute to compilations to insist on contracts, that full accounting should be made to all contributors for sales and costs, that mechanical copyright fees should be paid regardless of sales, as well as the traditionally accepted courtesy of at least one copy of the tape being sent to contributors.

Chris & Cosey are an interesting case, having been both home taping pioneers and artists who achieved a level of sales that few other homemade musicians would enjoy. It is unclear what compilations their claim to being owed £15,000 was related to. It was, however, widely advocated and accepted among hometapers that in most cases a complimentary copy of the finished product would be 'paid', and that the real profit would be any further networking opportunities the release would afford.

F/i founder and publisher of the *Uddersounds* contact list Richard Franecki was clear on this point when he spoke to the importance and benefits of being involved in the network. Franecki asserted that he contributed to as many compilation tapes as possible, despite no remuneration beyond a free copy, which Franecki considered a reality (*ND*, Issue 8, 1987, p. 6).

Compilations covered the gamut of music that hometapers were creating throughout the 1980s and a survey of several hundred could easily warrant a book of its own.

Interactions among hometapers inspired close personal bonds and a strong sense of community. Artists were pleased to have fellow travelers to share their recordings with, even if bonds of friendship did not result.

Don Campau recalls how most responses he received from reviews in *Sound Choice* or *Option* were requests to trade tapes: "And I was always fine with that. Plus, people seemed to be happy to trade with me because they would also get radio play." Campau traded with fellow hometapers, but also enjoyed taking the chance that others outside the network might appreciate his music by gifting his tapes: "Occasionally, I would give out tapes to people at my day job or folks I would run into not connected to the cassette scene. I also used to give my tapes to the public library, and it was fun to see them there in the racks" (personal communication, 2007).

Barry Lamb expresses the feeling of community he experienced within the hometaper network that was lacking in his local music scene: "We were a community and there was a great desire to help each other. It's quite sad but the local gigging scene was fraught with rivalry and ego issues between bands. But in the DIY cassette network there were hardly any ego or rivalry issues, not that I noticed anyway. We just wanted to help each other get heard. We'd swap contacts and share resources. It was deeply encouraging. I think the fact that we communicated by letter helped establish deeper relationships and left less room for assumptions as quite often happened in local band rivalry. The DIY network was real people communicating in real terms with each other. The amount of expressiveness in a letter or even on the pages of a fanzine really helped build a community" (personal communication, 2009).

Lamb's sentiment about the nature of communicating via letter speaks volumes. People are considerably more thoughtful and reflective in letter writing. Whether handwritten or typed, letter writing differs significantly from email, texting and social media posts, which over many years of widespread use has encouraged quick and impulsive elucidation of thoughts. Letter writing requires time and encourages thought, which is in sharp contrast to the simplicity of banging out emails or texts on a smart phone, a form of communication that people have learned to take for granted.

When asked in a 1986 interview if he had considered having his tapes handled by a distributor rather than selling them himself, Tom Furgas explained his preference for the establishment of relationships, even when someone is interested in his music yet not necessarily a prospect for exchange:

"I really prefer to have control over them. There are several fine distributors around and I've considered it but I prefer to have a one-to-one relationship with the people who hear my music and since I do a lot of trading, it's the only way to work it. I'm willing to send a tape to anyone who's willing to trade with me. I will even send out music if someone will send me a blank tape and return postage" (Kissinger, 1986, p. 27).

Jeff Chenault recorded as Jeff Central and in 1983 founded the International Terrorist Network (ITN) label in Port Huron, Michigan. Chenault formed the label as a vehicle for his recordings, those of his friend Pat Grafik, and recordings they made together. He fondly recalls Port Huron as a haven for underground artists and musicians like Hunting Lodge, Shame Exposure and John Wright: "Lon C. Diehl of Hunting Lodge also happened to manage the local record store, Full Moon, at the time and he made sure the store was well stocked with all the latest industrial, punk and any other kind of music that tickled his fancy" (personal communication, 2019).

Chenault and Grafik soon relocated to Columbus, Ohio where ITN functioned for most of its existence. Chris Phinney, who ran the Harsh Reality Music label in Memphis, Tennessee, was an early collaborator who Chenault credits, along with the zines, for helping spread the word about ITN:

"After trading tapes with Chris Phinney, he sent customers my way who were interested in strange homemade electronic sounds. I had pretty good sales for a while but also traded a lot of tapes too. One guy purchased about 30 tapes from me! I sent tapes out for review as well and my first review was in *The Other Sound*. This generated a lot of interest as well and soon I was trading tapes with people all over the world. I sent tapes to *Sound Choice* and *Option* as well. No distribution as I made everything by hand as needed. Dubbing, artwork and shipping!" (ibid).

In a 1991 interview, Ken Clinger described an affinity for the relationships that can result from monitoring the evolution of a fellow artist's work: "My favorite cassette artists tend to be ones that I develop an ongoing relationship with in some manner or other. I rarely enjoy tapes 'just as tapes' in some kind of objective sense. I used to strongly dislike the idea of considering the artist when I experienced a work of art. Somehow I thought that every work of art was its own universe, where the artist was merely a 'manifesting machine'. But then I started to enjoy watching the evolution of someone's tapes from one to the next, which inevitably reflected things like new areas of interest, new equipment, etc. This led to an awareness of 'creative personality' which would dovetail with the usual 'correspondence personality' that would often accompany the tapes in word form of some type. So now I consider a tape as a special kind of communication by the person or people who made it, that is concentrated or controlled by in a manner that takes it beyond usual human interaction" (Fioretti, 1991, p. 31).

Richard Franecki emphasizes the benefits of being an active participant in the network. In the 1980s Franecki would write to every artist reviewed in an issue of *Op*: "With few exceptions, everyone was willing and eager to swap tapes. I amassed a very large collection of tapes, as well as the addresses of those who made them" (personal communication, 2010).

Franecki endeavored to propagate his name as widely as possible and advised others to send out as many review copies of their tapes as they could afford: "Sometimes you may feel like you're single-handedly keeping the U.S. Postal Service afloat, but in the long run, it pays off. One of the most exciting things I've discovered about mail networking is that the more you get involved, the more things will present themselves" (*ND*, Issue 8, 1987, p. 6).

Many hometapers were active contributors to the publications, writing reviews and conducting insightful interviews with one another. From the mid-1980s, increasing numbers of hometapers can be seen authoring reviews and articles. In a

1984 issue of *Op*, Tom Furgas contributed a *Cassettes Through The Mail* article, inspired by his experiences trading with other artists:

"Though I've only been trading tapes with other home-tapers for the past year or so, I've been astounded by how much good stuff is out there. So much, in fact, that I feel compelled to turn in this report. All of the following are highly recommended, so get in touch and discover the joy of trading" (Furgas, 1984, p. 31).

Trading tapes often led to postal collaboration projects, where original works were created with contributions from two or more artists. There were various methods of achieving this. Some artists sent tapes with source material that others would add to, while others manipulated the source material they were sent.

Bendle recalls networking with people wanting to form a band through Throbbing Gristle's *Industrial News*: "The band was called Chain of Dots and we made music (initially) by jamming by post. Each of us had two cassette recorders. One of us would initiate some noise - record it and send it on to a second person. They would play along with the tape and record it onto a second cassette, then post it to another participant. If two or more members could get together to perform then they could use the band name. We liked the possibility of there being two gigs by the same band, on the same night but in different places" (Bendle, 2015, p. 10-11).

Two or more artists adding tracks that would comprise a single collaborative work was a common method of collaboration. Ken Montgomery offers thoughts on the artistic possibilities to be found in the collaborative process:

"I got into all kinds of experimental music in the direction of avant-garde music like Cage and Stockhausen and all that kind of stuff. And I kind of left behind my 1970s Tangerine Dream electronic interest. And at some point in the early 1980s I was weeding out my record collection of things I was no longer interested in and I put on an early Conrad Schnitzler record, and it didn't fit in with all the electronic music that I was talking about. It was dark, it was complicated, it held my interest in a way that a lot of the stuff that I had known before did not. And on one of the records he gave his address on the back of the record. It was called *ConSequenz*. On the record was an invitation for people to record the record and add their sounds to it and send it back to him. I did that. And apparently there were only a couple of other people that actually did that. But that was my first connection with Conrad, which led to much collaboration with him in the future" (personal communication, 2007).

Montgomery goes on to describe how one's music could be an inspirational source while not being a part of the finished work: "In 1988 I made a tape called *Collaborations II*. I sent a cassette of sounds I composed to six or seven different artists and asked them to record music to it and send it back. I then mixed their works together, taking my original music out, so that the end result only contained the musical reactions to what I had sent them" (ibid).

Zan Hoffman recalls how he sought collaborative opportunities to overcome the limitations of the equipment available to him at the time: "I realized early on that I didn't have any studio equipment to save my life. Never had the money for it. And so, if I didn't have varied equipment my own material would get repetitive and boring, and I was nervous about that. So, collaborations seemed a way out of that. An honest way out of it. Everyone has their own studio. I collect worthless photographs. It goes along with the mail art obsession. I came up with the idea: What is it that everyone has that they're willing to get rid of? Not your best photographs. Just shitty ones. Ones you find on the streets. Anything, it doesn't matter. And people will always have studio material sitting around that they haven't finished. Why can't I get at some of that stuff was one of my early thoughts" (personal communication, 2008).

Hoffman would then obtain recordings from artists that were incomplete, works in progress, or ones that had been unused because the artist didn't know what to do with them: "Because collaboration isn't like, here's something finished and do something with it. It's sort of like, here's some broken things, and some stuff that's not finished, and some other stuff I can give you to play around with" (ibid).

In a 1996 interview, Frans de Waard explained how the level of complexity could vary from one collaboration to the next: "Every collaboration is different, but the first step usually is to get a communication between both parties going and to discuss in detail what we'd like to accomplish and how we would like to realize this. It also happens someone will send me a tape with the request to do something with it. Collaboration projects can be very short, the tape just goes back and forth only once, and is released immediately after, but they can also be spread over a very long period of time. When I collaborated with Merzbow for instance on the LP *Continuum*, we exchanged stacks of tapes. My final mix has been unrecognizably merged in the record. With some projects it takes years before something will actually happen, and some projects never result in a release. This is for instance the case in my collaboration with Abo of Yeast Culture. I am still sitting on heaps of sound material I received from him in many unfinished stages, and which I have not touched so far. There is a chance there will be a release for this material someday, but it may also remain shelved forever" (Tanz der Rozen, 1996).

Andy Xport recalls his Noise Collective project, which required the minimum participation of three collaborators: "I thought it would be cool to send a tape to a person with a track on it, then they would record over another sound and then send it to a third person, the rule being at least three people had to collaborate. The result was a 90-minute cassette release called *Hello! Hello! Can Anyone Hear Me?* All the pieces I received back I mixed together to create one whole piece. I actually think this was one of my best releases. Very experimental stuff, but something that really does have a feel of its own, and something I would call true mail art" (personal communication, 2008).

Hometaper and head of the Audiofile Tapes label Carl Howard was a dissenting voice in his opinion of mail collaborations, feeling that artists should interact in the same physical space: "I was someone who was not really a fan of you send me your tape and I'll dub something over it. I felt that was, if not an affront to the live tradition of music, then at least misguided. I always felt that whether it came from a jazz mindset or not, that face to face is the intuitive way to performance. And I was always someone who said, Ok, I'm going to take a weekend, I'm going to go down and we'll jam out. And I always felt that that way was better. And there were other people who did that, although there was a heck of a lot of collaborating, there's still a lot of collaborating by mail. But in terms of live improvised performance, I thought it should go the other way. That people should be face to face" (personal communication, 2009).

While Howard's points are well taken, the fact is that most hometapers had neither the resources nor the inclination to travel to record in person. Furthermore, the insistence on live interaction disregards the boundless artistic possibilities of taking the solitary time necessary to work with another artist's source material.

Tom Furgas supports this viewpoint in a 1986 interview describing his collaboration with a guitarist who lived down the street from him: "We haven't gotten together and played together at once. We both feel more comfortable working by trading tapes back and forth and adding overdubs to each other's material. That gives us time to experiment, work out things and see what works and what doesn't" (Kissinger, 1986, p. 27).

American hometaper Sue Ann Harkey provides insight into both the collaborative method and the bonds of friendship that can result. Harkey sent a tape of her band Audio Letter to the UK based magazine *Adventures in Reality* for review. The reviewer was sufficiently impressed to pass the tape on to the band Attrition, who then contacted Harkey requesting a trade, which led to the decision to collaborate.

Harkey expressed the creative excitement of the iterative process of exchanging tapes as the artists from different countries assembled the recordings: "You can imagine the suspense and surprise each time the masters were mailed back with new tracks added to them" (Harkey, 1987, p. 38).

Harkey continues, describing the joys and challenges of cooperative exchange: "Improvisation played a key in inspiring new methods of responding to the challenging opportunity of working with one another's styles and instrumentation. This cooperative exchange between two bands is an exercise in adaptability. The overdubbing creates a learning environment in the building of songs, like any composition, but collaboration tapes offer a refreshing variety of elements just by sharing the construction with another group whose technique you may know very little about" (ibid, p. 40).

The artists exchanged tapes back and forth until they concluded by each producing their own version to be distributed in their respective countries. Harkey went on to meet the band in London, as well as others in the UK and Belgium with whom she had been corresponding. Summarizing her feelings about the benefits of collaboration, Harkey says:

"Collaboration tapes can develop the communication necessary in the furtherment of the alternative music network. Such cooperative and participatory endeavors between mail contacts can extend those relationships as well as add a creative dimension to existing long distance friendships" (ibid, p. 39).

Home recording and exchange was international in scope, though there were countries that benefited from conditions unique to their experience. The Netherlands is a small country, only 16,000 square miles and slightly less than twice the size of New Jersey. Nonetheless, it enjoyed a thriving and creative hometaping scene with support from radio, government and mainstream press coverage. Moreover, because of its small size, the actions of individuals had a more profound impact.

Limbabwe Records is an interesting example. Based in Venlo, a town in the southern Netherlands on the German border, the label was founded by Mat 'Matski' Aerts, and in its brief 1982-85 existence issued 42 releases featuring a stylistically varied assortment of bands. While the artists were not necessarily people who participated in the global exchange network, the label succeeded in documenting a creatively robust music scene, representing a specific post-punk place in time.

Matski explains: "In the beginning of the 80s, the 'underground culture' was very alive. To get a good moving culture you have to create facilities. A small but very active group of local hippies in the late 60s and early 70s managed to get recognized by the city council for their cultural needs. A building to organize cultural events was the result. With the organization of concerts other needs came and got fulfilled in the same building. A rehearsal space, a PA (sound equipment) and after some time even a studio. The building got the name OOC - Open Ontmoetings Centrum - (Open Meeting Center). The OOC was very important for what came out of the next generation. As a teenager in the 70s I was a frequent visitor of the OOC. I met many people with similar creative ideas, became an active volunteer working at concerts and later with the technical equipment. In 1980 a house in the center of Venlo got squatted by a group of people. The reason was the eviction of another squat in town where I was living. We had to find a new place to live. This became Martinusstraat 24, aka Pand 24 or simply the 'Martinusstraat'" (Aerts, online).

Matski goes on to describe how the rich and varied Venlo arts culture led to the formation of the Limbabwe label: "I noticed there was a lot of good and different music going on in Venlo. I went around to rehearsing spaces, basements, and back rooms with a tape recorder to register the 'sound of Venlo'. It was a very diverse thing, from very industrial noise to very ultra jazz to very fast punk" (ibid).

Limbabwe's first release was a compilation called *Vlaaikots* (translation: Cakepuke), which represented the town's musical diversity. *Vlaaikots* is a cauldron of creativity that stands the test of time, featuring plenty of raw yet passionately executed punk songs, but also more intricate avant-progressive rock meets abrasive punk-jazz, Beatnik performance art jazz, twisted spoken word angst backed by free-wheeling progressive punk-jazz, impressively complex post-punk with offbeat progressive and jazz influences, experimental sound, rhythm and ambient rock explorations, and much more.

Matski expands on the label's successes and vibrant Venlo arts culture: "The tape was a success and got attention of the national press. Many tapes of bands followed. Also records got released. Venlo had the most creative period ever. Art nights with industrial punk rock, poetry and paintings. Movies were made. Reviews in international magazines. So much variety in music and art in such fast progress that a big German music magazine declared Venlo 'The New York of Europe' in that moment. The front basement room of the Martinusstraat became the Limbabwe space" (ibid).

The Netherlands benefited from a supportive press and radio that covered Dutch underground music and cassettes. Frans de Waard recalls two publications in 1981 - *Oor* and *Vinyl* - as well as Willem de Ridder's influential radio show:

"*Oor* ran an article about the Dutch version of No Wave which was called 'Ultra'. It mentioned a new magazine that was coming called *Vinyl* and maybe a month later there it was. In *Vinyl* there was an article in one of the first issues about a radio show Willem de Ridder did, where he would play any tape that people would make without listening or selection. I tuned into that program, thirty minutes on a late Friday night (i.e., when nobody listens to the radio), and heard all this crazy stuff. My father had a reel-to-reel recorder. I had a microphone which I banged on an acoustic guitar, slowed it down and sent the tape off. I think it was very hiss based, but it was played. Then the show would send you their newsletter with addresses from everybody and about tapes being released. So, the Willem de Ridder radio show and their newsletter were important, but also *Vinyl* printed addresses of cassette labels, so I started writing and asking for information. The local record store carried tapes too, and the odd fanzine, usually Dutch, but also perhaps foreign ones" (personal communication, 2009).

The combination of radio promotion, publications that covered cassettes and shops carrying tapes was a critical convergence of factors in this small country, and de Waard was inspired to index and publicize the many cassette labels and artists he was learning about:

"My encounter with this new kind of music was like a revelation to me. Then I also heard about a 'movement' issuing all sorts of tapes by people who were experimenting with home-recorded sounds. The first couple of years I mainly bought and listened to a lot of tapes, but gradually the idea came to mind to do something with sound myself. In 1983 I thought I should do something with what I had learned about the tape scene, so I issued *De Nederlandse Cassette Catalogus* (Dutch Tape Catalog), listing an overview of all the tapes that had been released in Holland in those days" (Tanz der Rozen, 1996).

de Waard says the catalog sold well and eventually found its way to Graf Haufen in Germany: "Haufen was intrigued by my initiative, and he wrote me saying: 'Well, if you know so much about industrial music why don't you compile a tape for me with some of the best Dutch industrial music?' Eventually he released my tape as the third volume in the *Katacombe* series, and to this date I still see it as the best tape in the entire series, because it does not include senseless industrial experiments and is very varied. When I was compiling the tracks for the tape, I wanted to include some of my own music too. This was the first Kapottte Muziek piece ever. There is still an earlier recording of Kapotte Muziek on the *Finger In The Dike* tape which dates back to 1982 and was recorded under a different name, but this is nothing but an extremely lousy experiment with sound" (ibid).

de Waard would go on to form his Korm Plastics label and release many tapes, recording under a variety of pseudonyms both solo and with other artists.

Hessel Veldman is a Haarlem based hometaper who was active throughout the 1980s, ran his Exart label and published a catalog that would enjoy a measure of success. Like many Dutch hometapers, Veldman was influenced by Willem de Ridder's radio show and was also involved in the Staalplaat shop in Amsterdam:

"It was the moment Willem de Ridder started his *Radiola Improvisatie Salon* on Dutch Radio. In one of the first broadcasts, he played my stuff. Amazed by my sounds he asked me for a radio special. The Dutch Radio company VPRO issued a special C90 cassette with my first compositions. Many were sold. Willem asked me to do a live tour. Willem and I started doing improvisations on stage with more and more guest musicians. We became aware of a cassette selling record shop in the center of Amsterdam. Geert-Jan Hobijn, the owner of Staalplaat, was inspired by all kinds of strange cassette releases. My wife (Nicole) and I, encouraged by the success of the VPRO tape, started Exart in 1982 and inspired Geert Jan Hobijn to do more and more with cassette releases. Nicole started working for Staalplaat. You understand, a shop, a label, live performances (even doing the Holland Festival), our own recording studio, all inspired people to come around and record with us. All contacts worked as a spiral and people started sending us tapes from all over the world" (personal communication, 2007).

Veldman became increasingly aware of the hometaping network and expanded his contacts, exchanging tapes both by mail and in local shops and markets. Through Staalplaat he became aware of hometapers and labels in other countries:

"From 1983 until 1988 contacts were constantly growing. Exart issues were partly exchanged and partly sold in local shops around the Netherlands and nearby countries. As we traveled a lot we took copies with us to Belgium, France and Germany. But the exchange by mail was also big. Most contacts we had were in the US, but also in the UK, Poland, Norway, Germany, France, Italy, Spain, Portugal and Japan were regular mailing contacts. By selling 50% we could pay for all those network contacts. Exchanging for me was inspiring. New, unknown exclusive material was dumped in my mailbox, and I even started collecting cassettes. And still, I have this amazing tape collection with hundreds and hundreds of weird compositions and artwork. I can't remember the first serious foreign hometaper contacts, but contacts from that period with Hal McGee, Charles Goff, Al Margolis, Chris Phinney, Mike Honeycutt and Tom Sutter still exist. But in the 1980s there were many more. A good friend and a big inspiration was Alain Neffe (Insane Music, Belgium)" (ibid).

In 1987, Veldman published the *Tapes for Dying* catalog, which was a small booklet illustrated by a Polish painter and featuring cassettes released by Exart and The Radio Art Foundation. "There was a special page about my solo work, the work of Enno Velthuys (the son of a famous Dutch children's book writer/illustrator) and experimental radio works with Alvin Curran, William Levy, Annie Sprinkle, Jon Rose and others. We printed 1500 copies and they were spread around our networks in one month" (ibid).

Tapes For Dying (1987)

Dutch Radio Staalplaat also reached out to international publications, seeking contacts and hoping to inform their listeners about the hometaper network and how to make their own tapes. An announcement in a 1985 issue of *Unsound* illustrates:

"During the past two years we have presented radio program Staalplaat which is a weekly broadcast of two hours on the illegal radio station G.O.T. Radio. G.O.T. is a station situated in Amsterdam with a variety of programs broadcasted in stereo. The aim of our program is to inform the listeners about the alternative cassette circuit and independent releases. We want to present our growing number of listeners with more up to date information. To realize this we are going to set up an independent release-list and an information telephone line during the program in order to inform the listeners about labels, bands, releases, etc. To realize this we need your cooperation. We therefore ask you to send your recent tape release and to continue to send us future releases. In that way your tapes will be repeatedly broadcasted. The listeners calling in during the program will amongst other things be told how and/or where they can obtain your tape. Our program also has a technical section. Would you be willing to write down and send us your experience with technical equipment, e.g., recording equipment and your findings with copying tapes, etc.? In that way we can give the listener some tips and advice on how to make their own tapes. So if you're interested in providing the audience with a birds-eye view of the ever growing tape market and give them technical information, then please send us your latest tape release and especially as much background material as possible" (*Unsound*, Vol 2 No 2, 1985, p. 47).

Belgium is an even smaller country with hometapers who created stunningly adventurous music. Acknowledged in hometaper circles as one of the godfathers of the 1980s network, Alain Neffe created music with multiple bands simultaneously, launched the influential Insane Music label, and was a tireless advocate for the home recording scene in Belgium and abroad.

Neffe had been recording since the 1970s and by early 1980 became aware of others creating their own recordings and forming labels. After the experience of producing his first record in 1981, Neffe took a similar approach to what the earlier UK punks did and sought to inform others that record contracts were not a necessary condition for recording their own music:

"I helped the scene a lot because Pseudo Code, my 1980s band, when we issued our first EP in 1981, I wrote to the music press explaining how I did it. Because in Belgium it was impossible to have a record pressed if you went to a pressing plant with a tape coming from a normal reel-to-reel. You had to have a certain speed, a very high speed, and a full track one. So, I decided to make it my way. We recorded the songs with my small recorder. And there was no mix. It was taken in the room with two microphones. And I booked a recording studio for one hour only to copy my tape to a big reel-to-reel tape. And I had it pressed myself. And so, it was very cheap. And I explained that to the press and I was telling them how much money it was costing, and that I could give all the information to anyone that asked, for them to be able to release their own material themselves. I said go ahead and do it. You can do it. And they printed that part of the letter I sent them. And so, I had a lot of people asking me how I did it. And they did it, which is something I'm proud of, because I think that I helped Belgian bands to dare to do this and do so in a very cheap way" (personal communication, 2007).

Neffe also produced a radio show which he used as a bullhorn for educating others on how to make cost effective recordings. He evangelized about the cost of professional studios who produced inferior products and what he considered expensive managers who provided poor services: "I couldn't stand all the thieves robbing people who lacked experience. So, it was in the 1980s that I met other people making their own home recordings" (ibid).

Negative experiences with independent labels that he assumed he could trust would be the catalyst for the formation of Insane Music: "I wanted to release the works of my bands. I was playing in seven different bands with seven different styles. Mostly experimental, but some based on French poetry and some a little bit more commercial. And I decided to make a compilation of these bands to make them known to other people. And so, I made *Insane Music for Insane People Volume 1*. But I didn't know what to do because I had no trade register. I was not ready for that. In the end we were signed to a label called Sandwich Records and our first EP was issued by these people. The band put up one half of the money and the label the other half, and we would share the benefits or the loss (it was a benefit). So, I asked the label, because he had the distribution, he had a shop in Brussels, and he had a lot of customers - this was in 1980 - and I asked him if I could release my cassette compilation tape on his label. I said I will put up the money and I will put Sandwich Records on it and you distribute it. And he said ok. But I had a problem with Sandwich Records because they didn't pay me back the benefits, so I decided to stop with them" (ibid).

Though *Insane Music for Insane People Volume 1* featured music by Neffe's various musical projects, he was receiving submissions from around the world: "Very interesting stuff. Things by The Legendary Pink Dots and such. So, I decided to make an international compilation. With my Belgian Insane groups I was playing in, but also a lot of these foreign musicians that I thought had great potential. And I wanted to help them be broadcasted. And so, I made *Insane Music for Insane People* compilations *Volume 2* and *Volume* 3. I made all the photographs, the layout, the cover sleeves, the plastic bags, the labels, I copied all the tapes. Everything. And I asked Grafika (Airlines) if it could be on their label because they had the distribution and so on. And they accepted. So, Volumes 2 and 3 were released on Grafika" (ibid).

Unfortunately, Neffe's experience was once again less than advantageous: "I decided I had three compilations with nobody to distribute them so I decided I must now do my own label. And I got the trade register. And my first task was to release the first volumes on my Insane label. I didn't change anything except the label's name. And I went on with the fourth volume because I was receiving more and more cassettes" (ibid).

Belgium benefited from the existence of free radio stations which Neffe says were playing hometaper cassettes, as well as shops and local music listening scenes: "We had shops that were defending our work. And people were forming clubs. They would meet and listen to music. It was very underground, and I suspect for a while a little bit trendy. But it was very strange because I remember one day I was in Brussels in the apartment of a friend. And suddenly I heard a track from one of my cassettes and I thought it was my friend in the living room who was playing it. But it was a young girl of maybe 16 or so playing it on her cassette player with her windows open. It was strange because I could not tell you exactly how they obtained it sometimes. But they did. It was distributed so it was possible to get it if you wanted it" (ibid).

Though he would become active in international communication and exchange, Neffe recognizes his country's early role in the network that developed in the 1980s: "I know that people in Belgium and Holland were very much ahead of their time. So first it was these two countries. After that came Germany, England and the US. And two or three years later France and other countries like Norway, Denmark and people like that. But I think in Belgium we were really in a good position in that period" (ibid).

Hometaping thrived throughout Europe and beyond. Releasing home recordings on cassette spread quickly in early 1980s Germany. Newsstand magazines like *SPEX* focused on punk but also, at least through the middle of the decade, included information on cassette releases, fanzines, and published addresses, before eventually transitioning to a more mainstream approach.

As was so often the case, it may have been the interest and activism of an individual that led to this coverage. The *Program Notes* in a 1983 issue of *Op* lists: "Michael Tesch of *SPEX Magazine* in Germany would like to receive cassettes for review. He does a monthly column for *SPEX* much like I do here" (*Op*, Issue R, 1983, p. 11).

Berlin based Karsten Rodemann ran the Graf Haufen label and recalls the value of the newsstand publications in early 1980s Germany: "There were a few big music magazines that also devoted some space for DIY artists, be it fanzines or self-released records or tapes. The bigger one was *Sounds* and later came *SPEX*. These were newsstand magazines, so a tiny review with an address definitely brought some interested correspondences. There was no network structure yet, it all developed only through one-on-one mail contact." (personal communication, 2010).

Rodemann explains how through publications and even shops, the network in Germany and abroad expanded: "Some independent record stores were open to sell fanzines and tapes, so the network got bigger and bigger. I was one of the first people to attempt something of a distribution for tapes and fanzines, so interested parties just needed to write to one address to access the products of various artists/labels/producers. It wasn't done for commercial reasons, although it helped expand my private collection quite a bit. Later I expanded to a few self-released vinyls as well as international products. But that was a lot of work that I was doing while still preparing for my school diploma. After I finished, I had a bit more time and branched into art performance and traveling more. At some point, I gave up distribution and the tape label and ventured into the art area" (ibid).

Rodemann would go on to start a zine, publishing twelve issues from 1981-84: "I published a fanzine called *Die Katastrophe* which contained only info about bands that published themselves on tape and/or from/by tape labels. It was first published 1980-81 and relaunched in 1983. The first batch was black and white photocopied and pretty poorly done. The relaunch was offset printed in an edition of 250-300 copies each. One issue also contained a poster with addresses of mostly German tape labels at that time. It was somewhat similar to the British *Stick It In Your Ear*. As far as I know it was the only fanzine in Germany solely devoted to tape culture" (ibid).

Rodemann emphasizes that the German experience was more regional than unified: "There was no one 'scene'. Even regionally it was more of a network than something truly organized. I once tried to have all the Berlin based tape labels join forces to break new ground by publishing a booklet with pages from each label to showcase their program and offering a one-stop distribution for interested people. The project received good press, and the booklets were printed in an edition of 2000 copies just for Berlin distribution. But the internal structure between the labels was non-existent. We were in touch but not truly cooperating" (ibid).

Andreas Müller was based in Bonn and ran the Datenverarbeitung label and published the zine of the same name. Müller recalls his access to international sources like Rough Trade and other distributors:

"Magazines and fanzines were crucial. For the electronic/experimental end of things, the most important ones when I started were *Die 80er Jahre* from Germany, *Flowmotion* and *Neumusik* from the UK and *CLEM*, the *Contact List of Electronic Music*, published by a fellow from Vancouver" (personal communication, 2009).

Müller was another early German zine publisher, starting *Datenverarbeitung* in January 1980 and publishing seven issues throughout that year. The evolution of *Datenverarbeitung* reflects Müller's evolving interests, beginning with a punk/new wave focus and eventually transitioning to an industrial/experimental theme. Furthermore, Müller's expanding global contacts led to his distinguishing between local and international periods of the publication and label:

"The 'international period' of *Datenverarbeitung* was preceded by the publication of the eighth and final issue of the fanzine in 1982. This issue was mostly in English and drifted heavily into industrial/experimental/noise territory since my tastes had moved into that direction. For the purpose of gathering material for the fanzine I had started corresponding with numerous labels and bands from outside Germany. This provided a first set of contacts for the second period of the label, for example, with Spanish band Esplendor Geometrico, whose *EG1* cassette became the first Datenverarbeitung release of a non-German band" (ibid).

Müller's experience working at Normal Records would be an important source of growing awareness, as well as an opportunity to influence the company's inventory: "In spring 1981 I got involved even further with independent music when Normal Records moved their offices to Bonn and opened a retail store there. I was still in high school then and worked at Normal in the afternoons and on weekends, helping out in the store and in the mail order department. Through that I became more and more aware of independent labels from around the world and of the growing cassette culture. The fact that I was working at Normal Records also played a big role. I was increasingly acting as a buyer for the mail order department and pushed its repertoire more and more into experimental/industrial territory. This made it necessary to deal directly with many of the small labels around the globe since the big indie distributors hardly carried any of their releases" (ibid).

Datenverarbeitung 8 (1982)

The late Jörg Dittmar, known in the hometaper and radio world as Lord Litter, recalled how in 1987 a German contact list was the catalyst for what would become a rapidly increasing network of contacts:

"In a Berlin magazine I found a small article about the *Independent Kontakter*, a booklet that would offer 600 'true independent addresses' from all around the world. It was published by Thomas Pradel (who also released music as L'Edarps A Moth on cassette – that was how he had found all these addresses). Then it REALLY only took ONE address from the *Independent Kontakter* and I was 'connected'. It was Matthias Lang with his IRRE Tapes label from Germany. I sent him two of my solo tapes. He immediately wrote back, offered to release some of the tracks on his already existing compilation series and sent back a few more contact addresses from all around the world. One of these addresses was Andy Xport who was also producing compilation tapes in England. He immediately accepted my music for his tapes and put me on the forthcoming double cassette. He sent this compilation and on this cassette I found a track I really liked, which came with the info that the musician who did that track also hosts a radio show, which I got in touch with - DON CAMPAU! The rest is history. So, I think the people who had the desire to spread the word and to share were starting it all" (personal communication, 2009).

Lord Litter goes on to explain how international contacts were made via the addresses in compilation tapes, but also the multiple leaflets with addresses that were included in nearly all packages:

"The network we're talking about was absolutely worldwide! The focus surely was the 'industrialized' countries but worldwide I had contacts in the US, Japan, South Africa, Argentina, France, Spain, England and Norway. I even was in touch with the (cassette) label that released the first Sugarcubes/Björk recordings in New Zealand, and later also the ex-Eastern Bloc countries" (ibid).

Eastern Europe was a challenge in the 1980s Cold War environment. Nevertheless, there were pockets of communication and even exchange. Lord Litter took advantage of his Berlin based radio show to reach out to listeners in the East:

"I had a radio show here in Berlin - *Lord Litter's Tape Department*. And on air I announced that East German bands are welcome to send cassettes which I would broadcast and distribute - for each East German cassette sold I would send back a blank cassette (good blank chrome tape was rare over there). I even smuggled master tapes out of Berlin in my car to broadcast/distribute and sent them to the US" (ibid).

To put the cost to East Germans into perspective, twenty freshly baked bread rolls in this era cost one mark, renting an official apartment cost about 50 marks a month, yet one blank cassette cost 20 marks (Mohr, 2018, p. 236).

Lord Litter would develop a close friendship with the East German band Das Freie Orchester (DFO), a free improvisational rock band: "I immediately joined them the day the wall fell! We then had three great years touring and recording. The band became quite known in the US underground because everybody saw similarities to German krautrock. When all Eastern countries opened their borders, I had a short time of very fruitful exchange/communication with musicians from there - nights of vodka in my flat with musicians from Russia, for example. Looking back, most of this music was EXTREMELY adventurous because A) the culture of those countries was quite unknown to us, and B) the music always was somehow part of the 'resistance movement', even if only in sound and not in political ideas then it was quite shocking to realize how quickly some of these Eastern music scenes just wanted to join the western system" (personal communication, 2009).

Alain Neffe describes his experience attempting to communicate with artists in Eastern Europe: "Some cassettes succeeded in reaching people there, but it was forbidden. Because they had to transit via Hungary. For example, a band from East Germany sent me a very good, though very badly recorded track for one compilation. But we couldn't send cassettes to East Germany because it was forbidden. So, we had to pass through Hungary. Because from Hungary to East Germany it was possible. And from East Germany to Hungary it was possible. In Poland, for a while, we could trade cassettes. I had a small distribution in Warsaw. Czechoslovakia worked also a little bit. It depended on the year" (personal communication, 2007).

In some cases, contacts at foreign consulates facilitated smuggling. Joanna Stingray was an American who befriended musicians in Soviet Russia, visiting Leningrad on multiple visits starting in 1984. Stingray spearheaded what became the 1986 compilation of Russian bands, *Red Wave: 4 Underground Bands From The USSR*. She got the tapes out of Russia through a combination of her own smuggling and the Swedish embassy sending tapes in diplomatic pouches (Stingray, 2020, personal communication, 2025). Similarly, the 1983 *DDR von unten* (East Germany from below) split LP was released by the West German Aggressive Rock Productions label thanks to the efforts of a West German diplomat (Mohr, 2018, p. 104-106).

Poland appears to have enjoyed some liberties and even the ability to send to and receive packages from the west. The *Networking and Contacts* section of a 1986 issue of *Unsound* magazine includes three separate listings from individuals in Poland.

One offers to trade Polish hardcore, new wave and experimental records for music unavailable in Poland. Another gives the address for a youth culture club promoting independent music through radio, gigs, meetings and lectures. The third is from the host of a Polish radio show hoping to make contacts and exchange music. (*Unsound*, Vol 3 No 1, 1986, p. 64-65).

Rodolfo Protti of Italy ran the Compact Cassette Echo and Old Europa Café labels. In a 1991 interview he spoke about corresponding with musicians from Czechoslovakia, mostly through one Czech artist – Mikolas Chadima, the leader of the MCH Band, who sent Protti cassettes by various Czech bands:

"The main trick was to give those cassettes to people who were leaving Czechoslovakia, then they sent the music to me from outside Czechoslovakia. I sent them back blank chrome tapes because the quality of Czechoslovakian tapes was really bad and they were very expensive. But the music that I received was so very surprising/interesting and good that I decided to have a special Czechoslovakian section at my Old Europa distribution and I realized the *Czech! Till Now You Were Alone* compilation in 1984 and a series of cassettes with more artists and different styles. I think I have more than 30 hours of different Czechoslovakian music now on my label" (Litter, 1991, p. 38).

Chapter 13

Labels, Distribution and Promotion

Communication, trading and collaboration were leading characteristics of the hometaper network. Nevertheless, many artists, even those whose primary interest was exchange, were interested in making their work more widely available.

Making the means of creative production available to individuals was monumental. But to establish, or gain access to distribution systems, was an altogether different challenge that was, and continues to be fraught with barriers to entry.

Regardless of the obstacles, motivated idealists sought to make hometaper cassettes available through small labels and mail order services.

Though not dedicated to cassettes, Rough Trade's attempts at forming the 'Cartel' of regional members, with the goal of alternative nationwide distribution in England is instructive. As a label and distributor, Rough Trade had grown to impressive heights for an enterprise based on a genuine love of music and idealistic fervor. As founder Geoff Travis explains:

"It was a small handful of people. It was a cooperative collective from the beginning in 1981, '82, '83. It was collective in the sense that it wasn't a traditional workplace. There weren't bosses and a hierarchy. People were paid equal amounts of money. We didn't sit around and have endless meetings, which is peoples' image. We were able to be adult about it as the work is what kept us together" (Gross, 1996).

Travis goes on to explain how bands got involved with Rough Trade. Even if it was just packing boxes on trucks, it provided an opportunity for musicians to get to know each other in ways they might otherwise not have:

"Robert Wyatt was on the label and got to sing at a Raincoats show and it was the first time he'd done a show in a while. Mayo Thompson of Red Crayola was part of the organization. Mayo and I produced a lot of records together, like the Raincoats and the Fall. When Red Crayola made their record, they had members of the Raincoats, Essential Logic and Pere Ubu working with them. There was a lot of interbreeding and inter-mingling, which I thought was very helpful" (ibid).

Travis expresses a political purpose that underscored the Cartel. In his history of Rough Trade, Neil Taylor positions Richard Scott as the architect of the Cartel, a loose conglomerate of associated, regional distributive businesses, begun in 1980 and formalized in 1982 (Taylor, 2010, p. 14, 16).

Richard Scott explains the ideals that fueled the Cartel's formation: "It seemed very important to me from very early on that anyone who wanted to be involved in the music business should be allowed access and that it was part of our job to enable them. It started out with us being able to see someone's record in the shop, then being able to distribute it to other shops, then being able to put it out ourselves if we liked it. And when the Cartel was up and running, not only could we do that but we could help other people - people living in the regions - work in the music business as well, because they would then help distribute those records. Right from the start, getting rid of the London-centric attitude to the music business was important" (ibid, p. 104).

In addition to Rough Trade the Cartel included Red Rhino, Revolver, Backs, Probe, and Fast Product, the latter being a label and the only member without a shop, with each functioning as regional distributors. But while the Cartel enjoyed a measure of success, business realities eventually trumped ideals and led to its demise after a few short years. Among the complicating factors was Rough Trade centralization, cash flow among the individual members, and the need to function competitively in the marketplace. Richard Scott explains:

"Of course, it was always going to be short-lived - the idea of a regional digital model, once we moved into the digital age, although interesting, was never going to happen. What was wonderful about those initial Cartel meetings and arrangements was that they were all done without contracts, all done by consensus" (ibid, p. 217).

The Cartel's efforts are illuminating because they demonstrate how ideals and informality present challenges that are difficult to sustain in a long-term business structure. Still, as Neil Taylor reflects: "Now consigned to history, the Cartel epitomizes the finest spirit of Rough Trade's communal unselfishness in action. It is the one area where - in human terms - Rough Trade really did make a difference" (ibid, p. 173).

Inspired by the Rough Trade Cartel model but only associated by links to its regional members, the Satellite Network was an attempt by cassette label and zine publishers to establish a similar regional system in England. Barry Lamb of the Falling A label explains how the concept of shared resources among the members and tapping into each other's networks would allow the Satellite Network to provide multiple services in addition to distribution, including cassette duplication and fanzine copying:

"By 1983 we had our own shop and so were able to sell some cassettes there too. We didn't really advertise. It was reviews and word of mouth. The fanzine network was huge though. There were hundreds of fanzines emerging all over the country, networking with their local scene and with other fanzines around the country and even overseas. We saw an opportunity to try and harness this and create a broader cartel type network and attempted to do so with Richard Rouska, the Subway Organization and several others. There were about five or six of us working on this" (personal communication, 2009).

Lamb continues, describing the details of how the network operated and the members interacted: "We started offering to distribute fanzines and other people's releases via our contact networks and some of the other people releasing stuff did the same for us. We took stock on sale or return some of the time and other times we put some releases out on our own label paying a licensing fee per sale. There was a great deal of trust and goodwill involved. A few labels with a similar operational model to ours began to surface, the first being a label called Music for Midgets run by a guy called Frazer Nash, then an organization called Rouska run by Richard Paddison, the Subway Organization run by Martin Whitehead and several others. We found ourselves to be geographically spread out, so we talked about trying to regionalize the distribution and look after a geographic region each. Between us we managed to have the whole of the UK covered. We promoted each other and published a couple of fanzine type magazines with catalog and release info. I think between us all we also had influential relationships with all the major fanzines in the UK and key people in the established music press who would generously give DIY cassettes some coverage" (ibid).

Like Rough Trade's Cartel, the Satellite Network achieved impressive results. However, the venture lasted a mere nine months, which Lamb attributes to a lack of maturity, leadership skills and idealistic naiveté. With decades of hindsight, Lamb reflects on the specifics:

"We never realized anywhere near our full potential for three main reasons. First, our vision lacked clarity and unity. On the one hand we wanted to be a unified collective of independent organizations, but on the other the Satellite Network meant something different to each person you would talk to. Our second main failure, which is perhaps the cause of the first, is that there was not a defined leadership or operational structure. Everything was a bit ad hoc. Myself and Richard were the instigators but we knew nothing about leadership and focus at that time. I was a struggling musician trying to help other struggling musicians and Richard was a little more of an entrepreneur than me, but he was really a fanzine writer with a lot of energy and some very good ideas. Our geographic distance from each other meant that we rarely met together, and communication was not as straightforward then as it is now. We did not have mobile phones. Some of us did not even have landlines! The third reason was that Falling A began to struggle financially during that period. We had seriously overcommitted our resources and had planned to be the major financial stakeholder in the Satellite Network. At the same time, we were giving way too much product away for nothing and we had a shop which was making a significant loss. Without the money behind it, the Satellite Network went from a promising initial launch to a project that just seemed to limp along and after about nine months the whole thing just fizzled out" (ibid).

Despite its limited success, Lamb is upbeat in his belief that the venture did help them broaden their network of contacts and provided coverage in fanzines and the music press. Yet Lamb's experience reveals a distaste for the business realities which would, in the end, solidify his commitment to functioning in an independent capacity:

"We struck up a good relationship with an independent record distributor called Backs and they agreed to distribute some of our cassette releases mainly for the export market. Some releases were shifting between 300-500 copies. Two releases sold over 1,000 copies, which was quite remarkable for a DIY cassette release with photocopied cover. We talked about doing some vinyl with them and they offered to put up the money for the pressings, which sounded great, but in reality we would find ourselves supplying cassette stock to them and not being paid for sales on the cassettes because we would owe them money for the vinyl pressings. It was too much of a financial headache adding to our cash flow problem. We ended up in 1986 doing a joint venture with a small label called Waterfall which was a little more palatable, but as we got deeper into trying to get radio play and promoting records and trying to influence the music press, I began to realize that I actually don't like the music business that much. It's shallow, almost everyone is out to serve themselves and there is a considerable lack of humility out there. I missed the mutual trust, the relationships and the honesty that we had experienced in the earlier years (1977-84) when we were just trying to get our music heard. I didn't sign up to pretend to be a pop star. I just wanted to make some music with integrity and help other like-minded musicians. But when someone waved a contract in front of my nose which had been vetted by the biggest music business lawyer in the country at the time I just felt it had all gone too far. By the end of 1986 we were winding down" (ibid).

Economic realities would be a consistent challenge, or something to be disregarded, as increasing numbers of hometapers formed labels and mail order services. Individuals were commonly involved in various aspects of the network, including home recording, zine publishing, cassette labels and radio.

Chris Phinney, who recorded as Mental Anguish, started publishing his *Malice* fanzine of industrial music in 1979 and formed his Harsh Reality label in 1982. Carl Howard, who recorded as Nomuzic, published 12 issues of his *Artitude* zine from 1984-86 and formed his Audiofile Tapes label in the same period.

Zan Hoffman explains how it was necessary for artists to form their own labels, especially those creating more experimental forms of music: "You have people who are experimentalists and are just doing it because there's no way in hell, heaven or earth that someone's going to carry your shit if you don't release it yourself. And I think that's an issue that's overlooked. It's hopeless to think someone else is going to make you someone. That Warner Brothers is going to find you. That level of fame is completely out of your grasp. And when you kill that demon and realize that shit doesn't matter, then you realize your only option is your own label, and occasional distro by other labels" (personal communication, 2008).

Don Campau formed his Lonely Whistle label in 1984 as a vehicle for his own work yet quickly discovered more expansive possibilities: "Shortly thereafter, I realized that I could have a 'label' that could release other people's music" (personal communication, 2007).

Focusing on one's own recordings plus including others on the label became a common theme as artists found that the mere existence of a label name drew attention. Randy Greif formed his Swinging Axe Productions label in 1983 after learning about the growing music network in *Op* magazine, starting with recordings of his music he had accumulated since 1975:

"So I put together four tapes of music that I'd worked on at various stages and called them different band names: The Love Stumps, Screaming Dukduks, Max & Mel, Face Cancer, plus stuff that was under my own name. I was coming in sort of naïve and didn't really understand this networking thing that was starting then, and I figured I should have a label for it. I found that as soon as I got a little catalog together, and ran a couple ads, and put some tapes in for review, all these tapes and things were pouring into me from people who were basically interested in the same thing I was, saying, 'Hey, listen to this, do you want to distribute this?'. Then I started writing to people and it just took off from there" (Orford, 1990, p. 53).

The hometaper network enjoyed a mainstream plug in 1987 when journalist Jon Pareles published an article titled *Record-It-Yourself Music on Cassette* in the *New York Times*: "A new underground of musicians is composing, performing and releasing its music on cassettes, trading and selling them in a loose network that extends across North America and from Australia to Yugoslavia. The artistic freedom, low cost, privacy and spontaneity of cassette recording have encouraged thousands of performers to bypass the music business and do it themselves" (Pareles, 1987).

Pareles mentions American labels Ladd-Frith, Sound of Pig and Cause And Effect, and artists like Minóy, R. Stevie Moore and Cleaners From Venus. He also speaks with broadcaster Don Campau, who hosted the *No Pigeonholes* radio show on KKUP in Cupertino, California, and with Robin James, referencing his cassette show on KAOS-FM in Olympia, Washington and his forthcoming *Cassette Mythos* book. Pareles covers the fundamental bases and makes the crucial point that these are not demos and that for many they are non-commercial, art for art's sake enterprises.

The exposure was appreciated, as paid advertising was not frequently exploited by the typical hometaper with limited resources. Al Margolis reports having only done minimal advertising: "You'd advertise in *Sound Choice*. And the ads were pretty cheap, $25 or something like that to do a quarter page ad in *Sound Choice*, since that was the only place I was advertising" (personal communication, 2007).

Many, like Don Campau, saw no value in paid advertising: "I did run a couple of paid ads in *Sound Choice* but nothing came of them. I thought it was a good way to support the mag through. I have never had much in the way of sales and generally have given away most of my releases to friends and music contacts" (personal communication 2007).

R. Stevie Moore's ads for his Cassette Club appeared regularly in *Op* starting in the early 1980s. Moore recalls how he designed the ads to draw attention:

"The Cassette Club was just a banner title, name, concept, that's all. I didn't truly and properly make it an authentic club with membership rules, cards, fees, autographed 8x10s. I just called it that as a joke; sort of a splashy announcement that my full oeuvre up to that point became a real catalog. One couldn't officially join up though, other than to merely order something and then suddenly become an automatic member. I guess what made it official to me was my decision to print up a xeroxed catalog. I mailed out hundreds of them. Also, the explosion of the format itself. Cassettes were ideal for duping my original reel-to-reels. Consider the fact that for a short while prior I would send out my music on reel-to-reel copies! As far as 'distributing' cassettes before the club, no, it was always just supply to any demand, dubbed to order or request. No proper distributing through normal channels" (personal communication, 2009).

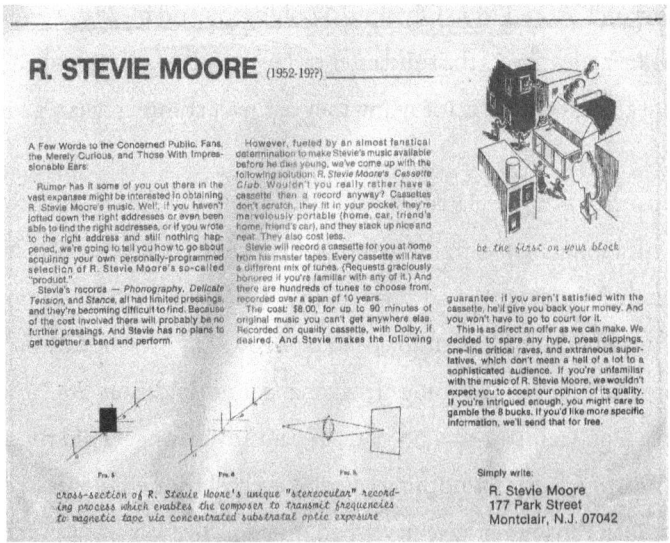

RSM Cassette Club (Op Issue E, 1981)

Frans de Waard explains how advertising for his Korm Plastics label releases could be obtained through the trade mechanism that was a routine characteristic of the network:

"Nothing was printed, but all was xeroxed - catalogs, covers. Every spare inch on a piece of paper was used to add small flyers about releases. I did a bit of advertising, only if it was possible to pay in product, rather than money. Also, promotion-wise a bit, to small fanzines around, provided I would get the fanzine in trade. That brought in new addresses" (personal communication, 2009).

Ken Moore's experiences highlight how exposure and becoming a known quantity through one's activities were the hometaper's de facto 'advertising'. In the late 1970s Moore advertised his cassette albums in a Baltimore, Maryland newspaper. The result was "no response whatsoever" and Moore decided there was no point in wasting money on more ads. He discovered that getting reviews of his music produced sales. This was augmented by distribution in the US through such sources as Archie Patterson's Eurock Distribution, including ads for his stock in *Eurock* magazine, and UK distribution by Alan and Steve Freeman and coverage in their *Audion* magazine (personal communication, 2025).

Moore soon connected with musicians associated with the International Electronic Music Association (IEMA) and its *SYNE* magazine. The team was also responsible for the IEMA Group Tape samplers started by Jim Finch. Voted in as Music Director by the staff, Moore curated five of the eight IEMA samplers released between 1981-85. By selecting the artists to be included, assemblage and distribution, Moore's role inserted him more deeply into the network:

"After I was voted to take over the project from Jim, my address was made known to all who wanted to buy and participate in the 'Group Tape' collection. I didn't have to solicit any of the material. More than what I needed was sent directly to me. I was certainly able to expand my active mailing list for my personal releases. And I guess I sort of just became 'known' in that regard because of my promotional activities" (ibid).

For many hometapers, their networking, exchange and label activities were tightly linked. For Al Margolis and his Sound of Pig label, there was a direct tie between promoting his releases and artist-to-artist exchange. In one year in the late 1980s Margolis reports that he mailed 3300 hand dubbed cassettes which represented a three-way split between sales, trades and promos:

"When SOP stopped, I had 302 cassettes. And there was a lot of radio. So, I was trying to trade with people. People were buying stuff. And there were a lot of radio people to send stuff to. I probably sent out 40-50 of every tape. When a tape came out you sent it to the artist, and you sent promos. But at that point there were more zines going around and you had some radio people, and trading with your friends - Hal McGee, Don Campau, Das, Zan Hoffman. There were probably 5-10 people who got almost every cassette that came out. So, I had a regular mailing list. These are my buddies who I'm trading with. And then there's a certain amount of zines and radio people" (personal communication, 2007).

Despite the man hours spent duplicating tapes and the effort dedicated to promoting his releases, Margolis is clear that he had no interest in becoming a distributor: "It's a hard thing to do. And you have to be really dedicated. The cassette thing was really nice because you could skip the business part. But the year I did 3300 cassettes, I also had to buy 3300 cassettes. So, how much money can you afford to lose? In the heyday of doing the cassette stuff I really couldn't afford to go out and buy music I wanted to hear in the store. So, if you didn't trade with me I wouldn't get your music" (ibid).

Margolis engaged in promotional activities, yet there was no 'business' component. He sent promotional copies to zines and radio, but sharing with friends was the primary motivation.

For some artists, the costs associated with their label and distribution activities were justified as labors of love because the participants could rely on paid employment outside of music. With their economic needs met by 'day jobs', these artists could fund their activities or take a dismissive view of the losses.

For those who ran the Italian TRAX label, employment gave them the freedom to engage in sales, promotion and business-related forms of exchange. There was no expectation of profit, and the participants were motivated to make available music they were passionate about and gain new contacts. TRAX cofounder Vittore Baroni explains:

"We tried all the usual routes. We circulated thousands of postcards and little ads and catalogs through our mail contacts. We participated annually to the Independent Music Meeting that was held in Florence, and to similar conventions for producers of fanzines and independent records. We sent out promo copies for reviews to all kinds of zines. We were usually able to sell out an edition of a TRAX item in a year or two, and I'm speaking of editions of 500 or 1000 copies, which is quite a lot compared to today's standards for micro-labels. We were able to ship out small quantities of items to specialized distributors like Rough Trade, UK, US and Japan, but we also often traded materials with other cassette producers. For example, I would send 20 copies of a TRAX cassette compilation to Ding Dong Tapes in Holland and pick as an exchange an equivalent value of titles from their catalog. In this way, your collection of cassettes would grow much faster, without all the hassle of having to collect money from creditors. I must add that TRAX was always for me, Piermario Ciani and the other main players involved a labor of love. We all had our different paying jobs and being realistic, we did not expect to make any money out of this. Rather, through TRAX we wished to find new contacts, to trade interesting materials and most of all to give life to an original experiment in mixed media and networking" (personal communication, 2008).

The benefit of steady employment similarly motivated Colorado based Kent Hotchkiss, who formed the AEON mail order service in early 1980. In addition to mail order and distribution, AEON was also a tape label, featuring cassette albums by such international artists as Human Flesh, Bene Gesserit, Merzbow, Het Zweet, Borbetomagus, Asmus Tietchens and others.

With a focus on experimental artists, Hotchkiss felt he could justify keeping his prices low because employment supported his commitment to eschewing a profit motive: "Distributors who depend for their living on selling records are trapped by the reality of economics. There are some distributors who are really concerned with the future of experimental music, but there are far more whose decisions are based on profit" (MFZ, 1983, p. 22).

Hotchkiss' comments in a 1983 interview indicate what he saw as a contradiction between selling experimental music and attempting to do so at a profit: "From a monetary standpoint AEON hasn't been worthwhile. Of course it was never intended to be. No one here has ever taken a cent out of the business. All of the profits have been put back into AEON to help it expand. The thing that has made AEON worthwhile are all the friendships we have made and the exchange of ideas and music" (ibid, p. 23).

Like so many others who attempted to promote hometaper cassettes, Hotchkiss shared the same motivations as the artists, enjoying the communication, music and resulting bonds of friendship. AEON would become an early casualty of the decade, lasting only until 1985 when he sold the remainder of his stock to Ron Lessard of RRRecords.

With the rise of global communication and collaboration, sending tapes in bulk was cumbersome and expensive, especially overseas. Many turned to a mechanism whereby a single master tape of an album would be sent to a distributor. Distributors would then make copies to order and pay artists a royalty based on the number sold. Frans de Waard explains the benefits of this arrangement, both for convenience and business simplicity:

"Very early on I thought it was a nightmare to do bookkeeping and especially paying people. There was no internet, so you got international money orders or checks. I was very young, so it was hard for me to get them. One thing that worked, however, was sending out good quality master tapes and original covers, say fifty, and asking distributors to make the copies themselves and pay for the covers. That worked quite well. RRRecords did that and did good sales" (personal communication, 2009).

Similarly, SJ Org Distribution in France, run by the band La Sonorite Jaune, partnered with Carl Howard's Audiofile Tapes in the US to establish a cooperative master tapes exchange deal in their respective countries.

Chris Phinney's Harsh Reality label engaged in a similar, informal mechanism with friends overseas: "I had agreements with overseas friends like Mitch Rushton at Alternate Media Tapes (UK) and Matthias Lang at IRRE Tapes (Germany) and a couple others where we sent each other masters of tapes. The tapes were released on both our labels and sold through each of our catalogs. No money was exchanged. It saved money for all of us on overseas shipping, plus we all reached a wider audience" (personal communication, 2025).

Mitch Rushton confirms Phinney's description of what both refer to as 'licensing' agreements: "I had no illusions about making money from it, just getting my own stuff heard by like-minded folks who would enjoy it. With that in mind, we set Alternate Media Tapes up as a cassette label that was based on distribution to other cassette labels and that any direct sales from us to customers would be priced to cover running costs only - copying, mastering, mailing, etc. No profit was made. As we became better known in the cassette community, musicians from other countries started sending us tapes and asking if we could distribute them on Alternate Media. We always made it clear to them that this was for distribution purposes only and that they would receive no money. We also pointed out that we may 'license' out a tape to other labels - again, only for distribution purposes. Most were happy with the arrangement. Those that weren't went elsewhere" (personal communication, 2025).

Some involved in cassette distribution functioned at the intersection of the individual operator and commercial realms. Andreas Müller leveraged his job at Normal Records in Germany to gain distribution for his releases. Müller distinguished between Datenverarbeitung's 'local' and 'international' phases:

"Stefan Colombier (who many years later founded Dauerblumen), a local punk legend, also worked part-time at Normal Records and released two cassettes in very small quantities on his Akrat Tapes label during 1981. In early 1982 we joined forces and Datenverarbeitung was launched as a cassette label. This began what in hindsight one might call the 'local period' of the label which saw ten or so releases, including reissues of the two Akrat Tapes cassettes. The idea was to give an outlet to New Wave (for lack of a better term) bands from Bonn and its surrounding region. Although some of the bands also released records, either on a local record label or on their own, they still had a lot of material that would not find its way onto vinyl for various reasons" (personal communication, 2009).

Müller describes how he moved on to releasing tapes by Esplendor Geometrico (Spain), Cultural Amnesia (UK) and Hunting Lodge (US): "The 'international period' of Datenverarbeitung was preceded by the publication of the eighth and final issue of *Datenverarbeitung* fanzine in May 1982. For the purpose of gathering material for the fanzine I had started corresponding with numerous labels and bands from outside of Germany.

Müller distributed his releases through Normal Records and others he was in contact with via his position with the company, though there were local and international components to this as well:

"With the exception of the *Die Fliegen* soundtrack the German bands' tapes were sold domestically only. When I started the label a network of small mail order companies specializing in cassettes already existed in Germany. I was fortunate in that the people running them liked the early Datenverarbeitung releases and stocked the entire early catalog. Thus, in addition to Normal Records my tapes were sold by Molto Menz in Munich, Graf Haufen Tapes in Berlin, Walters Lust in Frankfurt and 235 in Hennef near Bonn" (ibid).

Datenverarbeitung's international releases were sold by Ding Dong in the Netherlands, Front de L'Est in France, AEON in Colorado, Rough Trade in San Francisco, Wayside Music in Maryland, a record store plus mail order in Tokyo, Japan, plus Normal Records and 235 in Germany. Müller also shares sales figures, noting local releases typically sold 100-200 copies, with the *Die Fliegen* soundtrack being the only one to exceed 200 units in sales. The international releases, on the other hand, sold in greater numbers, with Esplendor Geometrico's *EG1* selling around 700, Hunting Lodge's *Exhumed* selling 500 and the *Sinn & Form* compilation selling in the 900 range (ibid).

Some enjoyed longer term success incorporating home recorded cassettes into more traditional record store business models. Ron Lessard of Lowell, Massachusetts opened his brick-and-mortar RRRecords shop on January 3, 1984, and would go on to distribute home recorded cassettes and release hometaper recordings on cassette and vinyl LPs through his RRRecords label. Lessard explains how he moved from dabbling in mail order to distribution through his shop:

"I was already interested in cassette culture before opening my shop and used to do small scale sales by printing up my own lists. Most of my customers came from adverts in *Goldmine* magazine. At that time, I was in contact with people like LAFMS, the Residents and Eugene Chadbourne. After opening my shop, I decided to try it on a larger scale. I started writing all the labels and artists I was interested in and picked up copies of their titles. Once I had a nice little stash happening, I published my first catalog - I advertised my wares in the underground mags and fanzines - and once the catalog started making the rounds, labels and artists started writing me and asking if I'd stock their titles" (personal communication, 2016).

Lessard mostly purchased titles outright from cassette artists and labels. But with European labels he also took masters of the tapes and covers and made copies at home rather than pay shipping on finished copies. Lessard also confirms Frans de Waard's claim that he "did good sales" with not only de Waard's recordings but the experimental/noise/hometaper artists he was selling in general:

"Oh yes, the tapes sold well, especially if they were good! Most of my sales were mail order but I also had in-store sales. A number of people from Boston and the New England area would drive to my shop to check out my wares. When you are specialized, people find you" (ibid).

For Lessard, the effort he made on behalf of hometaper recordings was fueled by the same motivations as the artists themselves: "It was all about the passion, sales were just the icing on the cake. I did it because I was totally in love with the whole scene. Trading is the life blood of the scene. I would often trade tapes I was distributing to get more tapes from other labels and artists" (ibid).

Archie Patterson published *Eurock* magazine from 1973-92, covering European progressive, electronic and experimental music. He also launched Eurock distribution which sold vinyl records, as well as cassette albums by hometaper artists. Patterson explains how Eurock Distribution was built from his experience in the 1970s import business:

"My entry point into the music business was the Intergalactic Trading Company (ITC) in Portland, Oregon. ITC was an adjunct to the record store, Music Millennium. At the outset the focus was on UK imports via Caroline Records UK and sporadic importing of German rock via Juliana Hopp of GMBH out of Germany. They had heard about Eurock and in September 1976 owner Don MacLeod hired me to run their mail order, and we soon began importing music from everywhere else. Due to my Eurock contacts over the span of the next approximately 3-4 years the floodgates were opened to France, Sweden, Finland, Italy, Spain, Japan, Australia. We did limited local wholesale and a couple stores in the northwest, but unlike JEM it was only me and one other person doing everything" (personal communication, 2016).

Patterson's experience sheds light on the challenges and pitfalls of music distribution in the revenue generating business world: "What happened at ITC was Music Millennium began doing 'parallel importing', which later became the big thing in the import music business that led to a more adventurous period in music importation and JEM's ultimate failure. In ITC's case they began bringing in import pressings from Japan of The Eagles, Steely Dan, etc., due to their superior pressings. As a result, my budget became limited for importing and selling fewer 'odd experimental music' titles from Europe. The result was I began offering my own parallel small section of things offered via Eurock Distribution" (ibid).

The first Eurock Distribution ad appeared in an early 1979 issue of *Eurock* magazine and included LPs by bands like Chrome, Univers Zero and Pascal Comelade, as well as cassettes from Palace of Lights and Zazen Zafaun, as well as books and VHS video tapes. Financial difficulties with the companies Patterson was working for would soon lead to his decision to focus full time on Eurock Distribution:

"Due to the ITC financial situation and budget constraints, I continued doing the multi-layered approach until one day I got a phone call from Los Angeles in late 1979 from people who were starting a new import music company called Greenworld. I flew down there and part of the 'business plan' was to have a direct retail arm of the company. They wanted me to come down and set it up. That was called Paradox Music Mailorder. I continued having Eurock Distribution adverts in the magazine through issue #17 selling only foreign EPs, books and magazines. After that point I simply reviewed all the indie cassettes and other EPs adding my personal contact at the end so people could write to me and buy things from me directly outside of the Greenworld business structure" (ibid).

Interest grew over the next few years for Eurock styled music and the market for US distribution of imports grew exponentially. This resulted in growth for Greenworld and Paradox Music Mailorder, though ITC had by this time faded away. Regardless, Patterson explains that the increasing payables began to outstrip cash inflow, resulting in his having to cut back on stock of European independent music:

"Ironically, a chief cause of this was once again the rapid expansion of parallel importation of mainstream music from Japan. It was déjà vu for me, so in 1981 I quit working for anyone else and began doing Eurock Distribution full time while living in Los Angeles. Its main focus was the exploding cassette music scene as well as various other releases on cassette, fanzines, indie LPs and EPs. A bit earlier in late 1979-early 1980 I began my own cassette only label. The first release was a tape smuggled out of Czechoslovakia via Canada recorded by the 'illegal' band, Plastic People of the Universe whose leader was then in jail. It was called *Hundred Points*. I released that followed by a series of original recordings by international artists from France, Eastern Europe and elsewhere" (ibid).

In 1984 Patterson moved back to Portland and Eurock expanded into many different areas: "One involved cassettes. I lectured for classes, grades 7-12, for five years in a Portland K-12 public school. I offered a *Listeners Guide to Experimental Music*. I recorded special 'mix cassettes' each week to use as musical background accompanying stories about my experiences in music overall. I ended up ultimately releasing them as a cassette series of taped music and lectures chronicling my personal adventures in the 1960s along with the creation of Eurock" (ibid).

Patterson was yet another example of someone driven by their passion for the music and the artists who were creating it: "While running Eurock Distribution I always dealt with artists directly as well as small indie labels. I never did wholesale of the cassettes as the retail price/cost was so low, or very high in the case of very special packaging. More importantly, cassettes at first were mostly all done in very limited editions. I'm sure it's hard to imagine a time now when everything wasn't ever present and mass marketed, available free as a download, or sold at ridiculously high prices. Most LPs were sold for around $7 via ITC or Paradox, with most cassettes I sold being $6. As strange as it seems, music back then was done for the love of creation by the artists. *Eurock* and Eurock Distribution were motivated by my desire to share it with people and form a personal link with other like-minded music lovers. In retrospect, I was blissfully naïve. Today it's all about capitalizing on and cashing in on everything, be it music or any other form of art or product being marketed. Not 'art for art's sake'" (ibid).

Patterson purchased tapes directly from such labels as DDAA, Bain Total, Ptose Productions (France), TRAX, ADN, MB (Italy), Marquee Moon, Vanity Records, YLEM, LLE (Japan), Mirage, YHR (UK), Via Lactea, Oxomaxoma Voldarepet (Mexico) and Agjtasjon (Norway). In many cases he was one of the only sellers of their music outside of direct sales by the artists and labels themselves. Patterson cites the Eurock label's 6-cassette *Kundalini Opera* set by Cyrille Verdeaux (of Clearlight fame) as a paradigm example of the 'indie' process in action:

"Those six individual tapes were all duped by Pat Baum, drummer for the legendary Portland all girl punk trio The Neo Boys. She lived in a big old rundown building on Russell Street that was serving as a series of ramshackle lofts at that time (now gentrified of course). Pat had 6 or 8 cassette recorders lined up on a couple shelves so she could dupe all the tapes in real time. I had a friend print the multi-colored j-cards plus color libretto, then gave them to her for assembly and she'd tell me - 'pick the order up next week'. It was totally cool, and she got to know my #1 son as I brought him along to her place sometimes to drop off or pick up the order" (ibid).

Of the artist run services that formed in the 1980s with an exclusive focus on cassette tapes, few better exemplified the excitement, accomplishment and sorrow of creating a distribution mechanism than Cause And Effect. Formed in Indianapolis, Indiana in 1984 by Hal McGee and Debbie Jaffe, Cause And Effect operated as a mail order, label and wholesale distributor for hundreds of home recording artists and labels. McGee and Jaffe were active hometapers, recording challenging works of experimental audio art as a duo in Viscera, McGee recorded solo as Dog As Master, and Jaffe recorded solo as Master/Slave Relationship.

The duo were tireless networkers, writing countless letters to hometapers around the world. McGee recalls writing 5-10 page letters describing the music they were creating, requesting trades and exploring interest in distributing other's work. It was the realization that there were not many reliable vehicles for artists and labels to make their cassette albums available that led to the creation of Cause And Effect, with the specific intent being to provide a centralized international distribution service.

The January 1985 Cause And Effect catalog presents a stunning array of over 100 tapes from all over the world, plus a variety of zines. McGee describes the process of producing tapes released on the label:

"None of the cassettes released on the CAE label were mass-produced or pro-printed. The covers were designed largely by Debbie and then xeroxed and hand-cut with an Exacto knife and then folded into the j-card and little labels pasted onto the cassette itself. Every so often a printed catalog was produced, with layout by Debbie who became quite adept at the Letraset burnish-on lettering. For more extensive typesetting a typewriter was used and blown up or reduced by Xerox machine and then physically pasted up onto the layout (no computers! no Photoshop!). They were xeroxed in bulk and mailed out, only to wait for orders to come back in weeks later. CAE also did not accept credit cards and PayPal had yet to be invented so orders had to also be sent via postal mail with payment by check, money order or cash" (McGee, online).

McGee and Jaffe's activities evolved rapidly, and both learned on the fly, expanding from mail order to label to distributor. McGee explains how the duo began by purchasing tapes outright: "We paid up front for all of the cassettes listed in the January 1985 Cause And Effect catalog. I'm pretty sure that this was unheard of at the time. Artists sent us one copy of each tape that they wanted us to carry in our catalog. We listened to each cassette, and if we liked what we heard I wrote to the artist and asked them for a wholesale price and told them how many copies we wanted. Then they mailed the requested amount of tapes to us and we would mail a payment for five or ten copies. If we sold all five or ten copies of the artist's tape we would send a payment for more copies if we thought that we could sell more" (personal communication, 2016).

It soon became apparent, however, that purchasing multiple copies in advance was a costly proposition. McGee continues: "By the time of the second catalog in May of 1985 we realized that paying for copies outright in advance wasn't a realistic business model for survival. With the licence (we used the Euro spelling) production method, in which the artist sent a master tape and several printed covers or a cover art master (from which we would duplicate/photocopy covers as needed), we could make as few or as many copies as we needed based on demand. This worked out well for a lot of overseas artists. I have numerous cassettes in my racks that were listed in the CAE catalogs that are labeled as 'master tape'" (ibid).

C&E Catalog (May 1985)

The May 1985 catalog listed three distribution methods: Outright purchase of tapes, license production, and release by the Cause And Effect label. The latter mechanism meant exclusive distribution by Cause And Effect, with McGee and Jaffe taking responsibility for manufacture and paid promotion. By the time of the third catalog the duo had dispensed entirely with purchasing stock in advance. And with the fourth catalog in Summer 1986 distribution was minimal, the lion's share of tapes being on the Cause And Effect label.

Unlike most artist run labels, McGee and Jaffe attempted to treat Cause And Effect as a business. McGee explains:

"We were seriously trying to treat CAE as a business. In fact, we registered with the IRS as a business. We kept business accounts and did all of the bookkeeping, sent receipts with customer orders, all of that stuff. There were a few months in 1985 when we even considered the possibility of future hopes that it might turn into a viable able-to-support-us-as-a-living business" (ibid).

But this was not to be. The magnitude of continuous activity – writing letters, duplicating tapes by hand, processing orders, packing and mailing, and creating their own recordings - eventually took its toll on the duo. Exhaustion, personal issues, and the impossibility of sustaining Cause And Effect financially resulted in its dissolution in 1988.

McGee estimates that over four years they mailed 5,000 tapes, 4,000 of which were sold and the rest given away or traded. As McGee says: "It wasn't a thing where you could live off of it. The kinds of prices we were charging, we weren't going to make a living off of that" (Kranitz, 2002).

McGee shares a further sentiment about the factors leading to his dissatisfaction with Cause And Effect and how its direction ran counter to his original ethic of supporting hometaper artists:

"I became disillusioned with Cause And Effect after we became label-only, because we more or less started releasing stuff that would SELL. This made us no better than what we originally reacted/rebelled against. In a sense we 'sold out' and forsook our original ideals. In other words, instead of continuing to support and distribute music by 'the little guy', we started only dealing with 'bigger names' like Merzbow, Nurse With Wound, Controlled Bleeding, etc. Huge mistake!" (personal communication, 2016).

The 'bigger names' that McGee calls out were indeed hometapers, and their recordings fell firmly into the experimental realm. But they were artists with a sense of marketing, self-promotion, or perhaps luck, who achieved a certain minimal level of popularity, with both tape and vinyl releases on relatively larger labels and sales that eluded the average home recorded artist.

Pascal Dauzier of the band La Sonorite Jaune and SJ Org Distribution alluded to similar concerns in a 1990 interview. SJ Org was based in France and distributing approximately 100 titles from the American Audiofile Tapes label. Speaking to the artists on the label, Dauzier says:

"European distributors like Staalplaat (Amsterdam) pick up and distribute mostly renowned and 'famous' people of Audiofile. They don't take risks with bands like Velvet Swines, Mars Everywhere... I found it interesting to promote such persons who are a good alternative to the 'industrial' and noise field" (Therer, 1990, p. 35).

It's astounding to think of any artist on the Audiofile Tapes label as 'famous', though bands such as the Legendary Pink Dots have, over the decades, produced a sizable catalog of tape, vinyl and CD releases and have maintained an ongoing tour schedule. Still, the notion of relative fame weighed heavily on artists like McGee and Dauzier, revealing sentiments for lesser known artists working in obscurity.

McGee says that he and Jaffe attempted to reconnect with the cassette community after transitioning to a label-only by releasing several compilations with a specific focus on the artists they felt they had abandoned. With the benefit of hindsight, McGee summarizes his feelings:

"We did what we thought were the right things to do at the time. It is significant that we felt the desire/need to do the CAE compilations to reconnect ourselves to the community. My later personal efforts, such as *Electronic Cottage* (magazine), the *Tape Heads* compilation series, and the five zillion other compilations I produced were all efforts to serve the community, which I personally felt I had abandoned during CAE's life. These are NOT examples of me wishing things had been different long after the fact. I set out to create *Electronic Cottage* specifically with the intention to rededicate myself to my ideals of serving the network, making connections, etc." (personal communication, 2016).

Economic realities and the rules of successfully operating in a capitalist market would be continually borne out as the 1980s wore on. In a 1991 interview, Carl Howard of Audiofile Tapes responded to a question asking if the label is self-supporting, if it breaks even, how many tapes does he sell, how many promotional copies does he send out, and how many does he trade:

"Self-whating? Break how? (laughter) All I can tell you is that I try to manage as best as I can, being reasonably frugal with unrequested promos, so that I don't cut into my rent and groceries and stuff. With regard to actual sales, if you figure that the total for an average month floats somewhere above the $100 mark and that tapes sell for $5 and $6 each, then do the division yourself. Regardless though, the promos ensure that I always wind up in the debit column" (McGee, 1991, p. 78).

In a 1988 interview Alain Neffe took a realists view by recognizing that product must be readily available and promoted: "We have had a lot of articles and interviews printed in the alternative and the so called 'normal' press in a lot of countries. We are also broadcast a lot on student and university radio. But for example, we had a three-hour broadcast in Chicago. A lot of people phoned in asking how they could buy the music. Of course we have no distribution in Chicago. Most people don't want to order by mail. They like to go to their favorite record shop and their favorite dealer. They can see the product, listen to it and then buy it immediately. They don't have to risk their money sending it by mail and waiting. It's a problem" (*ND*, Issue 10, 1988, p. 38).

Gaining listeners' interest through exposure means little if the music isn't readily available. Most consumers are not willing to make the effort to mail order for music when there are seemingly endless choices in their local record shops. Neffe continues:

"We have been well broadcasted on radio, but the problem is to have distribution in the area where you broadcast. People know the name, but they forget very quickly if they don't see something in the shop the day after they hear it" (ibid, p. 39).

Neffe recognized that while music fans may be open to alternatives, most understandably want mainstream, convenient methods of access. *CLEM* publisher Alex Douglas addressed this topic in a 1986 editorial:

"How does an artist in a small town create a need for his music in another small town in another country the other side of the ocean? If a listener has $20 to spend and has the choice of purchasing two records of known music at the local record store, or one record from another country that will take 2 months to arrive and take a lot of work to get, you've got a serious problem. Now sure there are dedicated listeners who will write away, but they're few and far between and soon they'll run out of money" (*CLEM*, April 1986).

This is the challenge that the hometapers and any independent recording artist faced. The popularity that artists like Merzbow, Nurse With Wound and the Legendary Pink Dots achieved demonstrated that there is a market for the type of music and audio art the hometapers were creating. But easy availability and, for many consumers, being a 'known' quantity speaks volumes to the fundamental rules of the market. This and the sheer volume of available music released each year were forces that hindered the ability of hometaper cassettes to become more widely available. Douglas' editorial continues on this point:

"All you need to do is open up *CLEM*, *Option*, *Sound Choice*, *Recordings*, etc. to see the thousands of independent records or tapes available. No one person can purchase them all and I wonder if any one person is interested in them all. Another way of describing this is, are you the listener happy with what you listen to or do you want to hear everything about the scene so that you can make a choice? And you, the artist, are the distributors, magazines, and networking system representing you the way you want them to? Looking at it one more way: The independent artist, what is he looking for? Do you expect to be popular? Do you expect to make a living from your music? To make a buck are you willing to do a more commercial sound or is it a case of you'll only play your music no matter if you never sell a thing. Is the music for you or the listener? And distributors, what about you? I've met guys with great ideals but once the reality of pay for produce, initial inventory, catalog printing, postage and handling, etc. come into play, things don't look so good anymore. I'll repeat what I said before and that's that most artists should distribute product themselves. If you don't do that who's going to know you've got something for sale?" (ibid).

Douglas concludes by saying he has no solution to offer, but does want to know if readers are happy with *CLEM*, and expresses the trademark sentiment of the independent music networker:

"Can it help, or does it open up too many doors? I love the friendship and music chat it brings but I'm also annoyed that I've not been able to deliver the product on time. Well thanks again to you all. I hope this editorial is seen in a positive atmosphere." Douglas adds: "The main objective of *CLEM* is communication, worldwide between the artist and listener" (ibid).

In a 1985 article, Tracy Hunker made a rare case for people in the independent music world to embrace components of capitalism. Hunker starts with observations about what he feels is a crisis of the new music scene:

"It stems from the scenario that most people would just as soon let the 'scene' be free and open, safe from the problems of finance and business procedure. However, regardless of the cavalier attitude of most consumers/producers in the field, there is still a strong need for service-related businesses in order for anything to succeed" (Hunker, 1985, p. 33),

Hunker points out that indie music people are dependent on several types of for-profit businesses, such as record and tape production houses and record stores: "Businesses like radio, fanzines, indie labels, booking agents, and distributors to an extent have the option of not being profit or income oriented. Nevertheless, people do need to earn a living, but ironically those businesses that are more likely to provide jobs in the field are also most likely to be rare in most parts of the US" (ibid).

Hunker puts forth numerous ideas, all of which he acknowledges require time, effort, organization and dedication. He concludes that change is possible "if we play a little more capitalism and get a well-informed grassroots movement going" (ibid).

Chapter 14

Radio

Radio remained a significant form of exposure in the 1980s and the subject of discussion and debate in the music publications. Listings of stations friendly to independent releases were common, and the challenges faced by artists and labels to get attention from stations were frequently addressed in letters columns.

Following the pattern of these discussions it becomes clear that, like much else in the vibrant DIY scene, airplay for independently released albums and cassettes was usually credited less to station policies than the efforts of knowledgeable and dedicated individuals.

Letters columns included the voices of both radio personnel and frustrated artists and labels. In a 1980 issue of *Op*, a DJ from WVCR radio lists some of the independent and non-commercial styled artists he plays on his show. A DJ from WACC in Arlington, Virginia writes in with greater ambitions, describing a plan to visit 'progressive' bands in the Washington, DC, Virginia and Maryland area. Matthew Moore reached out to *Op* readers because he didn't want to limit his efforts to his area and requested a list of radio outlets involved with *Op*'s Lost Music Network and asked for cassettes he might play on his show (*Op*, Issue A, 1980, p. 4).

Throughout the 1980s, increasing numbers of radio show listings indicated that they included cassettes in their airplay, and some were even devoted exclusively to independent cassettes. In an early 1984 listing, Rob Weisberg of WCBN (University of Michigan) in Ann Arbor "has been producing a weekly show featuring independent cassettes and he's looking for material" (*Op*, Issue U, 1984, p. 26).

An early 1985 report begins by complaining about the sad shape of independent radio but also includes a listing for *The Cassette Show* at Trent University in Peterborough, Ontario, "a weekly all-cassettes program that plays all styles of stuff they received. *Eer Meet* is their zine and has reviews and addresses" (*Sound Choice*, Issue 1, 1985, p. 11).

The Cassette Show stands out for the additional note about a zine with reviews and addresses. A radio station that also produced a zine and called out the availability of addresses suggests that the producers were intimate with networking activities and sought to exploit their radio access to spotlight independent cassette artists.

Show host Joanna Rogers sheds light on her activities and motivations: "*The Cassette Show* was started by Bill Kimball in maybe 1983. Bill was the artistic director of City Stage, the performing arts wing of ArtSpace, an artist-run center in Peterborough. He was an active member of Trent Radio and started the program to showcase local musicians and sound artists. I was the manager of Trent Radio, a campus/community radio station, from 1982 until 1987. At that time, I was making collages and became involved with the community of mail artists around the world by publishing a mail art zine called *Aborted Images*. Trent Radio was receiving a smattering of cassettes in the mail, and these interested me very much. When Bill Kimball was wanting to bow out of *The Cassette Show*, I took it over as a place to air these cassettes. This was in 1984, and I was able to tap into the self-tapers network through my mail art contacts. The cassettes kept coming. I used to open packages on-air and play them for the first time live on the radio. I wanted the program to be truly each cassette's show. I received cassettes from all over North America and Europe, and at least one from Japan" (personal communication, 2025).

Rogers continues, explaining how the zine intersected with the radio show: "*Eer Meet*, which became *Ear Meat* by the fourth issue, contained reviews of the cassettes received since the last issue along with contact information for the artists reviewed. The show and zine very much went hand in hand. To start with, I wrote most of the reviews, but I always had help from at least one person. Graham Longford became involved with the show as cohost and there were at least ten other people helping to write reviews over the life of the zine. John Farrell created occasional comic strips for inclusion. Ee(a)r Mee(a)t was a lot of fun to produce, and it gave us something to trade for other zines or for cassettes. The networks were all about reciprocity" (ibid).

Individuals commonly engaged in multiple interrelated activities. John Gullak had been a member of the San Francisco based performance art group the Mutants and cofounded the A.R.P.H. Tapes label, which also functioned as an in-house real time audio cassette duplicating service. Gullak also produced the *No Other Radio* show for KPFA Berkeley. In a 1985 interview, Gullak explained how the show grew out of a Public Hearing event in which Gullak set a P.A. system on the roof of a building in an industrial area of Oakland and 'broadcast' hometaper cassettes. Experimental, non-musical tapes were chosen for the purpose of fitting into the neighboring environment. (*Unsound*, Vol 1 No 5, 1984, p. 43).

The challenge faced by artists and labels in getting airplay for their music, and knowing if their music was played at all, was the subject of ongoing dialogue in the music publications. Zan Hoffman's frustration with radio highlights one of the key obstacles for all involved:

"I'm my worst promotion agent. I've realized that over the years. I would try to send stuff to radio and send stuff for review. And It's very frustrating work. And there seems to be so little return. After about 5-6 years you just burn out altogether. The only thing that seems to be worthwhile is to have your track on a compilation. Because you send something to a radio station and they never send you anything back. Except Don Campau, bless his pointy little head" (personal communication, 2008).

Campau did appear to be an exception among DJs: "Not only did I mail everyone a playlist (unless I did not know their address), but many times would often provide a cassette of the music on my show. I sent out thousands of these tapes. And for a time, I would also include a tape of my own latest music. I spent every day after working at my grocery store job doing this and had three kids at home at the time" (personal communication, 2025).

Other examples exist of stations mailing playlists. Jeff Chenault shares a detailed playlist he received dated January 1984 from WJHU (Johns Hopkins University) who played excerpts from the 'musicopsychological' tape Jeff had submitted. It's fascinating to see these examples. In this case we see underground artists like Hunting Lodge, Z'ev and Ramleh played alongside David Bowie, Camel and Cheech and Chong (personal communication, 2025).

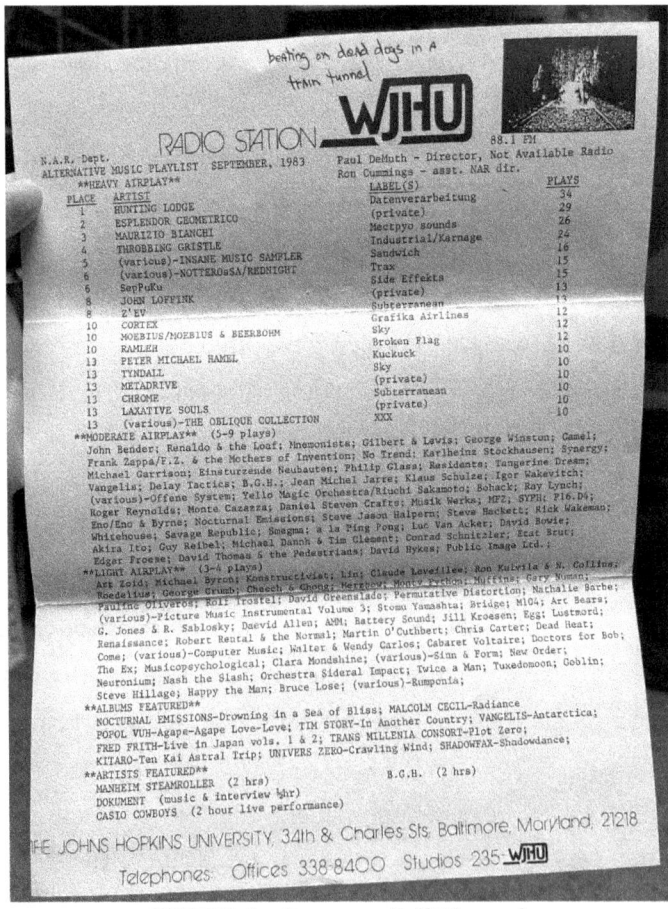

WJHU playlist sent to Jeff Chenault

Artists and labels continually wrote to the music publications bemoaning the lack of radio station response to their submissions. Yet along with these grievances were increasing numbers of stations listed as having been confirmed to play independent music and even singling out individual DJs and their shows. Those submitting music to stations outside their listening range would have no way of knowing if their music was played if the station didn't write to them. It's easy to imagine how cumbersome it would have been to mail a playlist to every artist or label who submitted music for airplay.

A 1984 letter from one-time WMUC music director Steve Kiviat points out that the job of being responsible for acknowledging receipt of submissions is by volunteer music directors who are usually students with many other responsibilities and distractions: "It takes a lot of dedication and altruism to write some of these letters when you're not getting credits or getting paid." Kiviat had no solution but ends his letter with, "Anyone have any ideas?" (*Op*, Issue U, 1984, p. 7).

Sound Choice publisher David Ciaffardini was combative in his criticism of college radio stations and traded barbs with station personnel who wrote in to protest his attacks. In one letter Ciaffardini accused stations of being "slaves to promotional propaganda" and playing a narrow range of music. "You're getting slagged in *Sound Choice* and you deserve it" (*Sound Choice*, Issue 4, 1986, p. 7).

Hometaper and cofounder of the Generations Unlimited label David Prescott had a show on WZBC (Boston College) on which he featured music he had acquired through his global networking activities. But when asked in a 1989 interview if he keeps lists of alternative stations to send his label's records, Prescott issued a warning to artists considering promotional submissions to radio:

"My problem with that is that the kind of music we do is so alternative that we don't bother sending it to radio stations. One of the DJs at WZBC actually trashed one of my records, although I guess that was more of a personality thing. I'm hesitant to give my records to my own station, because the airplay ultimately is nice, but you never know what's going to happen once your record gets to a radio station. Getting a response from a radio station can be extremely difficult. What I've wound up doing is just acquiring a small list of cool DJs" (Barr, 1989/90, p. 11).

Prescott's restriction of allocating promos to a small list of 'cool DJs' highlights the reality that airplay for independent music and, especially hometapers, was limited to individuals who were aware of the existence of such music and willing to make the effort to support it.

A 1989 issue of *GAJOOB* included in its Radio section an announcement for a directory of radio stations that would play independent music and the specific individuals to contact:

"On The Air is 52 pages of radio stations addresses and information. It costs $25, but you can get it for $20 if you mention you saw it here. Whenever sending tapes to radio stations for airplay, it's always a good idea to get as much information about the station and its programs, so that you're sending your work to the right people. Information this booklet includes on every contact: phone number, contact person, broadcast power, audience number, air time given (%), styles programmed, format (record, cassette, CD, etc.), interviews(?), live performances(?). So if you're wanting to get on the air, this booklet is indispensable. Write to Independent Music Services, Sharon, PA" (*GAJOOB*, Issue 4, Autumn 1989, p. 36).

Hometaper Mark Kissinger compiled the directory and explains his approach: "The idea was simply to compile information on the broadcasting habits of as many radio stations as I could get to play along. At that time, I was writing record reviews for *Option* magazine and was aware that they had a mailing list of around 500 radio stations that were presumably indie-friendly. I bought the list, put together a survey that touched on what I felt was useful information (what styles of music do you program, do you play independents, what recording formats do you accept, contact person/program director name, station wattage, etc.). I made it very easy to fill out (mostly check-the-box), and then I sent them out and hoped for the best. Eventually about half the surveys came back, which I considered a win. I got together with a graphic artist buddy of mine and we (mostly he) put it together. Very bare bones design but the useful information was there in an orderly, accessible fashion. I should mention that I never saw this as a big thing for cassette folks like myself. It was aimed more at the really small vinyl/CD labels. I don't recall how receptive stations were to receiving cassettes. When I began, I thought this might turn into an ongoing thing, with me compiling fresh information every year for an update. I made just enough money on it to pay income tax, after which I showed a net loss. I don't recall having ever heard back from any of the purchasers as to whether it had been useful or not" (personal communication, 2025).

A short-lived but energetically executed effort was *Pollution Control*, founded by Mark Edwards and Pennie Stasik at WCSB, Cleveland (Ohio) State University. *Pollution Control* functioned as a middleman to help independent artists get airplay. Edwards and Stasik's goal was to make it easy for sympathetic radio stations to acquire the music by supplying member stations with monthly packages of releases and a newsletter. Mark Edwards describes how the system worked:

"We solicited record labels/bands to send us copies of their releases and promotional materials, from which we built a monthly package to distribute to our member stations, who were charged a nominal monthly fee for the package. The service was free for labels/bands. I don't think it was ever more than $50 a month and the average package contained 20-40 records/tapes. The thought behind it was simple – we acted as a 'signal booster' for small bands and indie labels trying to break through the many releases sent to radio stations. In return, we provided the labels/bands guaranteed feedback on whether our stations played their release, including playlists and any reviews. In addition, we wrote our own 'reviews' for inclusion in the monthly *Pollution Control Newsletter*, which was sent free to all participants, and later on to subscribers, although I don't think we ever had more than 50 or so total outside subscribers" (personal communication, 2016).

Edwards explains that the maximum number of stations they signed up was 28, with about six in Canada, a couple in Europe and the rest in the US. Except for a few public radio stations, all were based at colleges and universities. However, the duo could only sustain *Pollution Control* for nearly two years. Edwards continues:

"The station revenues barely covered our costs, and it had turned into about a 30 hour a week job. We played around with a few things to try to increase revenue, but we could never get enough stations to buy in to turn a profit. We both juggled minimum wage jobs at the time, so it just became too much to keep up with" (ibid).

Pollution Control Newsletter

Edwards confirms the importance of establishing relationships with knowledgeable and dedicated individuals in any successes they had at radio stations: "One of the issues in maintaining station base was turnover of music directors. If we had kept every station we signed up we'd have had about 40. We figured it would take about 50 stations to make it viable enough for one of us to quit our jobs and dedicate full time to it" (ibid).

Edwards says that only a fraction of the subscriber packages included cassettes, and he doesn't believe they got much airplay, noting how inconvenient they were for DJs relative to records: "The main problem with them from a radio station standpoint was the time it took to queue a certain track. Even with the later 'find' technology it wasn't always that accurate as cassette makers often didn't leave enough space between songs or sent tapes with 20 songs per side" (ibid).

Yet *Pollution Control* did endeavor to promote cassette artists. One issue of the WCSB program guide included an article by Stasik targeting hometapers and providing tips to better their chances for airplay. Edwards also notes that WCSB had two shows dedicated exclusively to cassettes and encouraged their airplay, installing two cassette decks along with the turntables.

Those who ran labels supporting cassette artists were cautious in their willingness to send promos to radio stations. In a 1989 interview, Carl Howard of Audiofile Tapes responded to a question asking if he finds radio stations difficult in general or does he target stations that he knows give airplay to cassettes:

"It changes. You have to expect that. It depends usually upon the one person involved, whether he/she is soliciting for a station's library or for one particular show. I've generally found that if you try to deal to a whole station at once, you tend to get lost in the bureaucrazy of that station because there's no one person looking out for your interests. And some of the people you'd deal to directly have this habit of dropping off the planet for months at a time, while others are sweethearts who are always on the money and who you know are looking out for you. Some stations practice a politic which is so antithetical to the low-level independents, that there's no good in dealing to them at all. I won't even go into how bleedin' furious I got when Columbia University's station decided as a policy to drop cassettes from their printed playlist altogether... like we don't count, right? Bastards. So, I don't deal to them anymore. You have to deal with the individuals wherever possible. I mean, that's what networking is about in the first place, isn't it? Trying to defeat the impersonal megalopoly?" (*Pseudo'zine*, 1989).

Don Campau is interviewed in the same source and corroborates Howard's sentiment about the importance of targeting trusted individuals: "It's far easier for me to deal with specific individuals at selected radio stations. Since I work at one, I know how these things work. A tape comes in, gets ignored because it's a hassle to audition or cue it for airplay. Certain DJs who are into the idea of home tapes will take the time to listen to a whole tape and then play their favorite track. I would not send a tape blind to a radio station" (*Pseudo'zine*, 1989).

Looking back, Campau recalls: "I spent hours at home cueing up the songs I wanted to play and then hauling the tapes down to the station to air them. I would also take one of my own cassette machines to the station (because we only had one) and then I could segue from one tape to another" (personal communication, 2025).

Manny Theiner of SSS Productions explains how during the summer of 1986 he got his own show at WRCT, Carnegie-Mellon University in Pittsburgh, Pennsylvania, which became the cassette-only *Cooperative Anarchy* show, broadcasting on Sundays from 3-6pm. Theiner recalls how it took him two years to convince WRCT's DJs that cassettes are an equal medium to records, further highlighting the role of the motivated individual. Theiner concludes by saying, "finally they're doing it and not complaining" (*Pseudo'zine*, 1989).

Looking back at that era, Theiner further supports the importance of individual motivation and influence at radio stations, as well as shedding light on how stations functioned:

"The convincing was that cassettes existed not only in the cassette network but existed in the 1980s as a medium. If you were in a band you more than likely put out a tape before anything else. At some point you would call it a demo. But other people in our immediate region were putting out tape only releases. And these were being sent to the studio. I was also trying to encourage the hometaper/cassette network to send to the station so that their releases could be considered on the same level as other formats. But the problem was you didn't really have a convenient way to play tapes at the station. Or people didn't like to play tapes. If you were in college radio what you would do is 'cart up' stuff. You'd take a song from the tape and cart it up in the cart machine. Every station had several cart machines in the studio. So, instead of playing a cassette, technically you were playing the cart with the song from the cassette" (personal communication, 2025).

Theiner continues, describing how his goal was to encourage airing cassettes by making it easier for DJs to play them:

"In the studio was something called the new music bin. At WPTS (University of Pittsburgh) you were required to play a certain amount of those per show. At WRCT the requirement existed but it was a lot less. There was the new music bin for LPs, but there was no bin in the studio for cassettes. I cleared out an area and made sure that the newest tapes were there. People were able to claim them as new releases and play them in the studio. After that I cleared off a few shelves and had the kind of racks that fit cassettes that were old releases and people could go back and play them. I basically legitimized playing cassettes and recognizing them as legitimate releases, rather than demo tapes that you carted up a song or two from" (ibid).

Radio shows that included or were dedicated to hometaper cassettes were increasingly produced by home recording artists themselves. Milwaukee, Wisconsin based Richard Franecki of the band F/i and the Uddersounds label and contact list recalls his one-off opportunities to DJ shows dedicated to cassette artists:

"I called it the *Uddersounds Independent Tape Show*. The stations were WMSE (as of 2025 the only college station left in Milwaukee), WCCX (defunct, it was the college station for Carroll University, which phased out its radio station), and WYRE (the station of UW-Waukesha, which also phased out its station). I did all this stuff in the mid-1980s. My DJ friend was Paul Host who had shows on all three stations! Paul still has a show on WMSE, Saturday afternoons. He had an interest in the tape trading scene. He was the one who suggested I put together a 'canned' show that he would play during his own show. I was on the radio without actually being a college radio DJ myself" (personal communication, 2016, 2025).

Belgian musician Peter Bonne recorded with the Micrart Group and had a show called *Radio Progress*, which played what Bonne describes as minimal electronic or electro style music, with a touch of cosmic synth trance. Bonne explains how his networking activities benefited both the Micrart Group and the radio show:

"We did exchange a lot of tapes around the world and passed them to anyone we knew. With the range of projects and bands within Micrart Group, there was quite a productive series of tapes to be exchanged and tracks to be sent out. And yes, I played all that on my show on *Radio Progress*" (personal communication, 2009).

Radio was ideal for the heavily networked hometaper. Regardless of audience size, having a radio show seamlessly intersected with an artist's networking activities, with the prospect of airplay a bonus for anyone sending their tapes or trading with the hometaper DJ. Joe Schmidt had a show pointedly titled *Home Taper* at WMUH, Muhlenberg College in Allentown, Pennsylvania. Schmidt utilized the show as a tool for his trading with other artists but also sought to network with tape labels and other radio stations. A 1984 listing describes the show:

"Consists entirely of independently and privately produced cassettes. We get tapes from listeners, air these, and make copies which we then exchange for tapes by other Home Tapers, as well as with independent tape labels and radio stations. All exchange tapes also get airplay. We now have about 50 exchange contacts worldwide" (*Unsound*, Vol 1 No 4, 1984, p. 13).

Recalling the show decades later, Schmidt confirms the mechanism described in the 1984 *Unsound* listing and adds: "The difficult part of this process is getting started. You need to build up an exchange network from nothing. At first, we got only a few tapes from local artists, but gradually we made contacts with others having similar interests. The network grew rapidly and before long exchange material from overseas became the predominant part of the program - primarily from the Netherlands, UK, Germany and Japan. All tape exchanges and interactions were by mail, so it became a kind of international pen pal system, with each person or group sharing their contacts with others" (personal communication, 2025).

Some hometaper DJs had radio shows that lasted for decades. Though Don Campau's career in radio started in 1971, it wasn't until 1985 that he launched his *No Pigeonholes* show on listener supported station KKUP in Cupertino, California. Campau recalls how he planned his all-home recorded artists show:

"In early 1984 I got the idea to do an all-hometapers show but at first didn't have enough. I started a massive letter writing campaign and solicited cassettes from addresses in *Option* magazine. The underground scene was pretty fledgling in those days but gradually it really snowballed to where it is today" (Howard, 1991, p. 50).

Campau's enthusiasm for his work reflects the communal spirit of 'anyone can be an artist': "For me, the challenge has been with my radio show. Because of the amount of submissions, it has been difficult to get everyone on the air in a timely manner. Sure, I love quality music, but my *No Pigeonholes* show is more about giving people a chance to be heard and letting their music speak for itself. And although I do try to pick out what I think is the best songs from a person/band's submission, I give everyone airplay no matter the style, no matter if I think they suck. You do not have to be good, fashionable or professional to be on *No Pigeonholes*. That being said, I am always amazed at the amount of talent and creativity out there" (personal communication, 2007).

The debut *No Pigeonholes* show from December 1985 reveals an exciting range of genre bending music and audio art. Campau opens the show with a progressive-jazz pop instrumental, followed by a throbbing Frippertronic and acid-psychedelic inspired space-noise workout. There is a whimsical sound collage and electronica assault combined with spoken word to create an offbeat lysergic audio theater production. Campau follows this track with a description of tape packaging that includes a cardboard hat you wear on your head while listening to the tape. And the parade continues, detouring from high energy Devo-esque new wave electronica, to disorienting electro sci-fi rhythmic gymnastics, cool grooving bluesy jazz-pop with Beat poet narration, creative electronic ditties played on simple synthesizers and much more.

Campau emphasizes throughout the show that the music heard is primarily underground cassette artists and is not available in stores, only to be obtained through trade or underground publications. He explains the exchange network and encourages listeners to record the show and call him to get the names and addresses of the artists he played. Campau also plugs key American publications like *Sound Choice*, *Option* and *Unsound* as sources for the type of music heard on *No Pigeonholes*.

Lord Litter started broadcasting in 1987, focusing on an equally varied potpourri of music. He recalls his beginnings in radio:

"I became quite known here in Berlin for being a 'figure' in the tape movement, so I was interviewed for a show titled *The Tapedepartment Radioshow*. A bit later the guy who did the show needed to find a 'real' job so I asked if I could take the show. When Berlin's true alternative station RADIO 100 asked me if I would like to do a show presenting 'this scene' – that was in late 1987 – I kept the name *The Tapedepartment Radioshow* until the mid-1990s when it became *The Lord Litter Show*. Now it's *Lord Litter's Magic Music Box*. Right from the start I had the idea to present the variety that the freedom of this 'alternative' made possible, so I broadcast everything from punk to folk to electronic to jazz to space" (personal communication, 2009).

Lord Litter continued broadcasting until his passing in 2024. He would not accept digital submissions. CDs, vinyl or cassettes had to be accompanied by some form of personal communication, even if only by email.

The late Mike Honeycutt of Memphis, Tennessee recorded as Mystery Hearsay but was also active in zine publishing and had radio shows on various stations (though not continuously) from 1980 until 2015.

Honeycutt became aware of the post-punk legion of bands via local networking and obtaining Rough Trade distribution catalogs: "John Morgan was brother of Bob X, a local artist who lured me into the small press scene via a local comic shop review newsletter and later self-publishing in the mini comix realm. John was a major influence and would send us, among other things, Rough Trade catalogs/lists" (personal communication, 2016).

One of Honeycutt's 1982 Rough Trade catalogs reveals a variety of underground and mainstream bands. Noise warriors Whitehouse and Maurizio Bianchi have entries in the same column as Culture Club and Ultravox, showcasing the diversity of the innovative post-punk scene. Honeycutt's entry to radio was in 1978 when he introduced WLYX music director Mike Childress to Throbbing Gristle: "He started inviting me up to the station and we would slip the tracks into his playlist. Then by 1980-81 he finally talked me into applying for a show" (ibid).

Honeycutt started with shows on 3500-watt station WLYX from 1980-81, moved on to 10-watt WEVL from 1982-83, and back to WLYX for the next couple years, in each case giving airplay to home taped cassette recordings. He also tapped his Rough Trade contacts to obtain overseas distribution for *Malice*, the fanzine that he and Chris Phinney published.

Honeycutt describes how his zine and networking activities careened into radio: "My insight into that world quickly adopted the field for promotion for the radio station. I would write Rough Trade and any indie label we were interested in and the new file grew and grew. The whole industry was different back then. You had the majors and then the indie explosion. Sometimes there was crossover where one would influence the other. The use of flyers, zines, etc. was the gorilla, strong arm approach to DIY marketing. I started distributing copies of the Rough Trade catalogs even to share the info about, Hey, here's this new, different kind of music and you should check it out method" (ibid).

David Lichtenverg, who recorded and DJ'd as Little Fyodor recalls his gateway to radio at the University of Virginia in the late 1970s, shedding light on the volunteer student experience: "I broadcasted on two different college radio stations, both at the University of Virginia. The first one was a commercial station, although it was student run, if you can imagine that. That was WUVA. I got sick of that after a year as a result of the management putting pressure on DJs to follow various dumb rules that I was always breaking. You didn't get paid, I was just doing it for fun, no real plans to become a pro, so I said fuck that. There was another station on campus called WTJU (Thomas Jefferson University) that was much cooler, but I hadn't found out about it until after I had already joined WUVA, which was right in the basement of my freshman dorm. At WTJU I had total freedom. I don't remember a whole lot of specifics of what I played there, but I do recall having a show called *Miscellaneous Madness* on which I did thematic shows, often revolving around madness or other anti-social concepts, featuring the likes of the Doors and Jonathan Richman and Hawkwind. I liked interesting lyrics, and I liked weirdness, but I had only just begun to dabble in the 'avant-garde'" (personal communication, 2016).

Lichtenverg got more seriously involved in radio after relocating to Boulder, Colorado in 1981, becoming a volunteer at community station KGNU, and was on the air by 1982: "The music director, one Fergus Stone, was anxious to fill up the late-night slots, which were largely unfilled at that time. Most nights, the late-night show was called *Sleepless Nights*, which was supposed to be a rock-oriented show playing a wide variety of new rock and anything related. Fergus wanted something a little different and special for the weekends, and I was all too happy to delve further into the experimental side of things. I didn't want to be committed every Saturday night, so they found someone to alternate with me, whose name was Brian Kraft. The first time I met this interesting and solitary kind of fellow I asked him what he liked or what he was going to play, and he shrugged and said, 'Same stuff as you, Residents'. So, that gives you an idea of what I was playing back then" (ibid).

Yet it was his introduction to home recording and the hometaper network that fueled Lichtenverg's commitment to showcasing underground music, and his radio activities intersected with his recording and networking activities. Lichtenverg joined Evan Cantor and Ed Fowler in the band Walls Of Genius, who released several uniquely individualistic cassette albums from 1982-86. Walls Of Genius represented everything that was totally twisted and creatively cool about the era's homemade music underground. They were all over the map, recording songs, acid rock, spaced out excursions, avant-garde progressive rock, sound collages and abstract experimentations. And nobody did cover songs like Walls Of Genius. Their lovingly art damaged assault on songs by Steppenwolf, Credence Clearwater Revival, The Beach Boys, Captain Beefheart, Chuck Berry, The Beatles and others was akin to the Residents' treatment of the Rolling Stones' 'Satisfaction'.

Lichtenverg describes his radio show at KGNU: "My show had no name at first. Then I started calling it *A Show From Under the Floorboards*, after a song called 'A Song From Under the Floorboards' by the band Magazine. It wasn't long before I trimmed the title down to just *Under The Floorboards*. I was either right away or before long Little Fyodor" (ibid).

Under The Floorboards aired Saturday nights (Sunday morning) from 1-3:30am, with small timeslot shifts throughout the 1980s. Like other hometaper DJs, Lichtenverg's networking and exchange activities influenced his broadcasting choices:

"Walls Of Genius plugged me into the burgeoning cassette network and people started sending us all manner of cassettes, sometimes in trade for Walls Of Genius material and sometimes they just sent them. Sometimes they sent them because they knew I did a radio show. Anything that was weird or experimental (those aren't always the same thing) I would play on my show. Before long my show was predominantly cassettes, as well as predominantly from my own collection. How better to represent what was going on 'under the floorboards' then to play weird shit put out on a cassette by weird, extremely obscure musicians who mostly had little to no interest to outright contempt for 'making it' in the music biz?" (ibid).

Under The Floorboards showcased the home recorded tapes Lichtenverg was receiving, though he aways gave himself the freedom to mix in anything he liked. Some shows included such non rock artists as Frank Sinatra and Liberace. A playlist from 1984 lists cassette artists like Walls Of Genius, If, Bwana and R. Stevie Moore along with Hawkwind, Faust and Diamanda Galas. A playlist from 1985 features such hometaper artists as Ken Clinger, Minóy and Psyclones alongside Einstürzende Neubauten, Golden Palominos and The Work. And a playlist from 1987 is a cauldron of variety, with cassette artists like Master/Slave Relationship, Tara Cross and X-Ray Pop sharing the bill with Yoko Ono, The Shaggs and Patti Smith.

Lichtenverg eventually decided that some of the cassettes he was receiving were not 'weird' enough for his show, though equally deserving of airplay, and started a second show dedicated solely to cassettes:

"So, I started a second show that I hosted concurrently with the first called *The Cassette Underground*, which aired 12:30 in the afternoon for just a half hour and on which I toned down the weirdness some. Well, at least by my standards, though people still told me I played the weirdest stuff in the daytime. I remember playing Amy Denio on that show. She had sent a tape or two to the station before I had ever heard of her. I alternated on this show as well with a fellow named Phantor and another named Neil Parker. I'd say I did that show for about three years" (ibid).

The cassette recorder was used by many hometapers as a compositional tool. But radio too was being utilized for creative purposes, with DJs composing and/or mixing on air.

JERRY KRANITZ

An ad for Produktion QSL's shows described them as "A new series of radio programs began in April '85 dealing with radio 'Concrete'. Contributors were asked to send a cassette recording of radio, in various forms, manipulated, processed, etc. The recordings were then mixed and broadcast live to air from 2MBS-FM in Sydney, Australia. All the radio concrete pieces are to be edited into one cassette available from Produktion. Broadcast tapes are not for sale. But send a couple of IRC" (*ND*, 1985, p. 22).

Ron Lessard of RRRecords broadcast RRRadio on WZBC, Boston College. A listing in a 1989 magazine describes his show: "All shows are spontaneous record/tape collages with live musical accompaniment. All shows performed by Due Process. To participate, just send a good backing tape I can incorporate into the performance. I promise to send a dub of any show using your contribution" (*GAJOOB*, Issue 4, 1989, p. 36).

Lessard recalls: "I asked the artists to submit raw unfinished material, and I would use that as backing material for vinyl and cassette collages. However, I did occasionally have guest artists sit in and improvise along with the collages" (personal communication, 2016).

The *RRRadio 1-5* cassette is representative, featuring a continuous audio art collage. Multiple layers of voice samples, electronics, ambience, power tools, percussion and sounds intersperse and harmonize to create a seamless yet disorienting flow.

Peter Meyer began his *Nattovning/Night Exercise* program after joining the Swedish Radio Company's cultural department in 1982. In a 1983 article, Meyer described how he networked globally to solicit submissions for the show:

"The program *Night Exercise* was an attempt to renew and develop the radio medium. We advertised for mad sound artists in suitable newspapers. We also looked around outside Sweden. All the unconventional radio personalities that I had met during my years at foreign radio stations or at my annual radio analysis seminars at the Dramatic Institute were contacted. Thousands of letters with invitations to take part in *Night Exercise* were distributed in this way all over the world" (Meyer, 1983, p. 16).

Meyer and his fellow producers did not simply DJ shows of the submissions. They compiled the audio works into varied theme shows starting in January 1982 and broadcast the first Saturday of every month: "In *Nattovning No. 2 - Fire Souls* we chose to place the inserts on top of, instead of after, one another. This gave the program a more complex nature. The aim with *Fire Souls* was to depict an unidentifiable town with documentary sound effects from all over the world. The night exercises were therefore characterized by two levels of creating. Firstly, the artistic intention of the contributors and subsequently those of the production team" (ibid).

In the spirit of compilation tapes, Meyer sent cassette copies to all contributors. He reports that the publicity the shows generated resulted in interest from foreign radio stations in the US, Italy and Japan, and Canadian station CFFO broadcast the show.

GX Jupitter-Larsen, known as home recording artist The Haters, broadcast his *New Sounds Gallery* show on Vancouver's CFRO throughout the 1980s, "and was allied with other period shows such as Peter Meyer's *Nattovning* and Joe Schmidt's *Home Taper Show* (both of which traded broadcast material with New Sounds Gallery in order to further their own respective experiments)" (Bailey, 2012, p. 237-238).

Jupitter-Larsen describes *New Sounds Gallery* as a radio art show he did from 1984-88: "There was some tape trading going on, but mostly it was a venue for artists who wanted to do radio-specific pieces. Call-in shows, game shows, radio plays, all-night sound sculptures; stuff like that" (ibid).

With a similar focus on live mix and audio collage, *Over The Edge* debuted on KPFA in Berkeley, California in 1981. The show began when DJ Don Joyce invited the sound collage and appropriation band Negativland to the studio. Joyce explains how the band brought all their recording equipment and instruments, "and we proceeded to mix music and sounds together live on the air, also making use of all the regular studio playback equipment in simultaneous and over-lapping ways" (Joyce, 2005, p. 177).

Joyce explains how together with Negativland (who he eventually joined as a member) he created endless loops of their broadcast within the broadcast, mixed spoken dialogue, often captured from popular media, over various music by themselves or others, wrote phony commercials, and used the telephone to integrate listeners into the mix (ibid. p. 179).

Listeners were encouraged to call in: "We would like to invite you out there to contribute to this mix in any way you see fit over the telephone. If you would just pick your phone up and call, we'll get you on the air. And we'll take anything you can put through the speaker end of your telephone" (*Over The Edge*, July 6, 1981).

Joyce elaborates on how callers would be incorporated into the evolving mix: "The calls, which may include people playing music or tapes or making noises, as well as their rantings, ravings, criticisms, and commentaries, are all treated as just another element in a mix of sonic spontaneity. We can process calls with effects, and we 'edit' them in the same way we edit the whole mix going on around them, hanging up without warning whenever we've had enough" (Joyce, 2005, p. 184).

Part III:
Cassette 'Culture'?

Chapter 15

Was there a Cassette 'Culture'?

The late 1980s and early 1990s saw a more explicit identification as being part of a global 'cassette culture', with dedicated efforts to promote cassette culture identity, activities, education, and to solidify the distinction and cohesiveness of the network. These efforts were initiated by individuals in the global community who demonstrated a flag waving desire for unity.

Consequently, the short answer to the question of whether a distinct culture existed is: Once people self-identify as being part of a group with its own distinguishing characteristics, you have a de facto culture. There is comfort to be found in a community of people who share your interests and ideals. Promoting home taping as 'cassette culture' was noticeable in some of the newer publications beginning in the late 1980s, as well as in specific projects on the part of individuals.

These developments occurred roughly through 1992, intersecting with a period of dramatic technological change - and with technological change comes cultural change. The early to mid-1990s was a period of increasingly widespread access to online services and the internet, representing a sea change in the way people communicated.

Cassettes would soon be overshadowed by CDRs and digital formats. It became standard for computers to come out of the box equipped with CDR burning technology. Digital files, leading to the almighty mp3, would soon rise to a position of dominance. These digital music advances would result in the near elimination of the need to visit the post office. Collaborations could occur via file sharing, and finished works could be posted to websites and transferred through the internet.

These years also represented a generational transition. Many hometapers who had been active in the 1980s shifted their attention as life and priorities changed. Others became disillusioned with what they perceived to be an evolution in the characteristics of the community and the attitudes and motivations of its newer participants. Many more were unhindered and proceeded merrily with the transitional flow. And some just took a break, later reigniting their activities with renewed creative inspiration.

Magazines as rallying points for Cassette Culture

While music publications throughout the 1980s provided a showcase for hometapers and cassettes, they did so within a larger independent music context. Later, however, publications emerged that would focus on cassette culture explicitly, though these too would be subsumed into the digital realm, with internet websites, discussion groups, blogs and, eventually, social media taking their place.

One example is Hal McGee's *Electronic Cottage International Magazine*, with six issues published from 1989-91. After the dissolution of the Cause And Effect label, McGee had felt the need to reconnect with the hometaper community that he believed the label had strayed from, and founded *Electronic Cottage* "to re-dedicate myself to my ideals of serving the network, making connections, etc." (personal communication, 2016).

JERRY KRANITZ

Electronic Cottage Issue 1 (1989)

As McGee states in the first issue editorial: "Electronic Cottage is one of the first magazines to truly take the hometaper seriously. EC is also unique because it features writing by independent/underground artists themselves, telling all about what they do, their experiences, methods, ideas and philosophy in a highly personal, intimate fashion. Being a hometaper/artist is a lot more than just a hobby or casual pastime. It is a lifestyle, a way of looking at the world, a way of creating, a way of communicating" (McGee, 1989, p. 5).

The magazine featured artist and label profiles, interviews, reviews and various articles on topics of interest to hometapers. Reviews and articles were nearly all written by hometapers, and while accusations of communal back slapping would not be unfair, a close reading of the reviews show them to have largely been thoughtful and descriptive, and not without criticism.

The letters section was especially lively, with much feedback on the magazine's content and even debate. Letter writers, nearly all of whom were recognizable members of the community, were candid with their positive and negative feedback. Opposition to a review of the overtly racist band Terre Blanche was heated, raising controversial questions of censorship. A reviewer complaining about the pressing quality of an LP caused the head of the label that released the album to write in and decline to distribute the magazine, though this is followed by a second letter that arrived after McGee's efforts at diplomacy. There was much discussion around how hometapers might better help each other in tangible ways, with one suggesting the establishment of underground 'hotels' in different cities to ease travel expenses.

While being somewhat insular to the home taping community, not unlike an industry specific trade journal, *Electronic Cottage* was as useful and accessible to the public as any of the small press music publications had been. Its six issues stand as crucial documents of an era that was melting seamlessly into the next.

Another example is *GAJOOB*, launched in 1987 by Bryan Baker. Starting with a local Salt Lake City, Utah focus, Baker grew frustrated with the lack of local interest and as of issue 3 transitioned to an exclusive dedication to cassettes and the wider hometaper network:

"I got more response by writing to people I didn't know than I did with local people. So, that's where my attention went. I think part of it had to do with *OPTION*. By the time I got involved *OPTION* was discontinuing its cassette reviews. Whoever was editing the magazine just didn't seem as interested in covering them anymore. I thought, well I'm going to cover them and I'm going to be bold about it" (personal communication, 2025).

GAJOOB Issue 4 (1989)

GAJOOB's format was the same as other 1980s magazines. It had articles, interviews and reviews, plus the usual variety of resource listings including publications, radio stations, cassette labels and more. In one editorial, Baker casts his net toward the widely differing meanings cassette culture has for the hometaper scene and positions the publication as a rallying point for the community:

"These bands are Industrial, Punk, Post-Punk, Hardcore, Thrash, New Wave, Post-Wave, Heavy Metal, Punk Metal, Noise, Electronic, Hard Rock, Rock n Roll, Country and yes, even Pop. Cassette Culture is the name for this growing community that encompasses all these people in all their endlessly diverse occupations, with its own Statue of Liberty, proclaiming to the huddled masses its own standard of freedom. There is a currency in this community and its form of exchange is ideas and discussion. The discussion takes place by buying and trading tapes, writing letters and getting involved in magazines like *GAJOOB*" (Baker, 1989, p. 2).

GAJOOB's letters column showed Baker to be enthusiastic about the home taping scene, which he considered to be a 'budding revolution'. Like many of these publications, the letters section is illuminating. People wrote in about their experiences discovering and functioning within the cassette network. Hometapers asked for tips on everything from improving sound quality to distribution. There is much sharing of information, running the gamut from recording, to making contacts and communicating with fellow travelers, and reporting positive responses to trading.

Baker provided detailed responses to many letters. In one issue he responds to a reader's request for distribution advice: "Mailing Persistence is really the only key, actually. Other things are fairly obvious: send tapes to all the various magazines that review them - on a regular basis. As far as publications go, there are many things you can do, besides simply sending your tape, to get your work mentioned. Write letters, submit articles, graphics and ideas. We editors appreciate all this because it helps the make-up of our publications. Not everything you write will be published, but your efforts will certainly be noticed" (Baker, 1991, p. 5).

Baker's comments demonstrate not only an eagerness on his part to educate, but a desire to mentor those new to the home recording network. Baker is also encouraging one of the cornerstones of the hometaper community - offering advice on how people could make their recordings known by getting 'involved'.

Baker then goes on to acknowledge the different motivations individuals might have, whether they are more interested in communication with other artists or attempting to achieve more widespread availability of their work:

"But distribution really all depends on what it is you want to accomplish. Of course, getting compensated for your work allows you to produce more of it, but sometimes you may just want your work to be heard by someone somewhere. This applies more to the individual artist than it does to the independent tape label. In the case of just getting yourself heard, consider trading. The feedback you receive from this may be very valuable indeed and could help your work immensely. Another thing you might consider, as the number of tapes you have available increases, is to put together a catalog. It doesn't have to be very extensive. Many catalogs are just a single sheet of information. But this information can let people who are interested in your work know what else you might have available. It might also entice those who are not familiar with your work to try it out" (ibid).

Baker addresses several points in his response, even touching on sensitivity concerning the motivation to 'sell': "Some people will find all this talk about distribution distasteful. They might feel like distribution forces them to put a price on their work, and, thereby, sell out. I don't agree. If you have something valuable to someone they will appreciate knowing about it. And it's not wrong to be compensated for your work. I don't think many people work their 9 to 5 job for free. How much more or less is your creativity worth to you than that?" (ibid).

Baker is clearly an advocate for multiple inclinations, all of which he considers legitimate. He goes even further by warning readers of the economic risks of getting caught up in their passions: "A word of caution might be in order here. It's easy to get in over your head with expenses you might never match with income. It's easy because it's a lot of fun running a tape label and meeting all sorts of new people through the mail. But don't let your enthusiasm lead to your ruin. Take it slow. I say this only because there have been, very sad to say, many tape labels dissolved because they let their enjoyment dictate a little too heavily what they put into it, and certain financial realities (as damnable as they might be) came crashing down on their little empires" (ibid).

Baker clarifies that *GAJOOB*'s audience included more than just network dedicated hometapers: "A lot of *GAJOOB*'s audience was more music and rock oriented than some of the other zines. *Electronic Cottage* came out about the same time and Hal was more interested in experimental/electronic things. My background was as a songwriter, more rock oriented, song-based kind of thing. A lot of people sending me cassettes were the kind of bands who were looking to 'make it'. I spent a fair amount of time telling people they should just do it for the enjoyment of it. Most people aren't going to get picked up by a label and make it big" (personal communication, 2025).

Baker's responses condensed wisdom gleaned from his experiences into a capsule manual of advice.

Kentucky Fried Royalty

Kentucky Fried Royalty (KFR) was an attempt to create a global distribution and promotion system for home recording artists. Though short-lived, and doomed by its own ideals, KFR did, nonetheless, lead to in-person connections among its participants.

KFR sought to establish worldwide 'stations', manned by individuals operating under the mechanism whereby artists would send master tapes for reproduction. Bands were then encouraged to reach out to various stations. Lord Litter explains the concept:

"I think the original idea was by Steven Parsons in the UK. He was already distributing. He visited me here in Berlin and we had a serious discussion about how to make it all a bit more known and effective. The idea was to combine forces internationally, with one 'brand' KFR. First, was distribution: We asked for a master tape and a master copy of the cover. There were even printed catalogs in Germany and England. If someone ordered a tape, tape and cover master were copied and it was sold 'non-profit'. Second, was a label: KFR compilations, some of the tapes we distributed were KFR exclusive, some musicians would send several produced tapes for free for us to distribute, and more" (personal communication, 2009).

The first two 'stations' listed in a 1989 ad for Stephen Parsons of BBP Records & Tapes in Swindon, UK, and Jennifer McKinnis of Grievance Tapes in Van Nuys, California, who soon passed her responsibilities on to Don Campau.

KFR sought various promotional avenues. Radio shows willing to support KFR and its artists, all participants would make it a point to mention KFR whenever writing articles or being interviewed, and KFR newsletters would be included with all mailings.

JERRY KRANITZ

A 1989 issue of *Lord Litter's Out Of The Blue Informationzine*, sub-titled *an information service from Kentucky Fried Royalty*, highlights the idealism that drove KFR. In the Introduction, Lord Litter frames it as an opportunity to unite what he characterizes as a 'movement':

"So, right from the moment I discovered this I knew that this is not some kind of funny unimportant hobby by a few people - no this is a worldwide movement, which developed right out of the emotion from people. IT IS ABOUT TIME TO UNITE!!! We all have the desire to make more contacts and almost

Lord Litters Informationzine Issue 4 (1989)

every day I get to know about more addresses - so a very logical conclusion is that there is still an enormous amount of people who would be very interested in taking part in any way" (Litter, 1989, p. 2).

Lord Litter goes on to describe how KFR works: "The KFR stations will list the tapes in their catalogs and after someone orders - sell the tapes on a non-profit level. The first aim is to establish a worldwide network with real independent music - done for fun - not for money" (ibid).

Non-profit, done for fun, and not for money. Years later, Lord Litter reflected: "What we sure never thought of was - who pays us - the ones doing the work? There were some months I was extremely busy working for KFR because in my case it really increased the work. Before this period, I was only distributing my own tapes and some special compilations" (personal communication, 2009).

Once again, ideals ran afoul of the ability to sustain such efforts in the face of economic realities. Yet the KFR story is important from a networking community standpoint due to the organization of the *First International Cassette Makers Con-*

ference, dubbed *The Kentucky Fried Royalty Meeting*, held in Cologne, Germany during the week of July 11-15, 1989.

KFR participants from Germany and Belgium converged for meetings that combined conference, discussion and networking, tape fair and concerts. In his report of the event, Lord Litter said that for him the entire week was a non-stop talk and information exchange. As regards the opportunity to have met people in person, he added:

"People started to visit each other - so I have some kind of 'open house' now. My guest list is already very long, including friends from Norway and Japan. This is a whole new movement - people leave the 'isolation' of home recording and build a new cultural level of direct communication" (Litter, 1990, p. 16).

Reflecting on the event years later, Lord Litter focuses on the unity of the network rather than the 'isolation' of the home studio: "It sure was great. But to me it was just another step on a way we defined those years. There was no feeling of 'isolation' being a hometaper. We were part of a worldwide network, which brought daily food and thoughts and more. Everybody has an internet connection these days. Everybody can easily find ways to get connected with networking structures these days. The internet brought the element of networking into the world, so it's kind of normal these days. THEN it was like finding the key to a door that one thought one could NEVER enter" (personal communication, 2009).

Lord Litter expands on the resulting travel and visits he received from hometapers around the world: "In those years (1986-92) it was normal to travel the world, based on the people/musicians one got to know via the cassette scene. I had Toshiyuki Hiraoka from Tokyo here in Berlin as a visitor. We recorded at my studio and then kept traveling Germany to visit other musicians we knew" (ibid).

The conference received attention from mainstream press and radio: "Based on appearing in public via this festival, 'official' media showed some interest. We were interviewed on the radio. Everybody involved tried to spread the news into his/her 'official life'. I remember I had my tapes sold in a BIG music store in West Germany because someone who worked in this shop knew about the tape scene and liked my music. He convinced the shop to sell tapes" (ibid).

Lord litter sheds further light, however, on the challenges of sustaining a distribution and promotion mechanism, and to do so while holding true to one's ideals: "It would have been important to cultivate this, which means work with 'marketing ideas' and how to 'sell' the alternative idea to the public. And that was sure NOT in the context of our 'alternative'. A tricky situation because as soon as you try to sell/reach more people you start to see your art with different eyes. I NEVER wanted that so I decided that giving my music away for free would be one logical way to distribute my art. I still do it today. Sure, I take the money if someone wants to buy it. But all in all, 'spreading it' is the important aspect" (ibid).

Generator

Seeking like-minded music fans locally, hometaper Ken Montgomery (aka Gen Ken) drew on his global networking experience to establish a shop and performance space in New York City. The road to 'Generator' began with Montgomery dipping his toe in the waters of record production. A close collaborator of German electronic artist Conrad Schnitzler, Montgomery was frustrated that Schnitzler's records were seemingly impossible to find, especially in the US:

"A lot of his records were self-produced. He just sold them to people directly through the mail and there had only been one record that was produced in the US. In New York City record stores you couldn't find a Conrad Schnitzler record. I decided to try and produce a record to help get his name more known in the states. So, I talked to him about it and he composed a piece of music, a cassette concert, which we ended up calling *Concert*. He sent me four cassettes in a beautiful hand painted box with instructions to play them all together" (personal communication, 2007).

Encouraged by his experience producing and promoting the *Concert* LP, Montgomery decided to start a label, which led to the formation of Generations Unlimited: "It was at that time that I met David Prescott, who lived in Boston and hosted a great radio show on WZBC, a college station in Boston. David was very active in the cassette culture and was composing music himself and was collaborating with many people through the mail. David was extremely knowledgeable about all that was going on in the underground music scene as well as the avant-garde music scene. He heard the *Concert* LP and wrote me praising it and we began corresponding. Conrad Schnitzler and I conceived Generations Unlimited, and we decided that David would be a good partner, so we invited him to join us" (ibid).

Generations Unlimited would release a handful of LPs and approximately 30 cassettes from 1986-89. But Montgomery found that selling records in the US was challenging, especially the kind of experimental music the label was releasing:

"On trips I was making to Europe in the middle to late 1980s, I visited Staalplaat in Amsterdam and Gelbe Musik in Berlin, and loved the variety of independent, artist made productions and cassettes that were available in these places. There was also a little shop called Scheissladen near where I lived in Berlin that sold cassettes, including mine, and there was Zensor Records which also carried cassettes. So, there were these little shops that sold cassettes in Europe and hardly any places in New York City at this time. In the early 1980s there were several but by the late 1980s there were few alternative record shops in New York" (ibid).

With Prescott handling correspondence, mail and shipping orders for Generations Unlimited, Montgomery was free to ponder how he might address the scarcity of sources for the music the label was releasing, as well as music of the hometapers he had been exchanging with:

"My apartment was beginning to fill up with all these cassettes from people that I was trading and corresponding with. And at the same time, we were trying to get these records into the record shops. A lot of the small record stores that might have been interested had closed. Tower Records would take some records on consignment, but they would never be played, rarely seen, or sold. Nobody was carrying cassettes anymore. It was very difficult to try to get distribution for our music. We would make 500 copies of the records and have a very hard time getting anybody to buy them. Cassettes sold but we did so much trading that our sales were really minimal. I thought that if there was a place where people could walk in and hear them we might have a chance to sell them" (ibid).

Dreaming of a place where people could hear the music, Montgomery started scoping storefronts, eventually settling on a location in the East Village where Generator would be opened in June 1989:

"I rented one for $600 and my friend David Meyers helped me build shelves for the records and install speakers into the walls. I didn't know what I was doing when I first started Generator. I knew I wanted to have the music that I was interested in, and I wanted to have the cassettes, and I wanted it to be available for people to listen to. I wanted to be able to conduct Conrad's music in total darkness. And I also wanted to find out if there were people in New York City that were interested in the same music as me. So, when I first opened the space, I filled the walls with cassettes by attaching Velcro to the back of the cassettes and putting them on the walls in a grid. I had Walkmans attached to the wall so you could pick up a cassette and listen to it on the spot. I had a bin of records and a turntable to play them. I had cassette players in my desk area so that I could play the cassettes through the speakers, plus I had stereo speakers in the toilet room. I could mix four cassettes plus a record into the space and send each to different speakers. I had a very small basement, which eventually became a place where I would have sound installations. I had a rack of zines and books about art and music, sometimes to sell but many of them just to read and look at" (ibid).

Ken Montgomery at Generator

Montgomery embarked on a letter writing campaign to friends in the hometaper network, telling them about Generator and asking if they would like to send their cassette albums to stock in the store:

"I was already in touch with so many of these people, and most of them thought GREAT, there's a shop in New York where I can have my cassette on the wall for people to listen to! Many people would send me five cassettes and say, 'here, if you sell them keep the money and buy coffee'. Other people would send me an invoice for $3 per cassette or whatever it was. So, it started growing and I started developing relationships with people, not only individuals, but also labels such as Sound of Pig and Café Europa. I bought cassettes directly from more established labels like Touch, RRRecords, Staalplaat and Gelbe Musik" (ibid).

Montgomery goes on to describe the challenge of educating people about Generator: "In the beginning there wasn't much traffic. People didn't know what kind of store it was. Constantly people would walk by, turn around and walk past again, put their heads in and say, 'what is this'? It didn't look like a record store. I had a sign on the door that said 'experimental music, sub-independent music, art laminations, concerts, audio installations'. Quite a few people came in to ask me if I installed stereos in cars. I would always invite them to stay and listen to the music people were making from all around the world. People who were curious ended up spending hours at Generator, and occasionally I would sell a cassette or a record. Meanwhile I was spending hours a day on correspondence and going to the post office every day. To support Generator, I worked in a photo lab from 9 in the morning until about 2pm and then I would stop at the post office, order lunch from the Moroccan café next door and sit listening to music and answering mail until someone would drop in. I often stayed there until midnight" (ibid).

Montgomery immediately turned Generator into a multi-purpose space. In addition to the store, he began organizing concerts and performances by friends: "It quickly attracted a really interesting hub of activity. As the word got out I started getting more visitors, first in the mail, and then people coming from local radio stations and later from Europe and Japan because Generator would get mentioned in *OPTION* and other magazines. Not big articles or anything, just little things, although a film crew from Japan came in and did a special on Generator for a program about art in the East Village that was broadcast on a show called *ZIP*. Artists within a few hours of New York would stop in, show up for concerts and drop off cassettes. Soon there was a regular crowd of people who would show up for the different events I was producing" (ibid).

As exciting as developments appeared, sales were minimal and Montgomery would often spend an hour or more talking about the music to an individual, only to sell a single $4 or $5 cassette. Furthermore, music that generated greater sales clashed with Montgomery's ideals:

"There would occasionally be people who I knew were into record collecting and would snap up records I had traded with Merzbow and Whitehouse and other in demand artists. But my reaction to that was not to get more of that music in, because my focus was really on turning people on to music. And I had a big sign up in the space that said something like, Don't worry if you're feeling confused. If you're looking around and don't recognize any of the artists that you see, it's ok. Because you're not supposed to know who these artists are. Because these people are making their own music all around the world, possibly in their bedrooms or their kitchens, and there's no way you would know them. But if you have time to listen to them you may find something you really like" (ibid).

Montgomery looks back on Generator as a great experiment which allowed him to meet people, many of whom he continues to correspond with years later. He organized many events featuring musicians and audio artists from around the world. One of the more memorable events was an appearance by Conrad Schnitzler:

"I've said that Conrad was a big influence on opening Generator. He was very encouraging about opening a space in New York so he'd have a place in the world where people could hear his cassette concerts. Several months after I opened Generator he absolutely shocked me by calling me up to tell me he was coming in a week. This was an absolute surprise because Con hadn't left Berlin in years. He had made it very clear to me from the very first time I met him that he doesn't like to go out, not out in Berlin or anywhere else. So, it was a shock to hear that he was coming to New York. He would say he was doing a concert so I made an announcement that Conrad Schnitzler would be at Generator on a certain night and people came expecting a concert. Conrad entertained everybody telling stories and socializing all night. When people asked him when he would perform, he pointed to a sign we had made and hung on the wall which said, 'Now Playing'. At exactly midnight he put a black bandana over his mouth and didn't say another word. People slowly left and we closed Generator laughing about the night. Lots of people got to meet Conrad and experience his huge personality and creative generosity. Anybody who was at Generator that night won't forget it. And nobody complained that he didn't play a concert because it was so entertaining just hanging out with him. And he loved it as well. He had a great time. But at midnight he was like, ok, that's enough" (ibid).

Montgomery opened Generator to find a local audience that shared his interests in music, to showcase live performances of music not available elsewhere in New York City, and for his own enjoyment. It wasn't long, however, before the economic roadblock presented itself:

"I was having a good time. Until I got stressed out with the money situation, which became difficult for me because I wasn't making a living, not even close. If I sold five copies of a record or cassette I would consider that a big seller. I would tell people to send me two copies of their work and if I sold one I'd send them a few dollars and they'd usually send me more cassettes. I get really excited about the creative side of my projects but I'm a notoriously horrible businessperson. In the beginning all the concerts were free. I thought having concerts would bring people to the space and then they would hear great music and buy something. The concerts drew an audience, so they were successful in my mind. There were times when people were listening to the concerts on the street because they couldn't fit inside. Many performers were my friends and were performing for free, which was lucky, but they really deserved to get paid. We started passing the hat around but that never amounted to much. I started charging $2 admission but often started talking to people, playing music and forgot to collect the money. Plus, the audience was often mostly personal friends. There were lots of regular people who would just come over and hand me $2 without me asking. But there were plenty of people who didn't pay, and I didn't chase them down. So, at the end of the night, for a concert maybe I would have $60. I would give $30 to the musicians and $30 to the store" (ibid).

Realizing that he would need to earn more money if Generator was to continue, Montgomery scheduled four benefit shows. At the last benefit, he asked for $20 admission:

"It was a benefit to raise money. There had been so many free concerts. I sent out postcards saying I've given these many free concerts and all this stuff and now I need to raise some money. And there was this experience where you would walk through the space and I had sounds going on all around and Mariano Airaldi, a performance artist friend of mine, was dressed up in a crazy costume playing with dry ice and fire and smog machines. Conrad Schnitzler flew in and was secretly performing by banging on metal in the basement. It was a totally insane experiential event. The place was a wreck the next morning. I hadn't made nearly enough money to make a difference in my expenses. Con suggested I just close Generator. He said you did a great thing. People will always remember it. But just close it now and take care of yourself. I was shocked. It's not what I expected to hear. He said, you gave it a good shot. You had a benefit. You found out what it's worth to people in the community. It's worth $300 and you pay $600 a month. So, that's it" (ibid).

Generator lasted for one year. Exactly one year later, in June 1991, Montgomery opened a second Generator - Generator 547 - at 547 W 20th Street on the edge of the Chelsea district of New York. The new Generator focused on sound installations, live performances, and carried a curated selection of tapes and records for sale. Looking back, Montgomery is proud of his limited accomplishments at the first Generator and realizes that he addressed a challenge that people face, which is the effort involved in seeking out and discovering truly alternative music. Generator 547 closed in 1992 and by that time Montgomery had drifted from the cassette world, citing the increasing number of mediocre tapes he was receiving:

"There were more and more cassettes that I would put on and I'd be like, ok, I've heard this before. In the early 1980s, when I got a cassette in the mail it was more often than not very original. The artists making music in the early 1980s were aware that what they were doing was far out of the mainstream. In the 1990s, as technical production became less expensive, more and more people were making music that was more conventional and people who were suddenly making music without really having an experience of hearing what other people had done before. Of course there were exceptions. Some magnificent gems would still arrive in the mail. But overall, the creative content had gone down. And there were more and more people sending me cassettes with the hope of selling them instead of just hoping to have others listen to what they were doing. More cassettes came in that were slickly packaged too. I tend to like the lo-fi side of things. But there were people who were sending more slick products that were heading toward demos. And sometimes they would even come with a press release, or with a sheet attached to them as though they were sending them to a record company. At Generations Unlimited we always weeded that stuff out. We liked personal connections" (ibid).

Chapter 16

An Era in Transition

Around the same time as Generator's closing, many hometapers were moving on or transitioning for various reasons. For Al Margolis it was work related. In 1992 he started working at New World Records, a non-profit record label that produced such projects as a 100-record set for the American bicentennial. Margolis advanced from shipping to A&R administrator, gaining valuable record industry experience in the process. With priorities having shifted to career, Margolis no longer had the time he enjoyed at his former job where he spent entire days dubbing cassettes. Margolis contrasts New World Records with his previous job:

"I worked there about eight years. It was a learning experience, and I wouldn't trade it. But there was the other side where I used to be able to spend my entire day as a shipping guy, just thinking about music. My music. And I would record on the weekends. I would go home, and I had a piece worked out and BANG, it would happen. The longer I worked at New World, and I tend not to take work home with me mentally, but it's not like I could spend my entire day thinking about music. So, for a long time I'd come home and my thinking about my next piece was just starting in the studio instead of thinking about it all week. So, it was harder on the creative process in terms of my own music" (personal communication, 2007).

Margolis considers 1990-92 the period when the initial era of cassette culture ended for him. He hadn't ceased recording, but the time available to devote himself to his art had been impacted by career considerations. He cites additional changes that factor into his feeling that an era had ended: "Plus, over time, *OPTION* had just become this commercial magazine. *Sound Choice* had fallen apart. There were no zines" (ibid).

The winding down of the publications that had been so crucial to the hometaper network, without adequate replacements, surely contributed to the transition from one era to another. Margolis also brought his Sound of Pig label to a close and started a new one. Pogus was founded with David Prescott and Ken Montgomery, though it quickly became Margolis' sole responsibility. As of 2025, Margolis continues to record and tour.

Many hometapers got tired and simply moved on or took a break. Andy Xport left recording, only to return and embrace the internet as a mechanism for making his music available: "1989-90 was it for me because that's when I stopped doing it. I had had enough and was burned out, I think. My last cassette was *Turning Pleasantly Numb*, which was released in 1989. After that I took a break until 2006, when fueled by my hatred for Blair's Iraq war and the false flag of 9/11, I decided to make a comeback on Myspace. But this time using the computer to record and mp3s rather than cassettes" (personal communication, 2008).

There was also talk in the publications about an 'indie glut' - a market flooded with too many choices and its impact on individual artists. David Prescott pointed out that "there have never been more artists being heard at any time in history. Some independent labels are having such success that they are being noticed by the major record companies. The implication is that all of this bodes ill for the hometaper in that consumers are already bombarded with ever more easily available choices" (Prescott, 1989, p. 16).

Pascal Dauzier of the French band La Sonorite Jaune's experience with not only greater quantity of available music but also a lack of quality resulted in a finer focus on his priorities. Speaking to the responsibility and time limitations with the band and label he said:

"Accordingly, we are very selective with invitations we receive for compilations. I have stopped contributing to every compilation I receive an invitation for. We are also trying to contribute to the best ones, the ones that will be promoted correctly and which won't be poorly designed. We've got to get out of the ultra-alternative thing in order to offer more quality than quantity" (Plunkett, 1990, p. 9).

Diminished quality and changing attitudes on the part of newcomers reverberated throughout the community. Dan Burke of Complacency Productions and the band Illusion Of Safety spoke simultaneously to the quantity of participants, quality issues and lack of dedication on the part of those he was trading with:

"If anything, the fact that there is so much independent music actually hurts people's chances of reaching a larger audience, because distributors can only handle so much and it's hard to get attention. Especially with cassettes because there are just too many and a lot of them are bad" (Jerman, 1990, p. 43).

As regards trading tapes, Burke says that he has discovered great artists and made good friends, but he's grown tired of it: "When you get back work that's dubbed onto cheap cassettes, a cheap cover, it sounds like the music was made in one night with no thought behind it, you get tired of getting that. All my tapes are on chrome tape; I have color Xerox covers that are laminated. I take a lot of time and effort with each release and each piece of music" (ibid).

In a 1991 editorial, Hal McGee spoke to new challenges hometapers faced but also issues that call the 'culture' and 'community' into question. Speaking of the US postal service raising their rates and the shifting nature of networking, he says:

"To take, for example, three of my best friends in the network - Carl Howard of Audiofile Tapes, Al Margolis of Sound Of Pig, and Chris Phinney of Harsh Reality - have all remarked to me that tape sales are way down, and that the cost of operating such mammoth organizations has become downright discouraging. It seems like almost everybody wants Chris or Al or Carl to put out their tape, and they send them the master and cover art and with many people that's as far as their level of involvement goes" (McGee, 1991, p. 5).

A hallmark of citizenship in the network was the expectation that people would be INVOLVED, because if individuals are not involved then the perception is that they don't view themselves as being part of the community.

Don Campau recognized these shifts but was untroubled and continued his recording and radio activities with reality inspired optimism: "In the past I would trade with everybody. You could send me a one-song cassette and I would send you a full C60 of my music. Alas, those days may be gone, but I'm still open to people sending me blank cassettes and enough money for postage. Lonely Whistle is basically a money-losing hobby for me" (Howard, 1991, p. 52).

Campau is explicit in calling his activities a 'hobby', though the time and commitment he has dedicated to his art and promoting independent artists through his radio shows has carried him through the decades. Campau acknowledges the shifts brought on by the internet and that many hometapers simply drifted away after the various publications folded. He also speaks to sentiments that are shared by many who soldiered on or later returned with renewed creative energy:

"Cassette culture is also a state of mind to me as well and something that is larger than just the tape trading scene of the 1980s-90s. A lot of the sense of community went out of the scene once the magazines folded and CDs appeared. If anything, people are even more deluded now than they were then thinking they could 'make it' in the music industry. Even in the days of tape trading there were those who thought their slick, plastic sealed, professionally duplicated cassettes could give them a breakthrough to music success. That may only be amplified now because of the 'legit' status of CDs" (personal communication, 2007).

Nonetheless, Campau has embraced the internet as a benefit to hometapers: "The internet has been the godsend of the independent musician and artist. Quite simply, it is the best thing ever for what we do. The fact that 'birds of a feather' can connect so easily now is fantastic. There isn't a lot of wasted time or expense finding out if someone wants to deal with me. And the ease which people can transmit this information to others is an obvious big advantage. It is great to be able to post your own music for free" (ibid).

Lord Litter speaks to the transitions of the 1990s from a uniquely Berlin based German perspective but also acknowledges the internet's benefits: "In the 1990s, two aspects changed the whole world. The Eastern Bloc vanished (suddenly the

West no longer had an 'enemy'), and the internet became global. All is different now. I think this is very important to understand the difference between then and now, especially when people compare today's services like Myspace to 'networking'. Sure, the basis of Myspace is networking, but Myspace is mainstream - 'networking' in the cassette scene was the opposite: A true 'alternative'!" (personal communication, 2009).

Lord Litter echoes Campau's opinion about the advantages of the internet, proclaiming that "the new structure of communication it offers changed my life 100%. Ever since I earn my money by producing for the internet. Besides many other things, I produce audio for online e-learning programs, so I don't have to make money with my 'art', which keeps it free! I have the biggest library EVER on my desk! I can send information to whomever I like within seconds. I can offer information to anyone who has an internet connected computer and much more, which is excellent!" (ibid).

Frans de Waard is undisturbed by the changes that occurred in the network, having simply moved on with technology and the digital times. de Waard says that there were two distinct periods in the history of his Korm Plastics label. From 1984-92 when he started as a cassette label plus limited amounts of vinyl, and then 1992-2003 he partnered with Staalplaat records and released music on CD and more limited vinyl. For de Waard, 1992 began what was simply a new phase of his activities:

"For me personally it ended when I entered Staalplaat in June 1992. They had no more interest in cassettes, and also my own interest moved away. Looking back, it was a great but isolated hobby. Nobody in school understood what it was all about. Throughout I met some people in my immediate surrounding who tried a bit of releasing cassettes, but they all lost interest very quickly. It was perhaps too complicated" (personal communication, 2009).

Jeff Chenault experienced no disruption in his recording and networking activities, though he transitioned his International Terrorist Network (ITN) label for reasons of both caution and technological change:

"ITN ended with #53, *Port Sinister* by 10-Speed Guillotine. It was 1992. I changed the name of the label to Exoteque Music around 1993. Terrorism was starting to get popular in the US and abroad and after receiving a letter from a prisoner who wanted to help 'the cause' I decided to make the name change. It was a smooth transition because I was still recording like crazy and also doing multiple collaborations with people including Chris Phinney and Andrew Izold. I didn't think of it as an end of an era so much as a change in technology. Cassettes were being phased out and CDs were the preferred format. I left kicking and screaming because cassettes were cheap and so were the postal rates" (personal communication, 2019).

Zan Hoffman is adamant that while there may have been a generational shift, creative life was uninterrupted: "What happened was you lost your first major generation of people you traded with. And you had to weed through a second generation, and most people weren't willing to find an entirely new generation of contacts. A whole range of early 1980s contacts were just done, finished, you're over it. It had gotten big, it had gotten weird. But there's still interesting people. There always will be. You just had to take the effort to weed through another whole range of artists. I watched it morph into different iterations. But I know what its roots are. And if people aren't using cassettes, they're home taping. If they're not taping, they're home recording. A rose by any other name. These are home recording artists" (personal communication, 2008).

Bryan Baker experienced life changes that impacted his ability to publish *GAJOOB*: "A lot of it was cost. I was married in 1992. Then we had a baby on the way. Before then I was just a single guy and spending all my money on *GAJOOB*" (personal communication, 2025).

But Baker is also a poster child for the transition from cassettes as a format to online communication: "I would get a fair amount of CDs and records from people. And I explicitly refused to do anything but cassettes until the CDRs started to come into being. And I would say the area between 'indie' and a 'major' was starting to blur quite a bit. It became harder to determine what was a self-made release that maybe just happened to get picked up by a label. So, I think probably around after issue 7 and into issues 8 (1992) and 9 (1993) I started covering CDs more" (ibid).

Baker embraced the internet while attempting to keep the magazine alive, with the last printed issue being published in 1997: "I went electronic. I had an email newsletter with a lot more subscribers. I called it the *DIY Report*. I think the first one was in 1994. And I was involved in the early BBSs. Those were the kind you dialed into. They had a bank of modems. It was before the World Wide Web. I tried different formats doing it electronic" (ibid).

Mark Lo published 16 issues of his *File 13* zine from 1988-93 and was candid in his editorials about the changes that combined to get away from the DIY effort he began with. Reflecting on that era, Lo describes the confluence of reasons for discontinuing *File 13*:

"The zine morphed dramatically during its five-year run. It got too big and maybe too 'professional'. The initial idea was to just do it for fun, to not charge any money and not make any money. I would just review whatever records I happened to buy. And I'd send the zine to anyone who would cover the postage and maybe drop off a stack at the local record store, making copies as needed on the copier after work. Then people began to send me records to review, or wanted to take out ads, and initially I told them no. But as the zine grew in in size and circulation I had to take it to a professional printer and that cost real money. There were some publications like *Forced Exposure* and *Maximum Rock 'n' Roll* that were too big to read in their entirety. I didn't want *File 13* to grow to a zine where it would become a chore to read. I began to miss the days when I would just write about whatever popped into my head that day. That was the DIY, lo-fi, hometaper mentality that appealed to me. As I was looking to make my exit, another friend, Rob Galgano, was thinking of starting a zine. So, I basically transferred all of my contacts, my subscriber list, and my contributors to him, and agreed to stay on as reviews editor, enabling him to hit the ground running. It lasted from 1994 until 1997, about the time the internet really started to take over as the vehicle of choice for publishing. And soon there was Napster and iTunes and it was a different world" (personal communication, 2025).

In summary, the culture, characteristics, motivations and expectations experienced by those who were introduced to home recording in the 1980s had shifted, and on a certain level came to an end. Being an independent artist was no longer a new concept, and the sometimes militant desire to promote independent musicians was perhaps less communal.

Furthermore, the zine culture transition to the internet led to an explosion of websites which struggled to function with the sense of community that publications like *Op* and many others had. The internet and its mighty search engines made it easy to seek, find and share information. Finding information in the pre-internet age required a far greater, or perhaps different level of dedication.

As Das of Big City Orchestra simply stated, "The K7 culture didn't vanish, it moved on to the next format" (personal communication, 2008).

Chapter 17

Revolution?

The cassette recorder inspired people who may never have considered doing so to create their own music and audio art. Yet while the cassette recorder and the network of communication and exchange that emerged in the 1980s may have felt truly revolutionary to the participants, there was no revolution. There was no toppling of the major record companies, who became further entrenched throughout this period.

In a 1989 letter to *GAJOOB*, a reader makes points in response to a *Is Cassette Culture Revolutionary* debate in the previous issue. "To be revolutionary, I would expect to see a major transfer of power across society. Clearly nothing of this scale has happened. Instead, we have a small special-interest minority subculture that, while it has managed to survive and expand, has probably had negligible effect on the superpowers of the music world. When we witness the collapse of mass media as it is overrun by independent production and distribution networks, and when the media star system is decomposed - let's call that a revolution!" (*GAJOOB*, Issue 4, 1989, p. 7).

Editor Bryan Baker responded: "I don't think the independent recording revolution is about stripping power away from the Music Machine. And we'll never see that happen as long as our society is fueled by money. The independent recording revolution is a revolt against that very thing (money or any other outside interest controlling the creative process)" (ibid).

Baker is, nonetheless, calling cassette culture a revolution and equating it with revolt. While revolt is a necessary condition for revolution, a toppling and transfer of power is required for success.

The problem appears to be the ease with which the word 'revolution' is used, something that is by no means specific to 1980s cassette culture. The creativity and bonds of friendship in the hometaper network was monumental and tempting to think of as having been a 'revolution' in home recording. Mail art never made any pretense to revolution. They simply created an alternative for themselves, and that is what the hometapers did.

Carl Howard is resolute in his views: "I felt, and I have not changed my point of view, that the use of the word revolution was an insult to people who daily face danger and who struggle. When you take the teeth out of the word revolution, you cheapen it for everybody else. Not every change needs to be a revolution, and neither does every change qualify as one. Sometimes change is just change. In a sense I wonder if some people were put off from adding to that homegrown change because the bar was set too high by those who somehow felt a need to make themselves look or feel better by wrapping themselves in a word they ill understood. Did that make the whole community seem too insular or too insulated? Maybe. Who knows. Sometime change does simply happen organically, and people need to celebrate that too" (personal communication, 2009).

The conclusion of this book is that continued major record company entrenchment and minimal distribution of cassette recordings is immaterial and misses the importance of the hometapers and network of communication, collaboration and exchange. The participants in the hometaper network were able to create for the sake of being artists and functioned admirably in that capacity. Thousands of recordings were produced, a substantial number of which were creatively exciting and even innovative. If these recordings were only heard by those the artists traded with, the efforts were no less substantial than if they were million sellers.

A subculture of artists was inspired to record their own music and audio art. Given the available technology, cassettes and the postal service were wholly adequate means to creative and communal ends. When the technology changed, those who wanted to create for the sake of doing so changed with the times.

From Dada, to Fluxus, mail art and cassette culture, fringe artists will continue to be ignored or shunned by record companies and gallery systems. This occurs for a variety of often bewildering reasons, including the content of their work and the inability or unwillingness to market themselves or engage in the complicated process of securing an agent or manager. As Hal McGee says in the *Forward* to the 1992 *Cassette Mythos* book:

"We were linked together with people in every corner of the Earth because we shared a set of common ideals and goals. We believed in the idea that art and the creative spirit belong not just to an elite few, but to everybody" (McGee, 1992, p. vii).

Anybody can be an artist. Sales, or even an audience are not required. Anyone can participate. Anyone can create.

Appendix: Cassette Culture Reviews

Hometapers in the 1980s created a head spinning assortment of punk, electronica, industrial, free-improvisational, experimental, avant-rock, songs, and a wildly cross-pollinated array of styles on cassette tapes. In this coda to the book, I will review a selection of recordings produced through 1990.

Because the artists functioned with unlimited creative freedom, many of the recordings were exciting precisely because genre categorizations were so often rendered meaningless. Furthermore, hometapers commonly disregarded consistency and indulged their stylistic whims from one cassette album to the next.

I'll convey the content of these recordings by eschewing the review as critique and focus on describing the experience of listening to these works. I believe the reader is best served by freeing my mind and having fun with the descriptive process.

From a colossal candidate pool, I've chosen a small number of representative examples that I hope will provide the reader with an appreciation for the astonishing variety of music and audio oddities created throughout the 1980s. Readers will note in a few cases I've included vinyl LP releases. The artists were known primarily for their cassette recordings, though it wasn't uncommon for vinyl opportunities to present themselves or for the artists to make the investment themselves.

Many of these tapes were issued as co-releases by different labels in different countries or enjoyed subsequent reissues by other labels. Therefore, while the dates are accurate for the version in my possession, the tapes may have been released multiple times over a period of years.

I've divided the reviews into four sections. I selected three cassette labels based in different countries whose rosters of artists were international in scope:

- Alain Neffe and Insane Music (Belgium)

- Matthias Lang and IRRE Tapes (Germany)

- Al Margolis and Sound of Pig (US)

The fourth section features 'song' oriented hometapers. In some cases, these artists were known for both songs and more experimental forms of music, which in my view makes them of particular interest to the cassette culture story.

Note that this is not intended to be an index or artist profile. Readers will find a mixture of artists who were prolific hometapers and active networkers, and those whose output was minimal. The focus is on the content of the recordings. Furthermore, many of the artists developed and grew over subsequent decades, and some are still active at the time of this book's publication. This sampling focuses exclusively on recordings released through 1990.

Whenever possible I am writing based on the original cassette tapes, though many are digital versions obtained online. In the case of original tapes, which have survived remarkably well, it is difficult to tell in instances of questionable sound quality if it is a sign of tape deterioration. If not obvious, I chose to disregard potential degradation as a hindrance to the listening experience.

My hope is that this small sampling inspires readers to further exploration…

Alain Neffe and Insane Music

Belgium based Alain Neffe began home recording in the early 1970s. Always interested in sound, his motivation was to accomplish things he couldn't do live, such as adjusting tape speed and playing backwards. In 1980 Neffe became aware of others making home recordings and forming labels. It was in this creative milieu that he formed Insane Music. The label released a spectacular discography of recordings until Neffe and partner Nadine Bal brought it to an end in 1990.

Neffe founded the label as a platform for the simultaneous musical projects he had been juggling. The first volume of the *Insane Music for Insane People* compilation was largely a showcase for his various bands, collaborations and solo works, though the label would go on to produce 26 compilations featuring an international roster of artists.

The following overview covers the gamut of Neffe and Insane family of music, and touches on the variety of artists the compilations featured.

I Scream – *Tomorrow is Another Day* (1984)

Though released on cassette in 1984, *Tomorrow is Another Day* consists of early Alain Neffe electronic experimentations recorded from 1973-78. The A-side includes brief pieces from various years. There's an eerily alien kosmiche exploration that sounds like the soundtrack to a 1960s Dr Who episode. Neffe can be playfully experimental, blending multiple sci-fi sounds and voices in a montage style. But he surrounds the rapid-fire collage with a majestic mellotron atmosphere and an underlying syncopated rhythmic pulse that recalls Tangerine Dream. Another track features a beautifully ethereal dual flute melody. The electronic beats are elevated by swirly keyboard runs and dark repetitive synthesizer bass lines. It's simple yet compelling in an endearingly lo-fi way.

The B-side is comprised of *Cyclical Music*, a four-part suite recorded in 1976. Neffe brings together all the A-side experimentations into a thematic soundtrack that combines elements of early Tangerine Dream and minimal synthesizer explorations, BBC Radiophonic Workshop and dashes of the Residents. The entire side of the tape flows beautifully and often chaotically as Neffe's electronic brush paints sonic landscapes and moods.

Cortex – *Souvenir/Souvenirs* (1984)

Souvenir/Souvenirs consists of Alain Neffe music recorded from 1975-1982, with spoken word narration based on French texts by female vocalists who appear on various tracks: Tina Scatozza, Nadine Bal, Isabelle Yernaux and Mirella Brunello.

Neffe uses synthesizers, rhythm boxes and sound effects to create music that often has a lo-fi soundtrack feel and fronts the music with enchanting spoken narratives. The opener blends space exploration and John Carpenter styled soundtrack. Another piece is punctuated by a robotic synth melody. The following piece supports the vocal narrative with whimsical classical piano followed by a deep space synthesizer melody. One of the highlights showcases Nadine Bal's ethereal French spoken word backed by orchestral space electronica.

The B-side is comprised of a single 24-minute work with Mirella Brunello's vocals combining spoken narration and operatic/chant singing. The music ranges from swirling space-symphonic runs, Latin rhythmic grooves and Emerson, Lake and Palmer meet the Residents orchestral hysteria with mesmerizing chant, spoken and theatrical vocalizations.

Pseudo Code – *Potlatch Music Vol. 2* (1981)

This collection exhibits Pseudo Code's flair for tuneful industrial cacophony and harmonious noise, percussion and electronic experimentation. The fun starts with a blend of chaotic space excursion, industrial upheaval and an unbalanced sense of rhythmic drive. 'The Crook Of Your Heart' features droning vocals singing a somber song that is simultaneously tranquil and disturbing. The vocals and noodling guitar melody contrast sharply with the varied electronic waves that become increasingly loud and intense as the piece progresses. 'Works' is a noise-drone symphony that serves as the foundation for a Residents meets Throbbing Gristle sense of song.

The B-side stands in stark contrast, consisting of a series of pleasantly melodic keyboard, synthesizer, guitar, horn and vocal ruminations. Each piece is played at a slowly reflective pace, conjuring up a parade of pastoral imagery.

Bene Gesserit – *Best Of...* (1981)

Bene Gesserit were headed up by Alain Neffe and Nadine Bal, creating some of the best synth-pop that was never heard on MTV. The songs are fun and playful but are intricately composed and arranged.

Songs like 'Epitaph for a One-Way Love' feature zany, spaced out synth-pop, with delightfully corny keys, swirling and bubbling effects, prominent lead bass lines and excellent vocals from Bal. 'Hymne au ver' sounds like the soundtrack to a sci-fi children's television show. I like the combination of child-like instrumentation, wacky effects, playfully quirky beats and classic 1980s electro-pop sounds.

Bene Gesserit put an entirely new spin on the classic Van Morrison and Them song 'Gloria'. Bal spells G.L.O.R.I.A. with dual vocals that are child banshee fluttering and with a space whispery vibe that recalls Gong's Gilli Smyth. Other highlights include 'Kidnapping', which carries an electro-funky Tom Tom Club styled groove. 'Erg Habbania' craftily blends electro-pop, eerie ambient jazz and radiophonic sci-fi soundtrack. And 'Live in China' feels like a traditional Japanese tea ceremony.

Human Flesh – *The Third Human Attempt* **(1984)**
Neffe collaborated with several musicians and vocalists on *The Third Human Attempt*. Instrumentation includes synthesizers, saxophone, guitar, bass, percussion, rhythm box and effects. Voices and 'vocalizations' are key components throughout the set. Most of the 17 tracks are in the 2 to 4-minute range and feel like case studies that explore minimalism and phantasmal thematic soundtrack development.

Among the highlights is the set opening 'Saxual Intercourse', on which a minimal synth drone and ominous bass riff lay the foundation around which the saxophone and guitar explore. 'Betsy Don't Care' is an experimental soundscape infused blend of sci-fi soundtrack and industrial minimalism, with narrative vocals by Mirella Brunello. 'He Has Lost His Head Too' is a playful synthesizer and rhythm box tune with vocals that nod to the song's Robert Wyatt dedication. 'T.V. Kills/Victims Of The Tube' is a sprightly jingle that's like a cross between Bene Gesserit and the Residents. And pianet and rhythm box inject a cheesy charm into 'Reject', which is a spirited and melodically catchy electro space-pop tune that's like a lo-fi Kraftwerk.

Various Artists - *Insane Music For Insane People Vol. 2* **(1983)**
Like most compilations of this era, the participating bands were a combination of those who were prolific in their output and others who came and went with little network fanfare.

Among the non-Alain Neffe artists are the Legendary Pink Dots, an English/Dutch ensemble who over the decades achieved a greater level of success than most of their hometaper brethren. 'Time Dance' is a beautiful acoustic driven folk-psychedelic song with vocals by the inimitable Edward Ka-Spel. 'Vigil-Anti' is simultaneously razor sharp and frolicsome, with buzzsaw guitar blasts and other machine shop themed instrumentation, a whimsical synthesizer melody and Ka-Spel's threatening vocal delivery.

Storm In A Nutshell is a Belgian band who contribute a stripped down yet bouncy, good time rock instrumental. It's just strumming guitars, drums and an electro beat that adds a spacey edge. Also from Belgium, Nosy Parker play a comparatively straightforward but impressively performed and arranged brand of melodic rock with passionate vocals. Let's Have Healthy Children is yet another Belgian entry who contribute a playful, lo-fi punk song.

In addition to being a prolific recording artist, English musician Colin Potter ran the ICR (Integrated Circuit Records) label and collaborated with artists like Nurse With Wound and Current 93. Three of Potter's songs grace this compilation: 'I Am Your Shadow' is a classic example of quirky, robotic electro-punk that's like Gary Numan meets The Normal. 'For All You Know' is similar but more darkly industrial. And 'In Front Of You' is a hyper-kinetic blend of sped up electro rock and backward vocals.

Also from England, electronic, industrial, experimental band Portion Control were staples of the 1980s hometaper network. At over ten minutes, their 'Shift And Shuffle' morphs and mixes alien electronics, voice samples, bang and clang percussion, an off-kilter rhythmic pulse and angst-ridden vocals as the music marches along an ominously industrial path. The blend of music, sounds and vocals is well crafted, creating a frighteningly hallucinatory atmosphere replete with yelling and screaming as the music maintains a steadily grooving stride.

Various Artists - *Insane Music For Insane People Vol. 3* (1983)
Volume 3 introduces new bands from Belgium, the Netherlands and England, and reaching across the Pacific to Japan.

Berntholder is from Belgium and their song 'Toys' consists of swinging new wave with a sunshine pop vibe. I like the corny but effective synthesizers and wispy female vocals, making for an enjoyably catchy tune. Also from Belgium, Let's Have Healthy Children return from Vol. 2 with a guitar strumming and electro drumming singer-songwriter punk song.

Andre de Saint-Obin are from the Netherlands and contribute a lo-fi alien synth-pop song with soulfully edgy vocals. I like the pitter-patter groove of the synthesizers and electro beats that dance about like an army of alien insects and are offset by a dark, intermittent bass pulse. Van Kaye + Ignit are another Dutch ensemble who present a goth infused blend of electro-industrial and new wave synth-pop, with a darkly passionate singer and mesmerizing melodies.

Metamorphosis are an English band who contribute two live performance tracks of spaced out freeform punk-jazz, with wailing horns and punky male/female vocals. It's all very chaotic, though held together by an impressively fiery drummer.

Finally, Japanese sound artist Merzbow was another cassette culture veteran who achieved greater success than most in the hometaper network. Merzbow contributes excerpts from two lengthier pieces. The music is characterized by psychedelic sound exploration, clatter percussion, audio art jazz excursion, eerie Tiki keyboard melodies and much more.

Various Artists – *Insane Music for Insane People Vol. 5* **(1984)**
As the series progressed, Neff and Bal's networking expanded with contributors appearing from increasing numbers of countries.

Fetus Productions are from Australia and their 'Flicker Flicker Flick' has an underlying keyboard melody with a Beatles feel, the vocals sound like a dreamy soulful torch song, and it's all colored by a parade of spacey effects, making for a nicely surreal pop song. Their second offering is different, being a metal infused lo-fi hard rock instrumental.

Austrian band Empty Wien contribute four songs, including a playfully bouncy synthesizer melody with weird effects, a similar but more mainstream tune with electro drums, a video game flavored synth-pop ditty, and an imaginatively offbeat combination of electro drums, spooky synthesizer melody, and call and response poetic telephone conversations.

American hometaper Sue Ann Harkey provides creatively experimental songcraft, with dissonant guitars, ambient soundscapes, and vocals that are like Joni Mitchell in a Beat era coffee house.

We've also got four Belgian bands. Jezebel sounds like an avant-pop cross between a children's song and German beerhall band and colored by rumbling psychedelic effects. Let's Have Healthy Children return yet again with a guitar strumming singer-songwriter tune. Instead Of crank out jamming space rock with electronic drums and a cool dance groove. Twilight Ritual produce lo-fi, melodic and pleasingly edgy industrial synth-pop. And Dutchman Enno Velthuys plays a tune that feels like the Goblin credit rolling finale to a Dario Argento film.

Various Artists – *Insane Music For Insane People Vol. 11* (1986)

Vol. 11 continues with a Euro-American array of artists, reaching north and south of the American border.

From Norway, Areknuteknyterne's entry consists of slowly grooving space-punk with a lazily cool lead bass riff, ambient guitar licks, chipmunk vocals and whirring effects. Denmark's Poets Of The Signature indulge in fun-with-tape experimentation in which a spoken narration is accompanied by pulsating effects that are sporadically sped up to awkwardly oddball effect. Vanishing Family from the US is similar, creating a tape speed challenged flow of electronic patterns with a mild rhythmic pulse. (The tape may or may not be damaged.)

After a Sunday morning mass introduction, Belgian band Twilight Ritual launch into an excellent progressive rock infused sci-fi television sounding theme. Lelu/Lu's are from England and play punk-pop with a post-Be Bop Deluxe Bill Nelson flavor. Frenchman Jean-Louis Descloux plays rhythmically off-kilter synth-pop with a simple but catchy melody and a lightly dissonant edge. From Germany, Mullah offers majestically gloomy, gothic, industrial punk with an atmospheric aura. Also from Germany, Collectionism contribute a blend of deeply ambient experimental sound exploration and free-jazz.

From Mexico we've got Armando Velaso Torres who contributes two very different pieces of music. One consists of wildly rushing wind and tape dragging effects, and the other is a rollicking party time instrumental with impressively sophisticated guitar work and zany frenetic bee swarm effects.

California based Psyclones create a space journey by blending tape effects and Residents circa *Eskimo* exploration. Canadian artists Tanz Victims play high intensity space-industrial hard rock that recalls Chrome, with monstrously searing Helios Creed guitar and acid-demon vocals. Colorado based Walls Of Genius serve up an intriguing combination of repetitive organ riff, typewriter groove and harshly wailing synthesizer melodies. Scottish band The Horsemen contribute a lovely melodic guitar and bass instrumental. This is followed by an equally luscious acoustic guitar instrumental from Belgian musician E. Hembersin. And French band Los Paranos play the appropriately titled 'Waltz' with a whimsically hallucinatory organ grinder vibe.

Various Artists – *Insane Music For Insane People Vol. 18* (1987)
Belgian band Nicky Ricci's White Tracks opens Vol. 18 with standard 1970s styled bluesy strutting cock rock. Synthetic Products are an American band who contribute two songs. One features hip-shaking electronica with Bowie vocals and guitar licks that smack of Midge Ure era Ultravox. The other is similar but with a swaggering rock 'n' roll injection. Dutch band Trespassers W. contribute good time angular glam-punk with a Captain Beefheart edge to the guitar.

Mechanical Sterility are a fun American band who contribute a goofy lo-fi punk tune, a short bedroom cover of The Doors' 'Light My Fire', and an acoustic country-punk song with loony vocals. Kaoru Todoroki are from Japan and sound like an industrial noise take on the Residents, with interesting vocal effects, zany electronics and guitar that sounds influenced by Snakefinger. On the more meditative side are O Yuki Conjugate from England, who play floating space electronica. Similarly pastoral is Canadian musician Michael Kleniec, whose first piece consists of acoustic guitar and light orchestration. He gets more adventurous on the second, which adds quirky electronica with a bit of Caribbean lounge swing to the acoustic guitar.

Lady June from England offer up a rumbling noise requiem with poetic spoken word. Y Create is Dutch hometaper Hessel Veldman, whose contribution features a combination of soulfully robotic electronica and cool jazz jamming horns. Belgian E.T. Ben Souf offers two tracks, one a bit of staccato lo-fi Philip Glass minimalism and the other a synthesizer melody that sounds like he's mocking an old Wurlitzer organ demo.

Brooklyn, New York based Ron Anderson plays an intricately composed avant-progressive rock-jazz-punk rocker that's like a blend of Dr. Nerve, MX-80 Sound and Material. Finally, Swiss band Svatopluck contribute playful, lo-fi electronica with a retro video game soundtrack vibe and oddball vocals.

Matthias Lang and IRRE Tapes

Matthias Lang launched the IRRE Tapes label after publishing eight issues of his IRRE fanzine. Intentionally avoiding a stylistic theme, Lang released artists that he enjoyed, resulting in a dazzling variety of music.

Like many cassette labels, Lang produced numerous compilation tapes. My focus in this section is on the individual artists, some of which are 'split' tapes that feature different artists on the A and B sides.

Kratzer – *Irrtum!* (1982)

Kratzer are a German band whose distinctive lo-fi style is to be found in the combination of grungy rocking guitar and spacey keyboards that sound like toy instruments. The tape includes six songs and is barely 20 minutes in length, yet Kratzer manage to pack in an impressive variety.

'Hertha Punx' opens with clunky grunge guitar and a plinkity keyboard melody led by German language vocals. There's slightly more keyboard action on 'Keine Chance für Kratzer', with a spacey vibe accompanying the rocking guitar chords that propel the music into stoned yet futuristic Neue Deutsche Welle terrain. 'Ich 2' is injected with a dose of complexity as one guitar lays down energetic riffs while a second cranks out 1960s West Coast psychedelic leads. 'Motoroller' surprises yet again, being a danceable bit of grungy lo-fi bedroom pop with catchy melodies. '17 Jahre' is like MX-80 Sound meets the B-52s in space. And 'Der alte Mann und die Frau' is similar to 'Hertha Punx' but more spaced out. The guitar chugs along as the toy keyboard plays its childlike melody and the effected vocals inject a darkly gothic flavor. This brief set is a classic example of imaginative homemade charm.

Stress / Thomas Struszka split (1983)

The A-side of this split features Stress, who are the Coventry, UK based duo of Alan Rider on bass, xylophone, percussion, synthesizers and violin, and Phil Clarke on vocals, synthesizers, percussion and keyboards. The two create well composed, performed and arranged pop songs that easily rival their major label contemporaries.

Though Stress fall into the synth-pop realm, there is a tantalizing cross section of music throughout their set. I enjoyed the funky grooving electro rock pulse of 'Cut The Jive'. 'Down Through The Years' is a standout, with its quirkily flowing, keyboard driven new wave pop. 'Enigma' is one of the more elaborately constructed tracks. It's an instrumental with a mesmerizing bass and synthesizer groove, which lays the foundation for an avant-tribal parade of percussion. '4th Dimension' is another strong instrumental, being an atmospheric excursion with inspired use of percussion, electronics, violin, voice and effects to create a hauntingly cosmic and thematically rich blend of soundscape construction and drone soundtrack.

The B-side belongs to German musician Thomas Struszka. With instrumentation including Roland Juno, Drumatix, bass and other electronic gear, Struszka creates punchy and intricately arranged electronic songs.

Highlights include 'Flucht Aus Der Disco', a hyper-kinetic dancefloor burning synth-pop tune with blazing interludes of craftily inserted effects madness. Struszka eases the pace with 'Schranken' and its provocative blend of eerie new wave and alien effects. Kraftwerk are a looming presence. 'Leute Nach 84' is a freeform canvas of space-industrial-noise experimentation, with harsh cosmic pulsations and percussive bursts that paint a meteor shower landscape. And 'Heidschi Bum Bum' is a lo-fi space-symphonic trek with bleepy blurpy effects and an Ennio Morricone western soundtrack edge.

Attrition / Alu split (1983)

Formed in Coventry, England in 1980, Attrition were cassette culture fixtures, creating post-punk/industrial/experimental electronica. Their set opens with 'I Saw You, Slowly', an experimental sound exploratory piece with an avant-chamber music atmosphere. Stringed instruments groan and drone to a gradually evolving electronic sequence that builds in volume and potency, only to cut off abruptly as Attrition launch into the propulsive, tape manipulated, industrial dance number 'Monkey In A Bin'. This is high intensity electronica with nails-on-a-blackboard scratchy keyboards and dual male/female vocals that are like a dance club demon/banshee combo. One of my favorites is 'You Will Remember Nothing', which chugs along at a robotic pace, punctuated by howling ambient guitar, a banging rhythmic pulse and chimerical vocals that create a haunting tribal-industrial atmosphere and idiosyncratic groove.

The B-side features Alu, the Berlin based duo of Hannes Vester on synthesizers and guitar and Nadja Molt on vocals. Representative of Alu's sound is 'Chassa', which lays down a funky, oddball bass and percussion beat with strangely strumming guitar and Nina Hagen punk-chanteuse vocals. 'Unaba' is pure Kraftwerk meets post-punk industrial soul. Nadja's vocals are simultaneously poetic and possessed as she rant-chants, spitting and demonizing the words. 'Vendetta' is both tribal and alien, creating a quietly tense atmosphere. Nadja plays the bedeviled poet sorcerous as she soulfully scats and chants to the electro grooving percussive flow. And 'Intox' is like James Blood Ulmer with a dose of gothic funk and Nina Hagen vocals.

Der Böse Bub Eugen / GUZ split (1988)

This tape consists of two Swiss German bands. Der Böse Bub Eugen play short and energetically punky German language songs with a tasty balance of punk aggression and good time rock 'n' roll. The drums set a steady pace, anchoring what in punk terms are fairly sophisticated guitar and bass interplay. There's little variation across the 12 songs, but they're energetic and set the punk bar high in compositional and instrumental terms. Guitar and bass rock out but color the music with brief instrumental forays that transcend standard three-chord punk.

GUZ's songs are even shorter, with a whopping 17 filling up the 30-minute B-side. These guys are pretty wacky, with lyrics in both German and English and bring to mind a punk version of the Bonzo Dog Band. I hear lots of 1960s pop and novelty influences that GUZ insidiously destroy. Among the highlights is 'Mary Ann', which sounds like a country flavored 1960s novelty song that Kim Fowley might have produced. I like the awkward Ska groove of 'Egyptian Regie'. 'GBS is like a carnivalesque satire of Gene Pitney. 'Sisch schad um mich' is different, being a lysergic bit of psychedelic effects experimentation. 'Morlocks' is another surprise, bashing out grunge fueled, psychedelic industrial rock. My personal favorite is 'One Hand Left', which reeks of well digested Captain Beefheart.

Kronstadt / Toshiyuki Hiraoka split (1988)

Kronstadt are a Berlin based band who play a dizzying array of styles. Opening track 'In deinem Kopf' consists of skittishly driving new wave rock that strikes me as an XTC and The Jam blend with German language vocals. The musicianship is top notch. 'Weiter' is a hauntingly energetic yet floating tune. 'Denk an die Feuer' finds Kronstadt exploring cinematic realms with an eye toward symphonic ambience and interesting thematic development. 'Opening' begins as the most pastoral song of the set, combining lilting acoustic guitar and synthesizer melody before launching into a progressive-folk rocker. And 'Askana' pounds out relentlessly energetic dancefloor electronica with a banquet of hurtling effects that melt seamlessly into the frenzied new wave rocking 'E electrical'.

Japanese musician Toshiyuki Hiraoka is a good B-side pairing for Kronstadt in terms of musicianship. He serves up 14 short guitar and bass workouts that are nothing short of stunning. Most of the tracks feature progressive-punk guitar and bass jams, with fuzzed out but razor-sharp guitar leads, augmented by funky snappy bass leads.

'Funky' is a barely one-minute slab of smoldering guitar and bass punk. 'Beat' is a playfully helter-skelter experimentation with guitar and bass effects. 'Terao' stands out for its jazz inspired yet good old 1970s rock 'n' roll vibe. Overall, Hiraoka's set is a roller coaster cavalcade of guitar and bass studies, most of them punk inspired energetic, but a handful are quieter musings. Hiraoka went on to become a film composer.

Flagrants D'Eli – *Carnaval* (1989)

Flagrants D'Eli are a French punk band with vocals by Eli Perin, who excels at both ranting angst and edgy pop luster. Despite the English song titles the vocals are in French. Many of the 24 short songs on *Carnaval* feature thrashy punk, which are often embellished with spacey bleeping pennywhistle keyboards.

The set is a feast of variety. 'The Difference' starts off as folk tinged pop-punk with grungy guitar, before picking up the pace and rocking harder. 'Radio Blitz' is total punk thrash, though the music is merely background for German, French and English language radio samples. 'You Don't Know Anything Of Life' surprises with relatively polished and tightly played punk-pop. The guitar retains the dirty edge that's so integral to the band's sound, but the punchy punky chord blasts sound great against Eli's aggressive vocals. 'Home Made Rock' parts One and Two are like The Ramones with goofy whistling effects. 'The Walls' sounds like the Clash with Eli on vocals and a gloriously zany keyboard melody that seems so out of place yet so nicely enriches the sound. The set also includes a couple of melodic acoustic guitar songs. And 'Waltz Of The Truncheons' alternates between grooving thrash rock and befuddled dancehall waltz with punky Edith Piaf vocals.

Square Sun – *Same* (1990)

Square Sun is Scottish hometaper Dion Trevarthen, who also played in the space rock band Sponge. Trevarthen serves up an hour of instrumental music that's part minimal synthesizer electronica that combines beats, robotic melodies, soundscapes, drones and effects, and part jamming psychedelic space rock.

The music transitions through a variety of themes, beginning with a repetitive, mechanized electro tribal groove with a deep space cavalcade of effects that soar, dance and drone. This is followed by a soundscape journey that blends elements of early Tangerine Dream alien forest teeming with life soundtrack, and beautiful glissando space guitar melodies. Voice samples, loops and backwards effects add texture to the proceedings. I was later surprised by a space rock jam with cosmically fuzzed and darkly psychedelic improvisation, followed by a Pink Floyd meets Tangerine Dream space jam that is compelling for its blend of meditative 'Set The Controls For The Heart Of The Sun' space excursion, free-wheeling sound experiments and good old jamming space rock.

Almost Human – *No Style Music* (1990)

From Germany, Almost Human play an accessible brand of progressive rock that's reminiscent of early 1980s English 'neo-prog' bands like IQ, Pendragon and Twelfth Night. The musicianship is outstanding, and the compositions are often played in challenging time signatures. The band incorporates numerous influences. 'Disco Town' has a Caribbean meets Ska groove which rocks and swings while maintaining an underlying progressive rock complexity. 'The Account' feels like 1980s new wave with a progressive rock sensibility. I like the opening guitar on 'The Family Of Life' that injects a trippy Eastern vibe into the music before the band launch into a gorgeously melodic progressive rocker. 'Walk On Water' tugs at the heart strings, transitioning through a range of emotional themes with impassioned vocals and soothing melodies. 'Jingle' sounds like it would be at home on a Steve Hackett album. And I like the jazzy flavor of 'The Runaway'.

Solanaceae Tau – *Outdoor Expressions* (1990)

Solanaceae Tau are a German band rooted in darkwave and dark gothic folk-punk but also explore industrial punk and Throbbing Gristle inspired realms. But it is the German and English language female vocals that make this set such a treasure.

Tracks like 'The Wolf Song' feature haunting organ, breathy soundscapes, a slow, steady marching beat and seductively eerie gothic vocals. 'Ozonik Hunter' carries an energetic bouncy beat and vocals like a possessed siren singer. 'Ethnological Hazard II' creates a tribal gothic punk setting with smatterings of Eno experimentalism and seductively possessed vocals. 'Muzak Transmission Line' is similar but the voice garbling effects are even more bizarre. 'The Algorythm Dream' is beautifully introspective, but with electronic effects that add a contrasting machine-like vibe. Other highlights include 'Tanks Of Xiao Ping', a tribal slab of industrial dance electronica with harsh acid-metal guitar. 'Education Through Anarchy' is a robotically grooving industrial rocker with a Throbbing Gristle edge. I love the spacey effects and combination of spoken word and chanting siren vocals on the tribal electronic 'Teuton'. And the dreamily industrial soundscapes of "Submissioned By Machine' are a delight.

Mental Anguish – *Refescent* (1990)

Mental Angish is Memphis, Tennessee based Chris Phinney, who also ran the Harsh Reality label. *Refescent* is a 5-track, 60-minute set in which Phinney employs his arsenal of synthesizer, Korg and Casio keyboards, sequencers, loops and effects to create abstract space electronic workouts but also more rocking electronica.

'Modern Chemistry' is characterized by 20 minutes of bleeping, pulsating and hissing radio signals. It's all very minimal but in my mind's eye I could imaging sipping coffee as I monitored transmissions at SETI. M. Bramhall contributes guitar and effects to the 10-minute 'Train Runnin' Through My Brain', a drugged vocal number and noodling space effects excursion. The guitar leads and vocals are lazily bluesy, making for an interesting combination of trippy psychedelia and radiophonic fun. 'From The Cradle To The Grave' is a deep space and lightly melodic minimal synth journey with ghostly vocals. 'Flat Tire Mister?' deviates from the space electronica theme for an abstract sound and percussion focused improvisation with scratching, clattering and bell combinations that create an interesting rhythmic flow. And 'A Lower Ratio' combines sound exploration with space electronics to create a drunkenly whimsical sped up/slowed down tape manipulation and effects workout.

Herd Of The Ether Space – *Dada's Little Psycho* (1990)

California based Herd Of The Ether Space play a Dada inspired potpourri of sounds, samples and freeform musical zaniness that would be right at home on the 1980s Ralph Records label. The set opens with what sounds like a typewriter instructional tape. The voice is slowed and looped to the point where the single world 'space' is repeated and juxtaposed, followed by an LSD cautionary recording. This is backed by whimsically eerie soundtrack music and scraping sounds given carefully effected treatment. 'Mister Bojangles' is a good fun Radiophonic country-western song, intended as a Dadaesque tribute to Sammy Davis Jr, who had passed away at the time of these recordings. The Sammy homage continues with a delirious concoction of Sammy samples, musical chaos, voices and disparate sounds.

Other highlights include the sound of tape manipulated crying babies intermingled with soundscape enhanced orchestral strings, rattling percussion and electronic effects. There's plenty of humor throughout, notably on 'Tipper Gore Aerobics Lesson', which combines a lecture on Kegel exercises with space symphonics, rock and pop record samples, Frippertronic guitar, erratic percussion and effects. Overall, this is a premier example of meticulously produced collage, manipulation and effects.

Al Margolis and Sound of Pig

From 1984-1990, New York based Al Margolis released 301 cassette albums on his Sound of Pig label, showcasing a wide range of music primarily in the experimental/improvisational realms. Several of the tapes spotlight Margolis' work – solo, collaborations and live ensemble performances. He also released an assortment of artists from around the world.

This overview begins with a selection of Margolis' recordings, followed by my personal choice picks of artists, providing readers with a sense of the varied music the label released. Note that while Sound of Pig released numerous outstanding compilation tapes, my focus is on the individual artist albums.

If, Bwana – *Freudian Slip* (1984)

If, Bwana was the alias under which Margolis recorded solo and *Freudian Slip* was Margolis' first If, Bwana cassette album. It consists of 15 short tracks of minimal electronics, spaced out effects, soundscapes, bits of rhythm and lots of melody. The result is an enticing set of outside-the-box yet accessible songs with a hodgepodge of electronica, industrial, rock and experimental influences.

After a brief tribal introduction, we're whisked off on a short minimal space electronics and percussion excursion. Margolis takes a turn into stimulating electronica territory with a minimal synth tune, creating a catchy, toe tapping melody and rhythmic pulse, and embellished by spacey electronic banshee riffs. It's simplistic, but Margolis brings together contrasting elements in intriguing ways as he folds a diversity of soundscapes and noise into music that is accessibly melodic and rhythmic.

The Residents and their Ralph Records label were a powerful influence on the hometapers and this spirit is evident on tracks like 'Mourning Glory' and 'Lord Have Mercy On Us', which struck me as basement tape candidates for the Residents' *Commercial Album*. I like the cosmically Oriental vibe on 'Hip, No ?'. Other highlights include 'CSQ', which mines space-industrial-tribal territory for its noise-jazz brand of swirling electronic futurism.

Sombrero Galaxy – *Next Stop...* (1984)

Sombrero Galaxy was the duo of Al Margolis and Jay Hernandez, who previously worked together in the band Pigs on Parade. Sombrero Galaxy was formed after, Margolis says, "we got tired of looking for singers and drummers."

In contrast to most of Margolis' work, Sombrero Galaxy recorded songs, with vocals on this album by Tony Charneco. This is a fun set, characterized by catchy, lo-fi space rock and electro-pop infused songs.

The main riff on 'To Die Young' sounds like a dead ringer for Hawkwind's 'Assault & Battery'. Swirly keyboards and electro saxophone provide plenty of jamming fun, and Charneco's vocals are readymade for MTV. 'Run Run' is propelled by a classic electronic drum pulse, theatrical vocals and keyboards. I like the corny devotional vibe of 'Spirit'. The ethereally acidic and soulful aura of 'Misty Harbor' is a highlight, with its wailing sax and Beat inspired spoken narrative.

'Sci-Fi #1' is a spaced out funky instrumental that kicks off the B-side. 'Show Me How' is a dreamy, crooning space-pop tune with cosmic keyboards and a jazzy funky groove. 'Ah, The Name' has a mesmerizing, robotic space rock vibe. And the closing 'Reprise' is a gem, bringing in spacey noise horns to jam along with the strumming acoustic guitar.

Thick Slimy Whisper – *Live At Fashion Moda, 10/11/86* **(1986)**
Thick Slimy Whisper was the trio of Al Margolis, Paul Richards and Cheryl Sobas, who played improvisational music utilizing traditional and electronic instrumentation. For the *Live At Fashion Moda* performance, we have Margolis on voice, violin, saxophone, effects and bicycle pump, Richards on electronic percussion, and Sobas on voice, oboe, synthesizer, violin, tapes, percussion and effects.

The set opens with voice and instrument drone, and Sobas quickly reveals her lovely songbird singing. The vocals have an 'Amazing Grace' quality, which sounds beautiful next to the murmuring thrum of the droning instruments. This is followed by what begins as a frantically paced number that sounds like the avant-garde soundtrack to a chase scene.

The themes evolve steadily throughout the set, from ambient explorations to robotic rhythm and sound workouts, to wailing Eastern tinged drone-chant-jazz junkets that are simultaneously theatrical and tribal. I enjoyed the combination of varied electro percussive patterns and often hypnotic atmospherics, which together communicate an image inducing filmic character.

As If^2 Bwana – *Damp* (1987)

As If^2 Bwana was a collaboration between Al Margolis and Boston based David Prescott, who called himself As If for the project (hence the square^2). Featuring two side long works that each clock in at 45 minutes, Margolis is credited with synthesizer, guitar, violin, trumpet, drum and toys, and Prescott with synthesizer and radio.

The A-side opens with minimal, pulsating drone-scapes that lay the foundation for howling, cosmic guitar effects, bringing to mind a marriage of Hawkwind's *Space Ritual* and Fripp and Eno's experiments. The setting feels like a space station machine shop and the evolving parade of effects conjure up images of an alien jungle.

The B-side is equally spacey but more focused on freeform sound exploration. The mood is playful at first as the synthesizers soar while percussion, trumpet, whistle and miscellaneous sounds bang in a strangely off-kilter yet rhythmic flow.

There's also an element of musicality amidst the tumult. Additional sound, instrument, voice samples and electronic components are added throughout, creating a frenzied collage choir that challenges the senses with its incessant, multi-layered assault. But then there's the descent, which gradually melts into a still fiery, yet dreamy valium induced delirium.

XTSW – *Bridge* (1987)

XTSW was formed by Margolis and Paul Richards after Thick Slimy Whisper disbanded. Though ostensibly a duo project, Margolis says he sometimes used the name while touring during what he considered to be collaborations that fell outside of If, Bwana.

Bridge consists of pure ambient-soundscape adventurism, with drones, rushes of wind across barren landscapes and alien communication across cosmic radio waves. There's also a powerful orchestral element, as quietly minimal passages explode in symphonic ambient percussion and string blasts. The shifts from deep space pastoral to high intensity atmospheric continually rise and fall, creating a razor's edge feeling of stress. The quieter moments are brief, with percussive rumbling laying the groundwork for swelling tides and inevitable eruption.

The journey continues on the B-side, with loudly pulsating echoes that made me feel like I was drifting in darkness through an enormous cosmic cavern. The sensation is solitary yet expansive, like floating through the blackest regions of space. Overall, this is an emotional 60 minutes of space-ambient exploration and electro symphonic intensity.

Der Akteur – *Rockery* (1985)

The two side long works of 30 minutes each on this tape are classic examples of what happens when the creatively inclined are armed with tape recorders. The machine is indeed weaponized, as German based Der Akteur unleash a non-stop flurry of industrial collage fun. Varied sounds, noise waves and voice samples are surgically spliced to create a head spinning roller coaster ride. A pounding noise dirge is abruptly followed by a Dead Kennedys song snippet. A church choir chants alongside a political rant. Whirring sound waves are jarringly warbled to produce a disorienting ambient effect. A spectral voice speaks in German as a haunting horror melody lulls in the background and a water faucet disturbingly drips, drips, drips. Sometimes the setting feels like a factory, at others like floating through a cross dimensional limbo, and there is often a sensation of a sound barraged media assault. It's all about clever mixing, morphing and manipulating the sounds, electronics and samples to create what feels like an industrial-psychedelic montage trip.

D.Z. Lectric – *Russo-American Songs* (1985)

D.Z. Lectric is the moniker under which Frenchman Christian Dezert recorded. Originally released in 1982, *Russo-American Songs* is a punchy set of lo-fi electro rock and minimal synth-pop tunes.

At only 30 minutes, Dezert is short and to the point with his 13 songs. Among the highlights is 'Musique' which has a funky punk tribal groove. 'Planned Accidents' is an edgy industrial-punk song that would appeal to Chrome fans. 'Loudmouth' is a Ramones cover that Dezert sinisterly executes in lo-fi basement fashion. 'N.Y. By Night' is a spaced out and engagingly lopsided electro dance number. Dezert does a drugged electro cover of 'Fever' ("You give me fee-ver!"). I like the haunting funereal vibe of 'Le Chemin De Croix', punctuated by slow staccato electro beats. This is immediately followed by the dizzying electronic bee swarm of '(La Fonction De) L'Orgasme'. 'Chanson our Les P4' is similarly frenetic, though offset by a strangely contrasting accordion drone melody. 'Le Moine' dials the pace down again, being a mournful stroll through a deep space cemetery. 'Remember When You Ate All Those Trips' has a dreamy vibe and is one of the catchiest floating melodies of the set. And 'Villa Triste' closes the set with a brief minimal synthesizer finale.

Little Fyodor – *Slither Sloth* (1985)

Little Fyodor (aka David Lichtenverg) was one-third of the trio Walls of Genius who from 1982-86 released cassette albums of crazy songs, twisted rock, zany cover tunes and experimental music. His *Slither Sloth* solo album serves up two very different themes on the A and B sides.

The *Slither* side consists of Fyodor's trademark humorously self-deprecating songs. I love the punk infused rock 'n' roll of 'Ugly Girl', with its cool cheesy organ and Fyodor's zanier than Devo vocal style: "I want an ugly girl. Who loves nobody but me." 'Those Three Little Words' is both funny and disturbing with its siren blaring space synthesizers and the clatter of objects being tossed around as Fyodor repeatedly moans, groans, growls and crazily cries "I LOVE YOU!" 'Doomed' features darkly comical, acid rocking punk.

The *Sloth* side is more free-wheeling experimental. An introductory noodling space electronics segment leads to 'No Relief In Sight', which continues the electronic fun and includes an eerie organ melody and clattering tribal percussion. 'The Soap Seeps In' is a wacky tune that recalls The Three Stooges theme, with various radio/TV samples cut-in and a steady bang-on-a-can hammer blast to set the rhythmic pace. And 'Fried In The Shell' is an electronics and percussion, high energy robot rocker. Little Fyodor is definitely in a realm all his own.

Dog As Master – *Brash Pussy* **(1986)**

Dog As Master is the solo project of Hal McGee, who along with Debbie Jaffe recorded as Viscera and ran the Cause And Effect label and distribution service.

Brash Pussy is a combination of power electronics and audio art sound collage. There is a linear thread of primal noise that permeates throughout, with McGee periodically launching into a screaming tirade of sexual violence. But this is more than densely compacted white noise. Slicing in samples and effects adds thematic and emotional variety. Bits of sitar infuse the brutality of McGee's ranting with a curiously trippy edge. Breakneck electro beats flittering between the left and right channels add a deviant rhythmic quality to the caterwauling tumult. The wall of noise at times slowly phases, creating the contradictory sensation of calm amidst the raging storm. Similarly, a succession of keyboard melodies oddly offset the overarching noise assault. McGee has a flair for dexterously mixing seemingly antithetical components into his principle theme of high intensity volume and noise.

PBK – *Poetry & Motion* **(1987)**

PBK is Phillip B. Klingler, who at the time of this recording was based in San Bernardino, California. There's variety across *Poetry & Motion's* seven tracks, though a ghostly ambience pervades throughout. I enjoy audio art that subtly approaches the creation of seemingly trivial places in time. The blowing wind, slowly chiming church bells and phantasmal choral chants of opening track 'Sacrifice' are eerie yet pleasantly atmospheric. After a while PBK introduces light orchestral waves and symphonic bits that add a musical sensibility, and all the while the wind blows on like an unwavering drone. 'Big Thumb' lays down flowing soundscapes over which staccato percussion weaves an energetically rhythmic path. PBK mixes things up nicely, with the percussion getting frenetically rocking at times, and buzz blasts that are like machine shop guitar chords bashing, and colorful alien effects are sprinkled about.

I like the combination of early Tangerine Dream kosmiche ambience and the apparitional themes that permeate throughout the B-side opener 'Underground', which conjures up images of wandering the desert or foggy, nighttime streets of limbo. 'Saving Grace' is intriguingly unsettling in its blend of voices, space effects and orchestral passages to create a streaming collage of cosmic oblivion. In summary, PBK's sonic canvas is image inducing, frightening and enlightening.

Famlende Forsøk – *Herring Tales* (1988)

Famlende Forsøk are a Norwegian trio and Herring Tales compiles re-recorded, alternate versions, and remixes of tracks from earlier cassette albums released on the band's SHiT label. The fragrant note in the credits reads: "A collection of the fishiest songs from that foul-smelling Norwegian ensemble."

The band utilize both traditional instruments and electronics, creating music that draws on experimental and industrial influences, and I often sensed an avant-garde theater feel that recalls the Residents. Brt's vocals are in Norwegian and have a commanding narrative style. The vocals typically come in spurts, as if he is reciting something. Only one track features actual 'singing'.

The set opens with a spacey punk-jazz Ska tune, which is different than the rest of the tracks. There's a rumbling, eruptive space-noise dirge with saxophone that wails against the vocals and distorted space electronic psychedelic chaos, which continually gets louder and noisier but also more atmospherically ominous. I especially enjoyed the ethereal dissonant musical tunes, with guitar that plinks and strums to clanking rhythms and saxophone that wails and drones.

Famlende Forsøk excel at combining noise, clatter percussion, electronics and guitar/synthesizer/saxophone to create pieces that are busy, rhythmic, atmospheric and noisy, yet also sound exploratory and musical.

Amy Denio – *Never Too Old To Pop A Hole* (1988)
My introduction to Amy Denio was through her band Tone Dogs, which would appeal to fans of avant-progressive rock styles. Denio's *Never Too Old To Pop A Hole* defies classification, but I would describe it as experimental pop for progressive rock fans. She incorporates elements of progressive rock, jazz, folk, punk, Caribbean and more to create a uniquely and surprisingly accessible set of offbeat tunes. Imagine Slapp Happy or Art Bears for the post-punk crowd.

Denio plays all instruments. I love her vocals, which she has fun with bringing singing, chanting, operatic and choral stylings together in creative ways. Such songs as 'I O U A C D' showcase her vocal gymnastics by combining operatic squalls with a skittish choral accompaniment and an intricately grooving bass lead. Several songs have a Caribbean flair, like 'Spring Jingle' which is also jazz flavored and features a poetic brand of multi-layered vocal stylings plus beautifully intricate guitar and bass interplay.

'Muzak Blues' deftly intersperses warped covers of the Carpenters' 'Close To You' and 'Sing A Song' and the Beatles' 'Eleanor Rigby' with Denio's own music. 'Marshall Whitey Wipes' is completely wacky, dissonant and masterfully rhythmic. And 'Birthing Chair Blues' consists of madcap rocking blues-pop, like Captain Beefheart teamed up with Laurie Anderson. Denio's music is challenging yet eminently accessible.

Songs... and MORE
Hometapers recorded far more than experimental music. There were many gifted singers and songwriters who were content to home record their music. Yet some of the most exciting song-oriented artists were experimentalists at heart, recording amazing pop and rock music that was adventurously light years from the music their

major label contemporaries were making. Moreover, some artists recorded both songs and experimental music, often including dramatically different recordings on the same cassette albums.

In this final section I will review the work of a handful of creatively inspired artists who were prominent cassette culture networkers.

Don Campau

California based Don Campau has produced some of the most intricately constructed music that backs some of the best rock and pop music in the hometaper world. Campau's songs are accessible while being elusively complex and masterfully weird. But Campau is also a poster child for the hometaper aesthetic of complete creative freedom as he delves into the experimental world, creating improvised instrumentals, sound collages, looped experiments and more.

Don Campau – *New Monterey Road Sounds* (1984)

New Monterey Road Sounds was released as a 2-tape set of music recorded from 1982-84. One tape features rock and pop tunes and the second consists of all instrumental music.

The song set is a treat. There is jangly dual guitar rocking pop with a new wave edge, good time grungy rock 'n' roll, trippy late 1960s west coast psychedelia, acoustic driven guitar rock and much more.

Among my favorite songs is, 'Bird In The Parking Lot Bush', with its dissonantly rocking acoustic folk which is given an extra kick by strange vocal effects. I like the jamming psychedelic guitar leads against a complex instrumental backdrop on 'Key To The Riddle'. 'Call Of The Wild' is jazzily grooving, with funky guitar and playfully spacey keyboard runs. 'Buddhist Ceremony At The Burger Joint' is hysterical, featuring trippy psychedelic music while Campau sings about a group of monks' experience at a fast food take out. More wacky humor is heard on the bouncy, jangly 'I Know A Guy', as Campau sings about the "low down dirty disgusting little rip off... crazy wacked out psycho little sucker". Despite the zany lyrics the music is circuitously varied. Campau finds an oddball balance between jangly and herky-jerky robot pop with playful spacey effects on 'That's How I Feel'. And I love the guitar interplay on 'Messin' With Old DJ', as Campau grooves along like a humorous take on the Grateful Dead and sings about getting the dog off his lawn.

The instrumental tape is equally diverse. Among the highlights is 'Organ Concerto', with its minimal church organ accompanied by eccentric effects and potently fuzzed pulsations. I like the repetitively strumming guitar and bass groove on 'Fantasy Dub', which lays the foundation for guitar jamming with Frippertronic guitar. 'Possible Plan #6' cranks out cool grooving jazz-pop and Grateful Dead jamming rock, while 'Dark Highway' is similar but with a mesmerizing ambient-jazz angle. And Campau rounds out the set with some tape collage works and a free-improvisational nod to experimental guitar à la Derek Bailey.

Don Campau – *Pinata Party* (1986)

Pinata Party was Campau's first mail music collaboration (he played live with some participants), having partnered with the likes of Greg Gray, Dino DiMuro, James Hill, Ken Clinger, Mark Hanley, Brian Conroy, Allen Dancer, John Hayden, and Campau's children Nicole, Kevin and Caity. It's a sprawling 2-tape set of 43 fun and inspiring songs.

The set opens with the jangly and jazz-pop rocking title track, with Campau singing about the party he had in his yard. There are numerous excellent Campau solo tunes, but I'll focus on the collaboration highlights.

James Hill's trumpet adds a cool jazz flavor to several songs. 'Before The Neighbors' has a funky vibe but is quirkily offbeat and bluesy with freaky effects. 'Mystery Of The Hemphill' playfully blends toy sounding keyboards, metronomic electro percussion and tasty jazz trumpet. And Campau turns tape collage cut-ups into a seductively blues grooving tune with trumpet on 'Go Navy'.

Some of the most impressive music is heard on the collaborations with Dino DiMuro. I like the ripping guitar solos, intense strumming acoustic guitar and lusciously peaceful but jamming guitar and banjo interlude on 'What's The Reason'. 'Megan's Morning' is a rocking instrumental with a distinctive Captain Beefheart flavor and outstanding dual guitars. And the guitars, banjo and electro keys interplay are incredible on the bouncy 'Promise Dollars', with daddy Don and daughter Nicole duo vocals.

The collaborations with Ken Clinger are the most weirdly compelling. 'Joey Roo Goes Dancing' is playful and otherworldly in its approach to rocking jazz-pop. Clinger's narrative on 'Life With Mary Mayhem' gives a cleverly crazy account of Mary and her encounter with cows. 'What A Mess' is a witty mash-up of goofy music and Clinger shaming Campau for a horrible musical contribution and a growling voice repeating 'What a mess, what a mess'.

The tracks with Campau's children are as cute as cute can get. 'Stupid Stinkin' Day' is a diddly bit of experimental pop with Campau sharing vocals with his son Kevin. 'Your Constant Paradox' is a very personal song that ends with young Kevin telling his dad he loves him but goes on to say that he hates himself and feels that he is dumb. Nicole charms with her fake commercial and show tune songs. And Caity coos and shouts throughout the gracefully free-wheeling and appropriately titled 'Daddy'.

Don Campau – *Meteors And Pickles* (1987)

Meteors And Pickles is a classic example of hometaper stylistic free-for-all. Opening with a cover of Procol Harum's 'Homburg', Campau's unmistakable vocals are backed by dirty fuzzed guitar and a simple keyboard melody. Defying any expectations of what might follow this tuneful introduction, Campau launches into the 27-minute title track that he says was the most elaborate tape loop piece he ever did and caused so much wear on his 4-track TEAC 3340A that the heads had to be replaced. My favorite part is a strangely musical combination of harmonica, call-to-prayer horn, didgeridoo drone and jazz bass. Rock guitar solos along with operatic yodeling, hip-hop grooves and repetitive drumming and organ riffs. A children's song is mashed up and backed by harmonica, flute and bass, followed by a traditional African children's tune.

Campau returns to song form with the quirkily rocking 'They Warned Me'. He then swivels back into experimental mode with the samples and song montage of 'The Golden Years', a delirious mash-up of voices, scratching, music and guitar solos that Campau had created for the 'Dead Things' mail art project. 'Sandra is a cover of a song by hometaper Ken Clinger. And Campau rocks out with more tasty guitar solos on 'Possible Plan #9' and the high energy pop instrumental 'Major Minor'.

Lord Litter

The late German musician and radio personality Jörg Dittmar adopted the alias Lord Litter in 1983 when he needed a name for a music competition. A fixture on the international hometaper scene, Lord Litter's music was steeped in 1960s pop, pub rock, roots rock and good old rock 'n' roll, with plenty of electronic, experimental and progressive rock influences and amusingly twisted lyrics. He was an accomplished multi-instrumentalist and an imaginative creative force.

Lord Litter – *Tits, Zombies 'n Assholes* **(1986)**

The 14 songs on *Tits, Zombies 'n Assholes* are full of humor and satire, often drawing on trad pop and music hall influences that recall the Bonzo Dog Doo-Dah Band. The opening track, 'Open Your Brain', is a space-folk-electronica instrumental with whimsical flute and synth melodies that differs from the rest of the album. Among the highlight songs is the progressive rock infused pop of 'Sex Sells', with its lyrics: "Show them your titties. Show them your ass. Oh, go show it. Oh, that's a gas." 'Where Have All The People Gone' features swinging rock that sounds like a country barn stomper interpreted for a new wave audience. Litter does a rollicking cover of the Box Tops' classic 'The Letter'. 'I'm The Clown Of My Hometown' is like a Bonzos country parody blended with 1960s romance themed pop. 'The Theme' is a 1960s styled surf rock instrumental that holds up to the best of Dick Dale and the Ventures. 'He Is Just A Lonely Zombie' is my favorite song of the set, placing its sympathies firmly in the tragic zombies' court: "I can smell the Earth. The Earth that's stuck in my nose. And by the way, my left foot's been torn away." 'Artificial Asshole' showcase's Litter's flair for jazz and soul influences. And 'Crawling Next To You' carries a solidly executed pop and punky pub rock vibe that would have been right at home on Stiff Records.

Lord Litter - *A New Magic In A Dusty World* (1987)

A New Magic In A Dusty World is another collection of artful pop oddities, with Lord Litter playing all instruments except drums (credited to Thomas Tit).

The set opens with the high-powered rocking 'Hello', which could be the soundtrack to a 1960s film, mixing surf and comedic horror themes. But the last minute of the song consists of voices that throughout the album reveal what seems like the running theme of Mr. Pickinpepper and the search to figure out who Lord Litter is.

The title track is a good time country/folk/'Americana' song with superb playing by the one-man band Lord Litter. Once again he dispenses with pop conventions as the song unexpectedly ends with a synthesizer wash and strange narrative voices. 'You Was Made For Me' is swinging rock that's lightly country, though Litter's brand of conventional styles goes off the reservation with its guitar licks that are sometimes distantly atmospheric and at others raw and psychedelic. 'I'm Not Normal' is a thrashy but tight as a knot, manic punk and grungy hard rock angst tune that could be a Stooges outtake. Litter wears his humor on his shirtsleeve on 'It Was A Boring Party', with its disco vibe and madcap vocals. 'Ma Gal' is a mournfully drugged blend of the Beatles, Bread and sad country. 'Commercial Things' injects a bit of avant-garde adventure, with its tribal percussion and Arabic chanting intro, before launching into a goofily raw punk-pop song about Africa. And the amusingly off-centered country and novelty pop swing of 'Ma Buyba' is a fun finale to this wonderful set.

Das Freie Orchester – *Now* (1990)

Das Freie Orchester (DFO) formed in Communist East Germany and was forced to function in a dangerously unofficial capacity. Despite the risks, the band released several cassette albums that Lord Litter distributed in the west. When the wall came down in 1989, Lord Litter immediately joined the band.

Now is the first DFO album with Lord Litter as a member. It's a remarkable set of avant-rock drenched in numerous categorically challenged influences. The music is all improvised and DFO diffuse a free-wheeling improvisational feel while being an incredibly tight ensemble.

Some of the music is like Can comingled with King Crimson and Captain Beefheart and thrust through a post-punk grinder. The guitars recall the volcanic potency of *Red* era King Crimson and the bluesy angularity of Beefheart. The vocals are in English and consist of often anguished punk-poet narrative rants. Imagine Damo Suzuki clearly enunciating his lyrics and that would be the DFO vocals. At times they occupy an intensely energetic punk, funk, jazz and progressive rock realm, with insane guitars that alternate between sharp attack chord blasts and manically spaced out soloing. The dual guitars sound like a psychedelic-metal synthesis and mutation of Robert Fripp and Michael Karoli. The guitars whine and wail in anguished, psychedelic-metal hysteria, as the drums unleash in free-jazz tribal frenzy and the singer rants like a man possessed. This is inventive rock music that creatively fuses a hodgepodge of progressive, jazz and punk influences.

Tara Cross

Tara Cross is a New Yorker who formed punk bands in the Manhattan village scene of the late 1970s and early 1980s, later going on to home record with an Electro-Harmonix mini-synthesizer and a drum box. Cross released a handful of cassettes and at least one vinyl LP and contributed to numerous cassette compilations.

Tara Cross – *Limelight* (1985)

Limelight is a 13-track set of synth-pop vocal tunes, melodic instrumentals and experimental music. Cross cleverly and creatively finesses a complexity/simplicity balance. Her singing/spoken word narrative style is a mechanized poetic match for the bare bones beats of the drum box on 'When Will You?'. The simple melodies and beat on many of the songs are compelling, feeling like mechanical lullabies as Cross weaves together multiple melodies. I like the extraterrestrial gothic pop and choral vibe of the title track. A simple synth line and punchy electro beat zip along as Cross alternates between chant singing and poetic rap on 'Desperate'. And 'Hotel Midnite' is a haunting yet uplifting romantic song with droning choral synths.

Even at her most experimental, Cross is concerned with melody, like on the sound exploratory soundtrack piece 'Hot Wax'. 'Flight * 2' is one of the more complexly produced and arranged tracks of the set. A rumbling bass riff serves as the anchor for a rhythmic blend of rattling bells, breaths and claps, all of which Cross meshes into an energetic and smoothly rolling groove. She deftly combines cut-up collage and rhythms on the space electronic 'Long Distance'. And 'Hear Me' is a vocal exercise of dual wispy choral chants, underscored by a fuzzed droning electronic pulse.

Tara Cross & Stefan Tischler – *Searchlight & Torch* (1984)

Searchlight & Torch is a collaboration between Cross and fellow New Yorker Stefan Tischler. It's a short set, with ten tracks in 30 minutes. There are only three tracks with vocals, there being no singer per se, though these are very much instrumental 'songs'.

The music is beautifully melodic and engaging. An alien presence permeates throughout, as if these short pieces were incidental music in a sci-fi film. Tranquil cosmic melodies are embellished by flowing drone waves and rickety robot percussion. Motorized whirring synthesizers sound like flying saucer engines colored by bells. I love the celestially pastoral melodies on 'Arcadia', with its multiple synth passages intertwined to create a minimal sci-fi synthesizer ensemble. The mambo grooves of 'Porto Rico' inject a hip-shaking video game swing. 'Alien Code' is simultaneously playful and film noir electro cinematic and includes spoken word by Cross and Tischler. And I like the insect buzzing and swarming electronics and various vocalizations and chants on 'Silkworm'.

Tara Cross – *Tempus Fugit* (1988)

Tempus Fugit is a vinyl LP released by the French Permis De Construire label. Cross hasn't left the lo-fi world behind, though the production is clearly superior and she seems to have secured new keyboards that inject a heavily symphonic feel.

'Rain Sprouts' features spoken word poetry and an anthem-like chorus against a church organ melody, commanding march beats, sprinkled effects and strumming acoustic guitar. The searing synth lines and phased looped effects on 'PK-15' make for an intense B-film soundtrack over which Cross recites poetry. Though synthesizer driven, 'Shade Of Blue' is more sci-fi punk-pop than synth-pop, having the same feel as 'PK-15' but with acoustic guitar and passionate vocals. The title track is a standout, laying down a gothic electro funk groove with spoken and sung vocals and a dizzying array of effects. 'Days Fade' is an enchanting symphonic and lightly tribal instrumental. And 'Aalter Image' is like lo-fi Vangelis, being the most fully electro orchestrated track of the set.

Andy Xport

Andy Xport is a UK based singer-songwriter, punk rocker and sound explorer. In addition to releasing cassette albums of his anarcho-punk band A.P.F. Brigade, Andy recorded solo as Man's Hate. An ardent animal rights and environmental activist, Xport's songs commonly speak to the abuse of animals. A.P.F. Brigade's abbreviation stands for Animal/Anarchy, Peace and Freedom. Xport also curated 15 volumes of the International Sound Communication cassette compilations from 1984-89, featuring a variety of music and audio art by hometapers from around the world.

A.P.F. Brigade – *God The Tape* (1983)

A.P.F. Brigade was founded in 1980 by Andy Xport and Jon Hindle. The *God The Tape* album includes a drum machine which the duo named Livingston Seagul, though there is real percussion as well. Xport and Hindle may not have been the most proficient musicians, but they had a flair for catchy melodies and are textbook examples of heartfelt passion.

There's a lot of variety here as the band shift from punk thrash to Ramones styled punk rock 'n' roll to melodic, acoustic driven songs. The opener, 'The Dark Age' is one of the oddest songs of the set, consisting of steadily plodding guitar, bass and vocals rock, augmented by a continuous stream of harshly shrill whistling. There's plenty of high energy and angrily spewed punk thrash. It's hard to make out the lyrics, though the drum machine provides an appealing raw sound that is quirkily different from most early punk era thrash bands. 'Food For Thought' is also a bit different, having a tank rolling punk-metal drive.

Then there are songs like 'El Dorado', a choppy country-punk tune with acoustic guitar and bass speaking to the problem of moneyed people of power, evil politicians and their negative impact on the world. 'Slave To A Rolls Royce' is trademark angry punk that takes a swing at the rich. 'Atomic Dawn To Census Forms' is an acoustic folk-punk song that implores people to realize that they have only got one life to live and share. The swinging and dissonantly rocking 'Skin' takes an across the kneecaps swipe at rich people who adorn themselves with animal furs: "Skin that once was free, is now trapped on your back." 'Carve It Up' attempts to put a bad taste in the mouths of carnivores. And 'Paradise Lost' stands in marked contrast to the rest of the album, being an acoustic guitar, vocals and drum sticks song that brings to mind a 1960s Claudine Longet lounge-pop tune.

Man's Hate – *Suffer In Silence* (1984)

One glimpse of the photograph of a sad eyed dog peering from behind bars on the *Suffer In Silence* tape cover and songs like 'Burn The Flag', 'No Money No Rights', 'Animal Farming' and 'Meat Means Money', and it's clear where Andy Xport's sympathies lie.

This set of noise-pop songs is characterized by lo-fi drum machine propelled rock with a dual combination of dirty strumming and melodic riff guitars and Xport's emotionally yelling vocal style. Attentive listening through the coarsely jagged bluster of the guitars reveals an illusory pop sensibility and flair for melody. 'No Money No Rights' has a guitar attack like the Clash's 'London Calling' but is accompanied by riffs that recall a Squeeze style of pop. The choppily angular guitars on 'Work Experience' are like a jackhammer to the skull. 'Animal Farming' takes a break from the rackety rock to give a solo spoken word describing a visit to a slaughterhouse and graphic descriptions of how animals are killed and subsequently processed. And the title track is the most sedate and bouncy pop song of the set.

Man's Hate - *Turning Pleasantly Numb* **(1989)**

Andy Xport considered *Turning Pleasantly Numb* to be his most technically accomplished album and the one that summed up his sound and views on life. It was also the last album he would record until making a comeback on the internet in 2006.

The noisy edge of the guitars has been cleaned up without dispensing with the essential lo-fi rawness of his sound. 'New Song' has an electro Reggae groove during the verse, is bouncy rocking during the chorus, and has a melodic mid-section guitar solo. 'Got Myself' has a cool 1960s surf and garage pop feel and a whiff of Beatles in the guitar fills. Xport sings of inner turmoil, both negative and positive: "Drama every day, pain that comes my way. Feelings that are real, and the hate that I feel, is burning inside, and there is nowhere to hide. Giving me such spirit and pouring me with power."

I like the wailing keys and spacey synths on the new wave rocking 'Frying Tonight'. It's a merrily melodic tune, given the thematic focus on Xport's flag waving call for vegetarianism: "Medium rare. Do you not care? Blood on your chin. Drippin' in the kitchen." 'Let Them Be' is another animal rights song, with music that is both carnivalesque and funereal, while also having the 1960s pop vibe that permeates throughout the album. I love how Xport contrasts happy music with severe lyrics. The jangly folk-pop with searing synthesizer lines and merry whistling fills on '2009' is in sharp contrast to the lyrics that worry about a future of over population and pollution. And the punky ska groove and dual guitars of 'Cruel Operation' make for an energetic close to this album that was a coda to the 1980s for Xport.

Martin Newell

After negative experiences with record companies left him feeling jaded toward the music business, English musician and songwriter Martin Newell committed himself to the homemade life. Newell formed the band Stray Trolleys in 1979, and then the more popular and prolific Cleaners From Venus, as well as recording solo. One of the most brilliant songwriters to emerge from the 1980s cassette culture, Newell would later enjoy a modicum of recognition with an album produced by XTC's Andy Partridge, as well as writing and television appearances.

The Cleaners From Venus – *On Any Normal Monday* (1982)

Released when Cleaners From Venus consisted of the founding duo of Martin Newell and Lol Elliott, *On Any Normal Monday* is a 30-minute festival of pop craftsmanship. The credits state that all the songs were recorded to 4-track in a dining room. Given the astonishingly solid production, instrumental arrangements and vocal harmonies throughout, the album is a poster child for what can be accomplished with mastery over inexpensive technology.

Songs like 'Night Starvation' and 'I Can't Stop' are exemplars of jangly sunshine pop. 'Tukani (Monday Is Grey)' is interestingly varied, with dub propelled grooves, carefully placed effects, assorted vocal harmonies and poetic narrative. I love the guitar, funky bass and vocal interplay on 'A Girl With Cars In Her Eyes'. I love the jazz and soul infused pop of 'I Wanna Do That', the hints of 1960s garage and surf on 'F.U.N.', the Devo-ish quirkiness of 'Be An Idiot Pop Star', and the punky, electro effects splashed space-pop of 'Spirit Of Youth In Flames'. The compositions and arrangements are breathtakingly on par with the best major studio produced pop recordings.

The Cleaners From Venus – *Living With Victoria Grey* (1986)

At the time of Living With Victoria Grey, Cleaners From Venus consisted of Martin Newell and Giles Anthony Smith, with additional musicians on guitars and percussion. Songs like the title track are firmly in the Cleaners style, though with a more robust, full band, 1980s power pop sound. Newell is a master of seductively happy melody. I like the dynamic rocking potency balanced by sunny acoustic instrumentation and piano on 'Ilya Kuryakin Looked At Me'. Pop psychedelia meets romantic salsa swing on 'Clara Bow', an ode to the silent film era 'It' girl. I love the interplay between the dissonantly catchy guitars, strumming acoustic guitar and hip shaking percussion. Healthy doses of 1960s Motown and soul are injected into 'Stay On' and "What's Going On'.

Newell hints at a theme, as several songs are prefaced by 1930s big band samples and a goofy voice talking about Mr. Schmootie Patootie. There are other strange interludes, like the last two minutes of 'Stay On' that shifts to what sounds like a DJ making funny preview announcements.

The credits note that 'Pearl' is a song that Andy Partridge threw away. With the lightest of instrumentation, this is an impressively arranged, vocal dominated song with multiple voice parts, harmonies and 'doo-doot' backing vocals. Newell is indeed on par with and similar to Andy Partridge, with both striking me as being among the most progressive pop artists of their era.

The Brotherhood Of Lizards (1988)

The Brotherhood Of Lizards was Newell's post-Cleaners duo with bassist Nelson, who would eventually leave to join New Model Army. The band name may have changed but this is pure Martin Newell.

From start to finish the album is a treasure trove of mesmerizing melodies and pied piper vocals. Newell's lyrics shine on songs like the trippy psychedelic sunshine-pop tune 'On Planets Where I Was Young': "Not yet, space cadet. You've gone too far, and now you're out of your depth. The world isn't flat anymore. You're caught, cosmonaut. The planet's vanished in a crowd of thought. She isn't there anymore." The cheery rocking band theme song is like a jangly psychedelic jab at the Monkees: "Let me welcome you to the Brotherhood Of Lizards. There's a lot to do in the Brotherhood Of Lizards. We'll be coming soon to your living room. If we're not there yet, then we'll be there soon. And then say hello to the Brotherhood."

The album includes some of Newell's best acoustic driven songs. 'Carmosine' and 'In Fireglow' consist of jaunty acoustic instrumentation, sprightly folk-psych melodic drift, and wee dashes of trad Celtic that conjure up images of hippie maidens frolicking through meadows. 'Tinny Rain' is an acoustic beauty. And the bouncy 'Radiant Boy' includes flute and acoustic guitar passages that bring to mind Newell replacing Peter Gabriel in *Trespass* era Genesis.

X Ray Pop

X Ray Pop are a French band formed in 1984 as the duo of Didier 'Doc' Pilot and Zouka Dzaza, both having been in Bocal 5. The two recorded numerous cassette albums, many of them live performances and with a fluid lineup of additional musicians. There were also vinyl releases and X Ray Pop contributions were easily found on the countless compilation tapes produced in the 1980s.

X Ray Pop – *Poems From France* (1986)

Though no titles are listed, *Poems From France* consists of a series of short songs. Most of the tape features Pilot on acoustic guitar and Dzaza on French language vocals. The songs are classic lo-fi charm. Pilot's guitar rolls along on beds of shimmering strums and varied picking styles, with Dzaza's vocals sounding like a wispy Françoise Hardy. From song to song there are elements of folk music, 1960s flavored French Yé-Yé pop, spellbinding psychedelia and open mic night singer-songwriter tunes. There's an enigmatic ambient quality throughout that may be due to the way the music was recorded. Regardless, it's an appealing enhancement to the duo's sound.

Pilot trades his guitar for the Casio PT-20 keyboard and electronic percussion about halfway through the B-side of the tape and the music shifts to the minimal brand of synth-pop that X Ray Pop were mostly known for. The songs take on a playfully perky quality as Dzaza aligns her vocals to the electro patterns. The songs are enjoyable, the melodies memorable, and Dzaza has a psychedelically seductive voice that would shine in any context.

X Ray Pop - *Bronzing Bosoum* (1986)

Recorded only weeks after *Poems From France*, *Bronzing Bosoum* is characterized by X Ray Pop's simplistic yet good fun brand of electronic pop songs. The recording quality is better, and Pilot seems to have secured more instruments. And the addition of second vocalist Pamela Picrate nicely compliments Dzaza. In addition to electronics, Pilot plays electric guitar on some songs and even fires off occasional solos, which add a tasty rocking edge to the music. The trio blast through a rapid-fire cycle of 25 tunes.

I like the spacey vibe of 'Dream Of A Shadow', with its alien effects and electro cosmic jazzy grooves. 'Pamela' sounds like Kraftwerk playing 1960s world-of-tomorrow French pop. The trio vocals on 'Gomme' have a swinging scat quality. 'Albrecht Dürer' is hauntingly yet meditatively space age ambient. 'Jugar Contigo' is a strangely captivating blend of lounge-pop, lo-fi symphonic keys and brisk electro beats. Dzaza and Picrate are like call-and-response cackling kewpie doll sirens on the psychedelic punk rocking 'J'ai Faim'. Pilot's guitar shifts gears and goes razor punk on 'Oh Q'il Est Vilain'. And 'Le Suceur Fou' is an experimental sound exploratory electronics, guitar and vocals number that would make a fine avant-garde sci-fi soundtrack.

X Ray Pop – *Rabelais* (1988)

Rabelais is a full band live recording from December 1988, featuring Pilot and Dzaza and their live guitar, bass, drums and synthesizer lineup of that period, including 'Pam-Pam' on backing vocals.

This is a lively set, with many of the songs characterized by country ragtime psychedelic swinging rock 'n' roll, often accompanied by streams of showering, squealing and hissing electronic effects. The mood is fun and bouncy, yet the band can be just as punk blistering as they are jug band festive. 'Mes Beaulte's' is rockabilly punk amidst a Hawkwind meltdown of meteor shower effects. Add to that Dzaza and Pam-Pam's vocals and their 1960s French pop flavor and you have a very different sound indeed. I like the melodic screech of the violin on 'Fuzzy Christmas'. And rounding out the set are two covers: A space-punk version of 'Beck's Bolero' and a raucously blistering cover of the Stooge's 'I Wanna Be your Dog'.

Charles Rice Goff III

Charles Rice Goff III has been a prolific hometaper since the 1970s. Throughout the 1980s he recorded with the bands -ING, DISISM and Herd Of The Ether Space, as well as his solo cassettes. Goff also ran the Taped Rugs Productions label, which as of 2025 is still active. Many of Goff's projects consist of tape loops, cut-up collage and other experimental works. But he also records vocal songs, many of which intersect with his more experimental tendencies.

Charles Rice Goff III – *Might As Well Beyond Venus* (1980)

Goff's first Taped Rugs Productions release, *Might As Well Beyond Venus* is a mixture of Frippertronic style tape loops and other experimental works. The tracks alternate between experimental works and vocal songs with poems documenting the experiences and emotions related to Goff's summer love affair with Heather Maria McKim. Goff wrote some of the poems for McKim and others were penned by McKim.

Not a conventionally gifted vocalist, Goff's unmistakable voice sounds like a combination of folk singer, impassioned mullah conducting service, and Bill Murray's lounge singer, which he packs with a wallop of genuine emotional intensity. 'Ours' is a pastoral tune with lovely dual guitars and flute. 'Fly Away' is an acoustic guitar and vocals ballad. 'The Presence Of Her Absence' is similar, being a cover song with Goff's vocals backed by strumming acoustic guitar and serpentine psychedelic electric guitar solos.

The combination of Goff's vocals and experimental music style on several tracks makes for an unorthodox and compelling form of 'song' structure. 'Hallways Of Always' features Goff singing like a man possessed, backed by tape looped guitar and clattering found percussion. Goff sings the words of two poems by McKim on 'Truth Lies In Trust', with each poem heard simultaneously, one in the right channel and one in the left. The poems are backed by slowly soloing melodic guitar and intoxicating effects. At the conclusion, Goff loses control and falls into anguished crying which goes on for some time, emphasizing the pain of the breakup with McKim.

Charles Rice Goff III – *Noel Porter's Holiday Collection* (1983)

Noel Porter's Holiday Collection is what Goff describes as a medley of Dadaist interpretations of traditional Christmas songs. As is common with his work, Goff employed a variety of instruments and the Frippertronic style tape loop system to create these bizarre carols.

Goff jams on guitar, strumming and fuzz-drone soloing, eventually launching into a psychedelic freakout rendition of 'God Rest Ye Merry Gentlemen' with multi-layered vocals. The psychedelic Frippertronics and varied voices lovingly demolish the Christmas classic, making for a fun mixture of sonic insanity and comic relief. The music soon devolves into what sounds like the Residents' *Eskimo* album with 'Up On The House Top' lyrics, though it abruptly transitions to multi-layered street carnival madness. Goff layers in the singing with a creatively unhinged blend of kazoo chorus, whistles and demented chanting, yodeling, cackling and speaking-in-tongues vocalizations which turn Christmas into a surreal, ethno-tribal mash-up. I especially enjoyed Goff's frantically bizarre 'Jingle Bells' delivery. A cleverly outrageous Christmas album.

Charles Rice Goff III - *Vaporbar Basesheet* (1989)

Goff explains that he constructed the music on Vaporbar Basesheet by running his many source recordings through a no-frills mixer into a stereo cassette deck. Only Goff's voice, an acoustic guitar, an electric guitar, some effects pedals and a Frippertronic tape loop system were used to generate the sounds on the source recordings. In many cases the right and left stereo channels are completely distinct from one another, resulting in crazily contrasting components that create a uniquely twisted brand of avant-psychedelia.

'Union Blues' is a stellar example, being a guitar and vocals blues song made deliriously psychedelic by the accompaniment of a noise and voices reverse track. For 'Swim In The Water', Goff recorded his vocals, guitar and clapping through tape loops, creating a 13-minute, continually evolving combination of multi-tracked lyrics that expound on Goff's love of swimming, drinking, showering and other aquatic pleasures, dreamily sinuous psych guitar and rhythmic clapping. Goff covers Todd Rundgren's 'Born To Synthesize' with lysergic poise, using Frippertronic guitar, his trademark vocals and tape manipulation effects. 'Loaf' and 'You Are The Dream' are a medley track of strumming acoustic guitar and vocals that are both melodic and dissonant, accompanied by eerily bubbling and densely treated guitar effects.

The rest of the tracks are improvised, one-take recordings, including spontaneously composed lyrics. Goff frequently combines acoustic guitar and vocal numbers with wild electric guitar and effects excursions. Some tracks are like Captain Beefheart meets Frippertronic acid dosed folk songs. Others are effects mangled dissonantly bluesy love songs. The highlight is the 35-minute medley that is an art damaged stream of freeform jamming, tape manipulation, effects and songs, including some blissfully warped scat singing. The album is an outstanding example of skillfully and imaginatively blended songs, experimental music and tape effects.

Bibliography

PUBLICATIONS

Aerts, Mat 'Matski'. "Limbabwe history." Found at https://limbabwe.com/limbabwe-history

Bailey, Thomas Bey William, *Unofficial Release: Self-Released and Handmade Audio in Post-Industrial Society* (Belsona Books, 2012)

Barr, Tavis. "David Prescott: On the Passage of One Man Through a Few Years." *Knot Magazine*, Vol 1 No 3, Winter 1989/90, 8-11

Bendle, *Permanent Transience* (Muddycrow Publishing, 2015)

Bordowitz, Hank, *Dirty Little Secrets of the Record Business* (Chicago Review Press, 2007)

Bradberry, Brad. "Cleaners From Venus: Just Pop In A Cassette." *Option*, Issue 20, May/June 1988, 66-69

Braun, Reinhard. "From Representation to Networks. Interplays of Visualities, Apparatuses, Discourses, Territories and Bodies." in *At A Distance: Precursors to Art and Activism on the Internet*, ed. by Annmarie Chandler and Norie Neumark (The MIT Press, 2005) 72-87

Burroughs, William, *Electronic Revolution* (8th Edition 1994, Expanded Media Edition)

Chadbourne, Eugene. "My Recording Career: LPs and Cassettes". in Robin James (Ed.), *Cassette Mythos* (Automedia, 1992), 54-59

Ciaffardini, David. "Q&A with Op Magazine Publisher John Foster." *Sound Choice*, Issue 1, Jan-Feb 1985, 36-39

_____. "Dr. Eugene Chadbourne interview." *Sound Choice*, Issue 7, April 1987, 34-39

Davenport, William, *The Great American Cassette Masters* (Talk Story Films DVD, 2015)

de Waard, Frans, *America's Great Noise!* (KORM Plastics, 2024)

Drew, Rob, Unspooled: How the Cassette Made Music Sharable (Duke University Press, 2024)

Drew, Rob and Benjamin Duester (2024). A Mix for the Ages: As media forms come and go, why do cassette tapes live on? Retrieved from https://limn.press/article/a-mix-for-the-ages/

Duester, Benjamin, *Tomorrow on Cassette: Tape Jams in the New Media Age* (Bloomsbury Academic, 2025)

Duncombe, Stephen, *Notes From Underground: Zines and the Politics of Alternative Culture* (Microcosm Publishing, 2008)

Fioretti, Dan. "The Ken Clinger Interview." *Electronic Cottage*, Issue 5, January 1991, 30-34

Fisk, Steve. "Fred Frith Interview." *Op*, Issue F, Summer 1981

Ford, Simon, *Wreckers of Civilisation*, (Black Dog Publishing, 1999)

Foster, John. "Lost Weekend Success!" *Op*, Issue Y, Sept-Oct 1984, 3-5

_____. "OP, Castanets, and the Cassette Revolution." In Robin James (Ed.), *Cassette Mythos* (Automedia, 1992) 52-53

Frantel, Hans. "Home Taping: The Legal Issue Comes To A Boil." *The New York Times*, August 29, 1982

Furgas, Tom. "Cassettes Through The Mail." *Op*, Issue Y, Sept-Oct 1984, 31

Goff, Charles Rice III. "Herd Of The Ether Space in the 1990s." 2009-2010. Found at https://ia801308.us.archive.org/35/items/TheHistoryOfHerdOfTheEtherSpace1980s1990s/02HerdOfTheEtherSpaceInThe1990s.pdf

Gross, Jason. "Rough Trade – Trade 2." Perfect Sound Forever, November 1996. Found at http://www.furious.com/perfect/rt.html

Gysin, Brion, and Terry Wilson, *Here to Go: Planet R-101* (Re/Search Publications, 1982)

Harkey, Sue Ann. "Collaboration Tapes." *Sound Choice*, Issue 8, May-June 1987, 39-40

Harrington, Richard. "Record Rentals: Cashing in on Home Taping." *The Washington Post*, June, 28, 1981

Hegerty, Paul, *Noise / Music: A History* (The Continuum International Publishing Group, 2007)

Held, John Jr., *Mail Art: An Annotated Bibliography* (The Scarecrow Press, Inc, Metuchen, NJ & London, 1991)

Hensley, Chad. "The Beauty of Noise: And interview with Masami Akita of Merzbow." *EsoTerra*, Issue 8, 1999. Found at http://www.esoterra.org/merzbow.htm (no longer available)

Hill, James. "Creative Mailers." *Sound Choice*, Issue 4, Spring 1986, 19

Home, Stewart, *The Assault On Culture: Utopian Currents From Lettrisme to Class War* (AK Press, 1991)

Howard, Carl. "Don Campau Interview." *Electronic Cottage International Magazine*, Issue 5, January 1991, 49-52

Hunker, Tracy. "We Can Survive: New music and its culture: Independents are interdependent." *Sound Choice*, Issue 1, January-Februaruy 1985, 33

Jerman, Jeph. "Interview With Dan Burke Of Complacency Productions/Illusion Of Safety.", *Electronic Cottage International Magazine*, Issue 3, March 1990, 42-45

Johnson, Ken. "Beuys, Maciunas, Fluxus: Art that bends the mind and plays with perception." *New York Times*, April 20, 2007

Joyce, Don. "An Unsuspected Future in Broadcasting: Negativland." in *At A Distance: Precursors to Art and Activism on the Internet*, ed. by Annmarie Chandler and Norie Neumark (The MIT Press, 2005) 176-189

Kastov, George. "Fight The Power! An interview with the founder of 'The Coalition for Independent Artists (C.I.A.).", *Electronic Cottage International Magazine*, Issue 6, July 1991, 14-15

Kissinger, Mark. "Making Contact With Tom Furgas." *Sound Choice*, Issue 4, Spring 1986, 27

_____. "Tom Furgas Interview." *GAJOOB*, Issue 7, Summer 1991, 12-14, 92

Kranitz, Jerry. "Hal McGee Interview." Aural Innovations, Issue 19, April 2002. Found at https://web.archive.org/web/20081011193110/http://aural-innovations.com/issues/issue19/halint.html

_____. "Charles Rice Goff III Interview." Aural Innovations, Issue 22, January 2003. Found at https://web.archive.org/web/20080719201304/http://www.aural-innovations.com/issues/issue22/charles1.html

Kriebel, Sabine T. "Cologne." in *Dada: Zurich, Berlin, Hannover, Cologne, New York, Paris*, ed. by Leah Dickerman (National Gallery of Art Washington, 2005) 214-273

Ladd, Brian. "Home Recording." *Objekt Magazine*, Issue 16, Nov-Dec 1984

Litter, Lord. "Introduction." *Lord Litter's Out Of The Blue Informationzine*, Issue 4, 1989, 1-2

_____, "First International Cassette Makers Conference: The Kentucky Fried Royalty Meeting." *Electronic Cottage International Magazine*, Issue 3, March 1990, 16-17

_____. "Having An Open Mind... Rodolfo Protti's Old Europa Café." *Electronic Cottage International Magazine*, Issue 5, January 1991, 38-40

Manuel, Peter, *Cassette Culture: Popular Music and Technology in North India* (University of Chicago Press, 1993)

Masters, Marc, *High Bias: The Distorted History of the Cassette Tape* (The University of North Carolina Press, 2023)

McGee, Hal. "Hello Hello!! Yo! and welcome to the first issue of Electronic Cottage!!!." *Electronic Cottage International Magazine*, Issue 1, April 1989, 5-6

_____. "Artitude: The Audiofile Magazine." *Electronic Cottage International Magazine*, Issue 5, January 1991, 76-78

_____. "Hello! Hello! Yo! And Welcome To The Sixth Issue Of Electronic Cottage!!!." *Electronic Cottage International Magazine*, Issue 6, July 1991, 5-6

_____. "Forward." In Robin James (Ed.), *Cassette Mythos* (Automedia, 1992) vii-viii

_____. "Brief outline of the history of Cause And Effect." Found at http://www.haltapes.com/brief-outline-cause-and-effect.html

Meyer, Peter R. "In the beginning was the sound." *Unsound*, Vol 1 No 1, September 1983, 16-18

MFZ. "Aeon Import Records Inc." *Industrial Elitist Songbook*, #1, February 1983, 21-23

Miles, Barry, *The Beat Hotel: Ginsberg, Burroughs, and Corso in Paris, 1957-1963* (Grove Press 2000)

Minóy. "Mail Art and Mail Music (A Personal View)." In Robin James (Ed.), *Cassette Mythos* (Automedia, 1992) 61-62

Mohr, Tim, *Burning Down The Haus: Punk Rock, Revolution, and the Fall of The Berlin Wall* (Algonquin Books, 2018)

ND. "Mail Art Congress." *ND*, Issue 8, 1987, 22-24

_____. "Richard Franecki interview." *ND*, Issue 8, 1987, 5-6

_____. "Insane Music." *ND*, Issue 10, 1988, 38-39

Naylor, Tim. "Lost gems From The UK Scene." (November 7, 2012) Found at http://livingarchive.doncampau.com/feature_articles/lost-gems-from-the-uk-scene-by-tim-naylor

Nechvatal, Joseph (ed.)., *Minóy* (Punctum Books, 2014)

Negativland. "Negativland's Tenets of Free Appropriation." Found at https://hex.ooo/library/negativland_tenets.html

Orford, Andrew. "Interview With Randy Greif." *Electronic Cottage International Magazine*, Issue 3, March 1990, 50-53

Oswald, John. "Plunderphonic album notes." Found at http://www.plunderphonics.com/xhtml/xnotes.html#plunderphonic

Pareles, Jon. "Record-It-Yourself Music on Cassette." *New York Times*, May 11, 1987

Perkins, Stephen. "Tape-beatles interview for Tractor." 1994. Found at https://pwp.detritus.net/news/interviews/perkins-tractor.html

Pinsent, Ed. "Philip Sanderson interview." *Sound Projector*, Issue 16, Winter 2007-08, 78-86

Pittore, Carlo. "An Open Letter to Dr. Ronny Cohen." *ND*, Issue 3, 1984, 23

Plunkett, Daniel. "La Sonorite Jaune." *ND*, Issue 13, 1990, 7-11

_____. "Rod Summers interview." *ND*, Issue 17, April 1993, 45-49

Prescott, Dave. "Impact Of The Indie Glut." *Electronic Cottage International Magazine*, Issue 1, April 1989, 15-16

Rasula, Jed, *Destruction Was My Beatrice: Dada And The Unmaking Of The Twentieth Century* (Basic Books, 2015)

Rüch, Gunther. "Open Letter." *ND*, Issue 8, 1986, 25

Saper, Craig, *Networked Art* (University of Minnesota Press. 2001)

Savage, Jon, *England's Dreaming: Anarchy, Sex Pistols, Punk Rock, and Beyond* (St. Martin's Press 1992)

Schmieder, Karl. "Vittore Baroni interview." in *Unsound*, Vol 3 No 1, 1986, 26-31

Schrage, Michael. "The War Against Home Taping." *Rolling Stone*, Issue 378, September 16, 1982

Sheppard, David, *On Some Faraway Beach: The Life and Times of Brian Eno* (Chicago review Press 2008)

Sinclair, Mick. *MESSTHETICS GREATEST HISS: Classics of the U.K. cassette-culture D.I.Y.: 1979-1982 Volume 1* (Hyped to Death, Compilation CD booklet, 2008)

Smith, Owen, *Fluxus: The History Of An Attitude* (San Diego State University Press, 1998)

_____. "Fluxus Praxis: An Exploration of Connections, Creativity, and Community." in *At A Distance: Precursors to Art and Activism on the Internet*, ed. by Annmarie Chandler and Norie Neumark (The MIT Press, 2005) 116-138

Simon, Andrew, *Media Of The Masses: Cassette Culture In Modern Egypt* (Stanford University Press, 2022)

Stasik, Pennie. "How the Music Industry is Killing Music." *Artitude*, Issue Ten, Feb/Mar 1986, 3

Stingray, Joanna, and Madison Stingray, *Red Wave: An American in the Soviet Music Underground* (DoppelHouse Press, 2020)

Sulyok, Teresa E. "The Home Audio Recording Act: An Inappropriate Response to the Home Taping Question." *Fordham Urban Law Journal*, Vol 15, Issue 2, 1986, 433-479

Szava-Kovats, Andrew, *Grindstone Redux: The Story of the 1980s US Underground Music Network* (True Age Media, 2014) Book based on Szava-Kovats DVD documentary

Szwed, John F., *Space Is The Place: The Lives and Times of Sun Ra* (Pantheon Books, 1997)

Tanz der Rozen. "Frans de Waard interview", *Tanz der Rozen*, June 1996, Online, no longer available

Taylor, Neil, *Document and Eyewitness: An Intimate History of Rough Trade* (Orion Books, 2010)

Therer, Eric. "La Sonorite Jaune." *Electronic Cottage International Magazine*, Issue 4, July 1990, 33-36

Unsound. "John Gullak." *Unsound*, Vol 1 No 5, 1984, 43-46

_____. "Tim Yohannan interview." *Unsound*, Vol 2 No 1, 1985, 37-40

_____. "Church Of The Subgenius." *Unsound*, Vol 3 No 1, 1986, 39-47

INTERVIEWS AND EMAIL EXCHANGES

Al Margolis, 2007, 2025

Alain Neffe, 2007

JERRY KRANITZ

Andreas Müller, 2009
Andy Xport, 2008
Archie Patterson, 2016
Barry Lamb, 2009
Benjamin Duester, 2025
Brian Ladd, 2010
Bryan Baker, 2025
Carl Howard, 2009
Charles Rice Goff III, 2007
Chris Phinney, 2025
Das, 2008
David Lichtenverg (Little Fyodor), 2016, 2025
Don Campau, 2007, 2025
Frans de Waard, 2009
George Smith, 2009
Glenn Frantz, 2025
Hal McGee, 2016
Hessel Veldman, 2007
Jeff Chenault, 2019, 2025
Joanna Rogers, 2025
Joanna Stingray, 2025
Joe Schmidt, 2025
Karsten Rodemann, 2010
Ken Montgomery, 2007, 2025
Ken Moore, 2025
Leslie Singer, 2025
Lord Litter, 2009
Manny Theiner, 2025
Mark Edwards, 2016
Mark Lo, 2025

Mark Kissinger, 2025

Michael Ryan, 2025

Mick Sinclair, 2008

Mike Honeycutt, 2016

Mitch Rushton, 2025

Peter Ashby, 2009

Peter Bonne, 2009

Peter Bright, 2009

Peter Catham, 2025

Philip Perkins, 2016

Philip Sanderson, 2009

R. Stevie Moore, 2009

Richard Franecki, 2010, 2016, 2025

Richard Rupenus, 2025

Rob Drew, 2025

Robin James, 2008, 2010, 2016

Rod Summers, 2008

Ron Lessard, 2016

Scott Becker, 2025

Scot Jenerick, 2025

Steve Peters, 2010

Tom Furgas, 2025

Tom Sutter, 2025

Vittore Baroni, 2008

Zan Hoffman, 2008

Index

A.R.P.H. Tapes, 193
ABC, 112
Aborted Images, 192
AbySSS, 128-129
ADN, 182
Adventures in Reality, 118, 149
AEON, 175-176
Aerts, Mat 'Matski', 150-151
Agiasjon, 182
Akita, Masami (see Merzbow)
Akrat Tapes, 177-178
Alien Brains, 104
Almost Human, 257
Alternate Media Tapes, 177
Alu, 254
Amazing Stories, 116-117
Anderson, Laurie, 58
Angry Samoans, 139
APF Brigade, 24, 275-276
Arte Postale!, 97
Artitude, 170
Ashby, Peter, 100-101, 104, 106
Attrition, 139, 149, 254
Audio Evolution Network, 125
Audio Leter, 149
Audiofile Tapes, 148, 170, 177, 186-187, 199, 233
Audion, 118, 173
Backs, 166, 169
Bailey, Thomas Bey William, xxx
Bain Total, 182
Baker, Bryan, 215-219, 236-237, 239-240
Bal, Nadine, 244, 246-247
Ball, Steve, 104
Baroni, Vittore, 30-31, 62-63, 70, 73, 92, 95-98, 118-119, 175
Baum, Pat, 182
BBC Radiophonic Workshop, 54
BBP Records & Tapes, 219
Beatles, 57-58, 67, 70
Becker, Scott, 124-125
Bendle, 104, 108, 110, 146
Bene Gesserit, 175, 246-247

Bianchi, Maurizio (MB), 63, 95-96, 182, 204
Big City Orchestra, 72-73, 238
Bonne, Peter, 201
Borbetomagus, 175
Bordowitz, Hank, 6
Braun, Richard, 84
Bright, Peter, 141
Broken Skull, 113
Brotherhood Of Lizards, 279-280
Bunk, 64-65
Burke, Dan, 233
Burroughs, William S., 54-57, 60, 69, 82
Cabaret Voltaire (band), 4, 20, 112
Cabaret Voltaire (venue), 82-83, 85
Cage, John, 53, 70, 146
Campau, Don, 40, 131, 143, 162, 170-171, 174, 193-194, 199-200, 202-203, 219, 234-235, 268-271
Cantor, Evan, 206
Cartel, 165-168
Carter, Chris, 60-61, 141-142
Cassette Gazette, 118
Cassette Mythos, xxxiii, 37, 171, 241
Cassette Show, 192
Cassettera, 123
Castanets, 121-122, 124, 131-132, 137
Catham, Peter, 38
Cause And Effect, 85, 128-129, 171, 183-187, 213, 265
Cazazza, Monte, 20
Chadbourne, Eugene, 29, 30, 178
Chain of Dots, 146
Chainsaw (magazine), 139
Chenault (Central), Jeff, 144, 194, 235-236
Childress, Mike, 204
Chris & Cosey, 141-142
Chrome, 180
Ciaffardini, David, 124-125, 195
Ciani, Piermario, 98, 175
Clash, 111
Cleaners From Venus, 21, 171, 278-279
Clearlight, 182
Clinger, Ken, 145, 207

Clock DVA, 20
Cohen, Ronny, 94
Coil, 39
Colombier, Stefan, 177
Comelade, Pascal, 180
Compact Cassette Echo, 164
Complacency Productions, 233
Contact List of Electronic Music (CLEM), 126-127, 160, 188-190
Controlled Bleeding, 186
Cooperative Anarchy Show, 128, 200
Cortex, 245-246
Crass, 24
Croiners, 76-77
Cross, Tara, 207, 273-275
Cultural Amnesia, 178
Cultural Revolution (magazine), 106
Curran, Alvin, 154
D.Z. Lectric, 264
Dada, 10, xxviii, 81-86, 89, 94, 241
Das, 174, 238
Das Freie Orchester, 162, 272
Datenverarbeitung, 160, 177-178
Dauerblumen, 177
Dauzier, Pascal, 186-187, 232-233
Davenport, William, 120
Davison, William A., 65
DDAA, 182
De Fabriek, 74, 95
De Nederlandse Cassette Catalogus, 152
de Ridder, Willem, 151-153
de Waard, Frans, 28, 85-86, 138, 147-148, 151-153, 173, 176, 179, 235
Demure, Alan, 118
Denio, Amy, 207, 267
Der Akteur, 263
Der Böse Bub Eugen, 254-255
Desperate Bicycles, 101, 112
Die 80er Jahre, 160
Die Katastrophe, 159
Diehl, Lon C., 144
Ding Dong Tapes, 175
Disism, 73, 86
Dittmar, Jörg (see Lord Litter)
DK, 132
Dog As Master, 128, 183, 265
Door and the Window, 104, 108, 110
Douglas, Alex, 126-127, 188-190

Drew, Rob, xxxi-xxxii
Due Process, 208
Duester, Benjamin, xxxii-xxxiii
Duncombe, Stephen, 116-117
Dunn, Lloyd, 70
Dzaza, Zouka, 280-282
Edison, Thomas, 9
Edwards, Mark, 197-199
Edwards, Simon, 110
Eer Meet/Ear Meat, 192-193
Electronic Cottage International Magazine, 7, 133, 187, 213-215, 218
Elliott, Lol, 21, 278
Eno, Brian, 18-19
Ernst, Max, 82
Esplendor Geometrico, 160, 178
Essential Logic, 166
Eurock, 173, 180-183
Exart, 21, 153-154
Exoteque Music, 236
F/i, 27, 127, 142, 201
Face Cancer, 170
Factsheet Five, 119
Fall (band), 166
Falling A, 12, 100, 104, 167-168
Famlende Forsøk, 266-267
Farcy, Yann, 27
Farrell, John, 193
Fast Product, 166
Faust, 3
File 13 (zine), 237-238
Filliou, Robert, 91
Flagrants D'Eli, 256
Flowmotion, 118, 160
Fluxus, xxviii, 37, 87-91, 94, 98, 241
Flynt, Henry, 90
Forced Exposure, 237
Foster, John, xxxiv, 119, 121-124
Fostex, 9-10
Fowler, Ed, 206
Franecki, Richard, 126-127, 142, 145, 201
Frantel, Hans, 33-34
Frantz, Glenn, 16, 63
Frenzid Melon, 100-101
Fricker, Hans Rudi, 93-94
Fripp, Robert, 63
Frith, Fred, 3,-4, 74
Furgas, Tom, 19, 135, 144, 146, 149

GAJOOB, 61, 196, 215-219, 236-237, 239
Gelbe Musik, 223, 226
Generations Unlimited, 195, 222-223
Generator, 222-231
Gernsback, Hugo, 116
Goff, Charles Rice III, 64, 73, 86, 154, 282-284
Gong, 3
Gortikov, Stanley, 33, 36
Graf Haufen, 152, 158
Grafik, Pat, 144
Grafika Airlines, 157
Greenworld, 181
Greif, Randy, 170-171
Grievance Tapes, 219
Gullak, John, 193
GUZ, 254-255
Gysin, Brion, 53-54
Harkey, Sue Ann, 149-150, 250
Harrington, Richard, 33
Harsh Reality Music, 144, 170, 177, 233, 258
Haters, 96, 209
Hausmann, Raoul, 83, 85
Hegerty, Paul, 14, 54
Held, John Jr., 91-93
Henri, Pierre, 70
Henry Cow, 3
Hertz, Phillip, 122
Het Zweet, 175
Higgins, Dick, 87
Hill, James, 41-42
Hilltcab, James, 133
Hiraoka, Toshiyuki, 255-256
Hobijn, Geert-Jan, 153
Hoffman, Zan, 12, 61-62, 126-127, 131, 147, 170, 174, 193, 236
Holmstrom, John, 102
Home, Stewart, 90
Home Taper Show, 202, 209
Honeycutt, Mike, 154, 204-205
Host, Paul, 201
Hotchkiss, Kent, 175-176
Howard, Carl, 148-149, 170, 177, 187-188, 199, 233, 240
Huelsenbeck, Richard, 83
Human Flesh, 175, 247
Human League, 112
Hunker, Tracy, 190

Hunting Lodge, 144, 178-179, 194
I Scream, 245
If, Bwana, 138-139, 207, 260, 262
Illusion Of Safety, 233
Independent Kontakter, 161
Industrial News, 118, 146
Industrial Records, 19-20, 56, 92
Ingels, Graham, 121-122, 137
Insane Music, 11, 113, 141, 155-158, 244-252
Insane Picnic, 100, 105
Instant Automatons, 112
Interchange (zine), 118
Intergalactic Trading Company (ITC), 180
International Electronic Music Association (IEMA), 173
International Sound Communication (ISC), 15, 140, 275
International Terrorist Network (ITN), 144
IRRE Tapes, 161, 177, 252-259
Island Records, 18, 67-69
Izold, Andrew, 236
Jabon, 128
Jacklin, Nigel, 104
Jackman, David, 104, 108
Jaffee, Debbie, 85, 183-187, 265
James, Robin, xiv-xxiv, xxxiii, 37-38, 59-60, 119, 123-125, 171
Janco, Marcel, 83
JEM Imports, 2, 180
Jenerik, Scot, 50
Johnson, Calvin, xxxi
Jones, Bryn, 75-76
Joyce, Don, 68, 209-210
Jupitter-Larsen, GX, 96, 209
K Records, 129
Kapotte Muziek, 28-29, 85, 153
Karcasheff, Rick, 84
Kaswan, Killr 'Mark', 73
Kentucky Fried Royalty (KFR), 219-222
Kimball, Bill, 192
Kirk, Richard H., 20
Kissinger, Mark, 136, 196-197
Kiviat, Steve, 195
Klingler, Philip B. (see PBK)
Kluster, 57
Korm Plastics, 29, 153, 173, 235
Kraft, Brian, 206
Kratzer, 252-253

Kriebel, Sabine T., 82
Kronstadt 255-256
L'Edarps A Moth, 161
La Sonorite Jaune, 177, 186, 232
Ladd, Brian, 27, 138
Ladd-Frith, 27, 171
Lamb, Barry, 12, 104-105, 113, 143, 167-169
Lang, Matthias, 161- 177, 252
Leather Nun, 20
Legendary Pink Dots, 157, 187, 189, 247-248
Lessard, Ron, 127, 129, 176, 179-180, 208
Levine, James, 76
Levy, William, 154
Lichtenverg, David (see Little Fyodor)
Limbabwe Records, 150-151
Little Fyodor, 205-207, 264-265
Lo, Mark, 237-238
London's Outrage (magazine), 107
Lonely Whistle Music, 170, 234
Lord Litter, 15, 25, 161-163, 203-204, 219-222, 234-235, 271-273
Longford, Graham, 193
Lost Music Network, 122, 124, 191
Love Stumps, 170
Maciunas, George, 37, 87-91
Mail art, xxviii, 30, 37, 91-98, 141, 240-241
Malice (zine), 170, 204
Man's Hate, 130, 276-278
Manuel, Peter, xxviii-xxix, 5
Margolis, Al, 23, 65, 131, 138-139, 154, 171, 174, 231-233, 259-267
Marquee Moon, 182
Mars Everywhere, 187
Master/Slave Relationship, 183, 207
Masters, Marc, xxx-xxxi
Max & Mel, 170
Maximum Rock 'n' Roll, 119, 129, 237
McGee, Hal, xxviii, 11, 13-14, 84-85, 129, 135, 154, 174, 183-187, 213-215, 218, 233, 241, 265
MCH Band, 164
McKinnis, Jennifer, 219
McLaren, Malcolm, 99-100
McNeil, Legs, 102
Melody Maker, 99, 104-105, 109
Mental Anguish, 170, 258-259
Merzbow, 30, 85, 96, 148, 175, 186, 189, 227, 249
Meyer, Peter, 208-209

Micrart Group, 201
Miles, Barry, 55
Miller, Daniel, 107
Minóy, 64, 96, 171, 207
Mirage, 182
Monks, Jon, 106
Montgomery, Ken (Gen Ken), 57-59, 95, 146-147, 222-230, 232
Montgomery, Steve, 107-108
Moore, Ken, 173
Moore, R. Stevie, 12, 95, 171-172, 207
Moore, Thurston, xxxi
Müller, Andreas, 160-161, 177-178
Music For Midgets, 168
Music Millennium, 180
Muslimgauze, 75-76
Mute Records, 107
Mystery Hearsay, 204
Nash, Fraser, 168
Naylor, Tim, 106, 111
ND (magazine), 59, 93-94, 141
Nechvatal, Joseph, 64
Neff, Paul, 71
Neffe, Alain, 11, 24-28, 61, 154-158, 163, 188, 244-252
Negativland, 67-69, 71, 209-210
Neo Boys, 182
Neumusik, 118, 160
New Blockaders, 39
New Musical Express (NME), 99, 103-105, 109-112
New Sounds Gallery, 209
Newell, Martin, 21-22, 278-280
Night Exercise/Nattovning, 208-209
No Other Radio, 193
No Pigeonholes, 131, 171, 202-203
No Trend, 27
Nomuzic, 170
Normal Records, 161, 177-178
Nurse With Wound, 128, 186, 189
O'Brien, Robin, 131
Objekt Magazine, 10
Old Europa Café, 164
Oor (magazine), 151-152
Op, xxxiii-xxxiv, 26, 118-127, 131, 137, 145-146, 170, 172, 191-192, 238
OPtion/OPTION, 123-125, 143, 145, 189, 196, 202-203, 215, 227, 232

Oswald, John, 69-70, 73, 135
Outward Inward, 128
Over The Edge, 209-210
Oxomaxoma Voldarepet, 182
P-Orridge, Genesis, 19-20, 56, 92
Paddison, Richard, 168
Palace of Lights, 181
Paradox Music, 181
Pareles, Jon, 171
Parsons, Steve, 219
Partridge, Andy, 278-279
Patterson, Archie, 173, 180-183
Pavitt, Bruce, xxxi-xxxii
PBK, 265-266
Peel, John, 110, 112
Pere Ubu, 166
Perkins, Philip, 26
Perry, Mark, 102
Peters, Steve, 123
Phinney, Chris, 144, 154, 170, 177, 204, 233, 258-259
Pilot, Didier 'Doc', 280-282
Pink Floyd, 6, 57-58
Pittore, Carlo, 94
Plastic People of the Universe, 181
Plunderphonic(s), 69-70, 73
Plunkett, Daniel, 59
Pogus, 232
Pollution Control, 197-199
Pop Bus, 129
Portastudio, 9-10, 64-65
Powder French, 128
Pradel, Thomas, 161
Prescott, David, 195-196, 223, 232, 262
Probe, 166
Problemist, 120
Produktion QSL, 208
Protti, Rodolfo, 164
Pseudo Code, 156, 246
Psyclones, 27, 65, 138, 207
Ptose Productions, 182
Punk (zine), 102
Radio Progress, 201
Raincoats, 166
Ramleh, 194
Ramones, 13, 99
Rasula, Jed, 83
Rauh, Dave, 121

Real Shocks, 118
Red Crayola, 166
Red Nail Music, 64
Red Rhino, 166
Regicide Bureau, 133-134
Residents, 67, 70, 74, 179, 206
Revolver, 166
Riley, Terry, 53
Rodemann, Karsten, 158-159
Rogers, Joanna, 192-193
Rolling Stone, 34
Rose, Jon, 154
Rough Trade, 4-5, 101, 106-108, 110, 118, 160, 165-168, 175, 204-205
Rouska, Richard, 167
RRRecords, 127, 129, 176, 179-180, 208, 226
Rück, Gunther, 93-94
Rupenus, Richard, 39
Rushton, Mitch, 177
Ryan, Michael, 136
Sanderson, Philip, 12-13, 104, 108, 111-112
Sandwich Records, 157
Satellite Network, 167-169
Savage, John, 102, 106
Schaeffer, Pierre, 54, 70
Scheissladen, 223
Schmidt, Joe, 202, 209
Schnitzler, Conrad, 57-60, 73, 146-147, 222-224, 227-229
Schrage, Michael, 34
Schulze, Klaus, 25
Schwitters, Kurt, 83, 85-86
Scott, Richard, 166
Scritti Politti, 101
Senseless Hate, 27
Sex Pistols, 4, 13, 99-100, 111-112
Shemps, 127
Sheppard, David, 18
Simon, Andrew, xxix-xxx
Sinclair, Mick, 103-104, 109-110
Singer, Leslie, 133
SJ Org Distribution, 177, 186
Smersh, 27, 138-139
Smith, George, 138-139
Smith, Giles Anthony, 279
Smith, Owen, 37, 87-88, 90-91
Smolders, Jos, 28
Snatch Tapes, 104, 108

Sniffin' Glue, 102
Solanaceae Tau, 258
Sombrero Galaxy, 260-261
Sommerville, Ian, 54-55
Sonic Options Network, 124
Sordide Sentimentale, 27
Sound Choice, 120, 123-125, 128-129, 143, 145, 171, 189, 195, 203, 232
Sound of Pig, 23, 138-139, 171, 174, 226, 232-233, 259-267
Sounds, 21, 24, 99, 103-106, 109, 111-112, 141
SPEX, 158
Sprinkle, Annie, 154
Square Sun, 257
SSS Productions, 200
Staalplaat, 153, 155, 186, 223, 226, 235
Stabmental, 118
Stasik, Pennie, 36, 197-199
Stick It In Your Ear, 104, 106, 119, 159
Stingray, Joanna, 163
Stockhausen, Karlheinz, 53, 146
Stone, Fergus, 205-206
Storm Bugs, 104
Stray Trolleys, 278
Stress, 253
Struszka, Thomas, 253-254
Stupid Rabbit Tapes, 106, 111
Subway Organization, 167-168
Sulyok, Teresa E., 35
Summers, Rod, 95-96
Sun Ra, 7-8
Sutter, Tom, 133-134, 154
Swell Maps, 4
Swinging Axe Productions, 170
SYNE, 173
Szava-Kovats, Andrew, 27
Tangerine Dream, 3, 25, 57, 74, 146
Tape-beatles, 70-71
Tapes for Dying, 154
Tascam, 23
Taylor, Neil, 4, 110, 166-167
TEAC, 9, 23, 63
Tentatively A Convenience, 95
Terre Blanche, 215
Tesch, Michael, 158
Theiner, Manny, 128-129, 200-201
Thick Slimy Whisper, 261-262

This Window, 141
Thompson, Mayo, 166
Throbbing Gristle, 19-20, 56, 60, 92, 141, 146, 204
Tietchens, Asmus, 175
Tischler, Stefan, 274-275
Travis, Geoff, 4-5, 101, 108, 165-166
TRAX, 30-31, 96, 98, 175, 182
Trent Radio, 192
Turmel, JP, 27
Tutti, Cosey Fanni, 92, 141-142
Tzara, Tristan, 82-83
U2, 67-69
Uddersounds, 126-127, 142, 201
Under The Floorboards, 206-207
Univers Zero, 180
Unsound, 120, 122, 132-133, 203
Vanity Records, 182
Varèse, Edgard, 70
Veldman, Hessel, 21-22, 153-154, 252
Velthuys, Enno, 154
Velvet Swines, 187
Verdeaux, Cyrille, 182
Via Lactea, 182
Vice Versa, 112
Virgin Records, 3-4
Viscera, 85, 183, 265
Vortex Campaign, 39
Vox (zine), 104, 118
Vinyl (magazine), 151-152
Wall, Geoff, 119
Walls of Genius, 74, 138, 206-207, 251, 264
Wayside Music, 178
Weisberg, Rob, 191
Westwood, Vivienne, 99
Whitehead, Martin, 168
Whitehouse, 63, 204, 227
Wyatt, Robert, 166
X Ray Pop, 207, 280-282
Xport, Andy, 11, 15, 24, 130, 140, 148, 161-162, 232, 275-278
XTC, 278
XTSW, 262-263
YHR, 182
YLEM, 182
Yohannan, Tim, 129
Z'ev, 194
Za Dharsh, 128

Zafaun, Zazen, 181
Zensor Records, 223

Zig Zag, 141

About the Author

Jerry Kranitz is the author of *Cassette Culture: Homemade Music and the Creative Spirit in the Pre-Internet Age*, and the memoir *Putt-Putt Abuse: And Other Zany Tales of Growing Up in 1970s Kenmore, New York*. For 18 years he published the Aural Innovations space rock web zine and podcast. Jerry is a freelance writer who has contributed to *Shindig!* magazine and his essays have accompanied several archival reissues. He lives in Columbus, Ohio with his wife, records and cassette tapes.

I would love to hear from readers! My email is jerry@jerrykranitzwriter.com. I can also be reached on Facebook where I post regularly about music I'm listening to.

www.ingramcontent.com/pod-product-compliance
Lightning Source LLC
Chambersburg PA
CBHW060451030426
42337CB00015B/1545